From Tennessee to Oz

Books by Michelle Russell

The Deppe and Ganser Families (1790–1987)
Musical Memories: Songs the Gumm Family Sang
The Gumm Family Souvenir Song Book
Sabrina: The Autobiography of a Cat
Lily: Through the Eyes of a Child

From Tennessee to Oz

The Amazing Saga
of
Judy Garland's
Family History

Part I

By
Michelle Russell

Catsong Publishing
White Haven, Pennsylvania

Visit: http://www.catsongpublishing.com

First Printing 2009

Published by
Catsong Publishing
HC 1 Box 23Z-31
White Haven, PA 18661
570-443-8275

Russell, Michelle
    From Tennessee to Oz
    Includes bibliographical references, appendix and index
    ISBN 978-0-9800642-2-3
    Library of Congress Control Number: 2009911082

Cover design: Michelle Russell
Interior design: Michelle Russell
Typesetting: Marny K. Parkin
All photos with the exception of historic works © Michelle Russell

Printed in the United States of America

For Joe and Curry

Contents

Acknowledgements

THE VERY EXISTENCE OF THIS BOOK IS OWED TO THE GENEROSITY OF THE descendents of the Baugh, Gumm, and Marable families, as well as the historians of Murfreesboro, Tennessee; Grand Rapids, Minnesota, and Lancaster, California.

First and foremost, my thanks to Curry Wolfe. This book as it stands would not exist without her! Besides generously sharing her more than ten years of research, which put me way ahead, we spent countless hours, months, years(!), working together on research and discussing the lives of the people in this book. It was the adventure of a lifetime. I hope some of the excitement we experienced is captured here.

In Tennessee, my thanks to C.B. Arnette. When I was a stranger in Murfreesboro, Mr. Arnette introduced me to many people, and took me to rare places, including an old log house with a gate looking like something out of Dickens. On a stone post by the gate was a plaque stating that the property had been in three states: North Carolina, Virginia, and Tennessee, and that the top log had been placed there by Andrew Jackson. C.B. was of great support and inspiration in this project.

Further, thanks to Ralph Puckett who shared his Gum family artifacts and took me to the original Gum/Fulks homestead. Dee Dee Stockard, whose husband was a descendent of Ebenezer MacGowan, spent countless hours typing original family letters and history, which she graciously shared.

Great thanks to the extraordinary Martha Wright at the Rutherford County Records office, and Donna Jordan of the Linebaugh Library, both of whom gave me extra special support in my research. Additional thanks to Susan Daniels of the Rutherford County Historical Society for her dedication to the county's history, and for keeping an eye out for any information I might need.

Toby Francis of the Rutherford County Historical Society should also have special mention for his vast knowledge of the legendary Jefferson, which no longer exits. Toby and I trounced through mud and weeds so that I could experience standing on the mound between the prongs of the Stones River, making it a real experience. Thank you also to Ernie Johns for his help on many historical issues, as well as taking me through the woods to try to find the Crosthwait land, before Toby and I did find it! Thanks as well to Martin Rooker for generously giving a tour of his historic homes, Jerry Marable for helping me find the original site of Rev. Henry Hartwell Marable's home and family graves, Lucy Mae Lenoir for her information and photos on the Wade family, and the lovely lady in Statesville, who invited me into her home, and shared her knowledge of the history of the town.

Other special thanks goes to Jimmy Fox, who took Curry and I on a tour of Old Millersburg, and later gave me another tour, taking me up to one of the lookouts mentioned in the Civil War section. John Lee Fults also took me on a tour of the historical areas between Old Millersburg and Bell Buckle, as well as generously sharing his research on the *Millersburg 110*, and other historic information. Cousins John Fox and Glen Taylor both shared much of their family history and the history of the Christiana/Millersburg area. Without the help of these four men, I would have had little knowledge of this very rich, but barely written of area. Additional thanks goes to Sheri Thomas for sharing her White family photos, as well as Mary Elam Fox and Larry Hannah for so kindly sharing their Baugh family photos. All this has helped to make this story real.

In addition, I am grateful to the Tennessee State Archives, where I spent many a Saturday afternoon studying their treasures. Not to be forgotten as well are the wonderful historical sites of middle Tennessee: Carnton Plantation, The Carter House, The Sam Davis Home, Oaklands Mansion, and The Stones River Battlefield.

Without all the people and places mentioned here, and many more, this story would not have come together. I will say more in Part 2.

Thank you again and God bless!

Foreword

FOR MOST OF OUR LIVES, THOSE GROWING UP IN OLD JEFFERSON ONLY knew our parents, grandparents, and neighbors. Then, a new world began to open before us—a world of earlier generations—early immigrant families who found their way to a hill in Middle Tennessee, ideally perched above the confluence of the East and West Forks of Stones River. Looking north, these early settlers visualized an artery for transporting forest and farm products—an artery leading to bigger rivers and larger towns.

From Tennessee to Oz, Part 1 is a fascinating picture of these early families of Old Jefferson and other parts of Rutherford County. We are sincerely indebted to Michelle Russell for the in-depth research she has done to give life to these families. In her book, she artfully follows these individuals from long ago, as they move from place to place, influencing lives and communities throughout Rutherford County, and ultimately, Tennessee.

James R. (Toby) Francis
President of the Rutherford County
Historical Society (2005–2009)

Preface

Where the Gums came from, and who their European ancestors were is unknown. Family legend tells of three brothers coming to America via France. They arrived in Delaware, and eventually, each went his own way.* Until now, however, little has been known about the connection between the Gums of early Tennessee and Judy Garland.

TENNESSEE, SEPTEMBER 2003—AS I PARKED MY CAR ACROSS THE STREET from the Rutherford County Courthouse, my heart pounded with anticipation. I had come to Murfreesboro to study some court files concerning Judy Garland's family history. Judy's father, Frank Gumm had been born in this town, and author Gerald Clarke had mentioned these court papers in his book, *Get Happy: The Life of Judy Garland*. However, until now no one had really explored them.

Crossing the town square consisting mainly of two-story buildings—all at least 100 years old—I headed to the center of the square where the red brick, white columned courthouse stands. This courthouse is the crown jewel of the old town center, and one of only six ante-bellum (pre–Civil War) Southern courthouses in existence today. To the right is East Main Street, a tree-lined avenue of gracious mansions, and down this lovely street, only a few blocks from the square, is the home where Frank Gumm was born.

---

* Letter to Dave Richardson for Mildred Gumm Durham from Mattie Gumm Puckett, June 30, 1980.

Four hours after entering the courthouse and intensely studying the hundred year-old, handwritten records, I walked across the courthouse balcony and peered into the court room below. This is where they all were during the trial: Frank's mother and father, Will and Clemmie Gum(m), as well as all of Frank's aunts and uncles. The story I had just read was not fiction. It was real. I was in a daze over what I had learned. I wondered if Frank's father really was the terrible man he was accused of being, or were the accusations by his mother-in-law, Mary Ann Baugh, simply those of a paranoid old woman?

That night, I called Curry Wolfe from my motel room. Curry is the great granddaughter of John Mason Marable Baugh, Frank Gumm's uncle. We had met online earlier that year, and she had graciously shared her more than ten years of family research with me. "Curry, you have to come here," I told her. "You have to read this court case!"

~

Where did it all begin? How did I travel the road from fan of the great Judy Garland, to singer, producer, and now suddenly, author of this book?

I never intended to write a book—to add to the pages of speculation, gossip and picking apart every detail of Judy's life. That had been done enough. I only wanted to know who the Gumms were before Hollywood and legend took over. But somehow along the way, a gift was laid in my hands. Bit by bit, the past had been revealed, until even I agreed—the story must be told.

So, in September 2004, with the support of trusted friends, I packed my car to the ceiling (including my three wonderful cats—Sabrina, Theo, and Pennsy), and moved to Murfreesboro, Tennessee.

As it turned out, Murfreesboro was the perfect place to discover the past. There, a sudden turn off a country road can take you back in time two hundred years. For this, I might add, you need the help of the locals, but I was just in time to find this past. In a quickly vanishing landscape—swallowed by bulldozers and modern buildings—history was a questionable commodity.

The Pioneers

Introduction

Tennessee—Land of Dreams

L ONG BEFORE THE WHITE MAN CAME TO THE LAND BEYOND THE MOUN-
tains of Virginia and North Carolina, Native Americans roamed
these fertile plains. It is said that the Cherokees, Creeks, Chickasaws,
and even the Iroquois of New York on occasion hunted on the central
plateau which lies midway between North Carolina and the Mississippi
River.[1] Yet, by some unspoken agreement none of them settled there for
the land was too rich to be owned by one tribe.[2]

Then, in 1541, explorers from Spain and France began to find their
way into the heart of this territory. Each claimed the land for their own
county, but eventually, both countries were forced to give up their claims.

During this period, King George III of England ordered his subjects
not to go beyond the crest of the Appalachian Mountains and disturb
the Native Americans. Nevertheless, early settlers saw this territory as a
kind of Eden, and they would not be deterred.[3]

Following the American Revolution, President George Washington,
like his predecessor King George, asked the colonists not to disturb the
Indian lands, however, it was a hopeless request.[4] Increasingly, pioneers
traveled west, cutting down forests and farming the land.

In answer to the destruction of the lands they depended on for suste-
nance, the Cherokees, Creeks, and Chickasaws responded with violence.
Entire pioneering families were found dead and savagely mutilated, yet
even these brutal attacks did little to deter the pioneers. Finally, the state
of North Carolina, which for years had held the southwest territory as

her own, turned it over to the Federal government.[5] The territory had become too much trouble.

President Washington began to worry that the increasing confrontation between the settlers and the Indian tribes might turn to war.[6] If this occurred, it could irreparably weaken the newly formed country. With an eye toward this impending disaster, on August 7, 1790, the President commissioned co-signer of the U.S. Constitution, William Blount of North Carolina governor of the lands formally known as the "Territory of the United States South of the River Ohio," soon to be known simply as, "The Southwest Territory."

Upon receiving the President's commission, William Blount wasted little time. Immediately, he and his wife, Mary Grainger, made preparations for the move west, to the wild land destined to become the state of Tennessee.

Chapter 1

Pioneers in Knoxville

HIGH ON A BLUFF OVERLOOKING THE HOLSTON RIVER—NOT FAR FROM the rude shanties where local vendors sold their goods—Governor Blount built his home. Unlike the log cabins, forts and block houses in which most of the locals lived, the Governor's residence was a wood frame home with real windows. Mrs. Blount had insisted on a "proper wooden house," so wood and nails were brought in from North Carolina and window glass from Virginia. In the front garden, Mary Blount planted lovely, rare flowers, which the citizens often passed to admire. Amidst the muddy yards and wilderness surrounding them, the Blount home was a small oasis of civilization.

Three years later, in 1793, William Blount could reflect on the progress made in the short time since his move west. During the first year, he had met with 700 flamboyantly dressed Indian chiefs and pledged amity by negotiating the Treaty of Holston. Following this, he had procured the land on which this meeting took place, designating it the seat of government for the new territory. He named the place Knoxville in honor of Secretary of War, Henry Knox.[7]

Knoxville was little more than a wilderness at that time; a hilly plateau, high above the river, covered with "brushwood and grapevines." Soon the town would boast a courthouse, tavern, and newspaper, the *Knoxville Gazette*. Early settler, General James White sold lots for eight dollars apiece to anyone who would improve them. His son-in-law, Charles McClung platted and laid out the new town.[8]

*Figure 1. Governor William Blount's home in Knoxville, Tennessee.
(Permission by Blount Mansion Association)*

Mr. McClung, who had lived in Philadelphia for a time, made his town grid an exact copy of that city—even giving some of the same names to the streets: Philadelphia, Market, Locust, Walnut and Broad.[9] The place known as "Scuffletown"—for the wild fights of its soldiers—was slowly but surely becoming a place of promise.[10]

As news spread about the new territory and its capital, men began arriving by the hundreds. They were rich and poor, cultured and uneducated, veterans and outlaws. Among these men was Norton Gum. What his place of origin was and who his people were is unknown. He was simply one of the ambitious multitude dreaming of a new life. For the pioneers, life held adventure and promise that old class distinctions and money would not have allowed the common man. It was a new world and the possibilities seemed limitless for those with the courage to seize them.

Although Norton Gum's profession at the time is unknown, if one judges by his children and grandchildren, he may well have been an artisan—a stone cutter, or brick mason.[11] If this was the case, he would have had little trouble finding work; Knoxville was in need of builders. Many of the men who came to Knoxville did not stay long, but Norton Gum had no interest in moving on. He was in love.

On February 23rd, 1793, Norton Gum and his intended, Sally Clampet, went down to the courthouse to see the county clerk about getting married. In 1793, the first step toward marriage was to obtain a marriage bond. A certain amount of money would have to be laid down by a male person of respectable character, stating they knew the potential groom, that he was free of debt, and there was no reason why he could not marry the woman of his choice.[12] For this purpose, Norton brought his good friend, John Chism. (Chism may have been a relative as well. Some genealogy records suggest that a number of Gums and Chisms had intermarried.[13])

John Chism seems to have been a man of income, with rank a bit above Norton. He agreed to put up the money for the marriage bond and swore that Norton's character was above reproach.[14] Norton and Sally, as citizens of early Knoxville wore the clothing of the period. Mr. Gum was likely dressed in a blousoned shirt, gathered at the neck and wrist, with knee-breeches, long stockings, and shoes with buckles. His shoulder-length hair would have been tied back, and a black tri-cornered hat on his head. Sally would have worn a long, loose dress, gathered high at the waist, and a shawl tucked across her chest. On her head was a simple bonnet.

Norton and Sally Gum were married in the small one-room cabin of rough-hewn logs. Officiating at the ceremony was six-foot tall, 160 pound county clerk, Charles McClung—the same Charles McClung who one year earlier had platted the new town.[15] In the near future, McClung would work with Governor Blount, helping to write the first draft of the Tennessee State Constitution and designing the state seal.[16]

The Gums, like the majority of Knoxville's residents, probably began their married life in a fort.[17] Although a few settlers lived in log cabins, most chose to live in forts where they would be protected. The James White Fort, which can still be seen today, was the first and most central fort in Knoxville. Many others sprang up between the years 1792 and 1796.

White's Fort contained a good-sized two-story log house with two large rooms, and a number of smaller cabins, surrounded by a rough fence

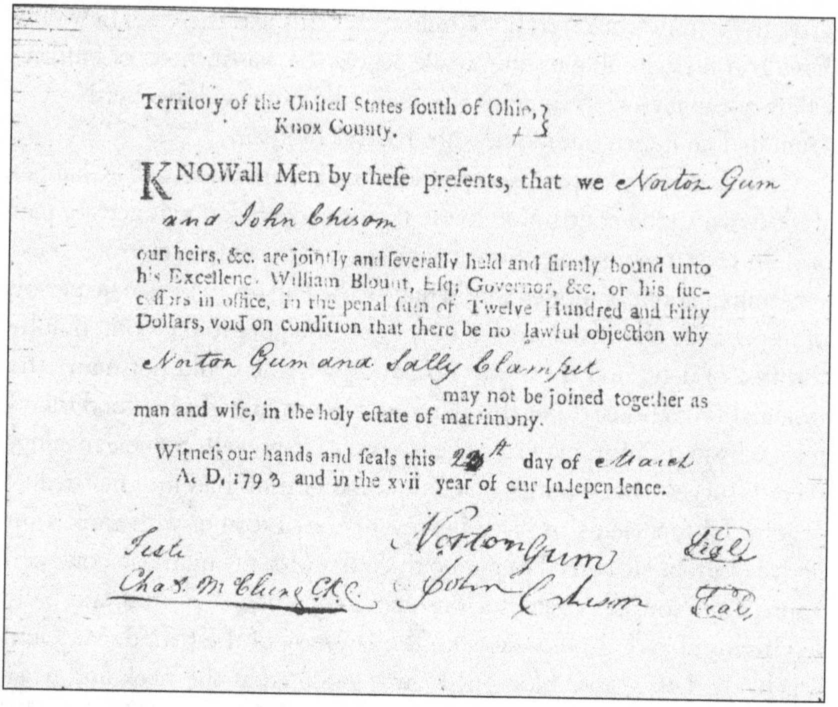

Territory of the United States ſouth of Ohio,
Knox County.

KNOW all Men by theſe preſents, that we Norton Gum and John Chisom our heirs, &c. are jointly and ſeverally held and firmly bound unto his Excellency William Blount, Eſq; Governor, &c. or his ſucceſſors in office, in the penal ſum of Twelve Hundred and Fifty Dollars, void on condition that there be no lawful objection why Norton Gum and Sally Clampet may not be joined together as man and wife, in the holy eſtate of matrimony.

Witneſs our hands and ſeals this 23th day of March A. D. 1793 and in the xvii year of our Independence.

Teste Chas. McClung CKC — Norton Gum (Seal) — John Chisom (Seal)

Figure 2. Norton Gum and Sally Clampet's Marriage Bond.
(Courtesy of the Knox County Archives—East Tennessee History Center)

approximately six feet in height. Inside the fence was a muddy yard with horses and other livestock. The fence was merely a deterrent, not only for the Indians, but for cougars, bears, wolves, and other wild beasts that roamed the surrounding landscape. Outside the fence, the fields were planted for food. An armed guard was stationed there at all times for protection.[18]

The cabins in the fort were made of criss-crossed logs with mud, clay, and straw filling the chinks. They had one window at most. The insides were dark and close. It took much effort to make candles, and they were too precious for extravagant use. People lived by the light of the fire, which was kept going day and night for cooking. Two families of ten or more members each might live in these 12′ x 12′ cabin rooms.

During the day, the center of the room was empty. Then, at mealtime several tables would be pushed to the center, allowing enough space for most adults to be seated. After mealtime, the tables were pushed back against the walls, and the beds laid out.[19] There was little privacy for anyone.

The pioneers existed on a diet of pork, grease, and cornbread. It was not an easy life, but those who survived were hardy people. On the frontier, people seldom bathed, waiting for spring or summer to bathe in a creek. One set of clothing was worn until it wore out. Conditions that would be unacceptable to most persons today were simply a way of life then. This was the way Norton and Sally Gum began their marriage.

Governor Blount's "mansion" was not far from the James White Fort. Behind his home, was a small, one-room office, where he conducted business for the territory. This business included taking the complaints of Native Americans, as well as negotiating with them. It was not unusual to see tall, copper-colored Cherokees with straight black hair and Indian garb walking the streets of Knoxville, though it cannot be said they were a welcome sight. In fact, one Indian, who came to see Blount was shot and killed outside the Governor's office.

Norton and Sally Gum had been married only seven months when an event took place that sent a chill through the heart of every man, woman, and child living in the tiny hamlet of Knoxville. Like an ominous wind, news swept through town that an entire family had been slaughtered by the Indians. The date was September 25, 1793, and as citizens soon learned, Knoxville had been the intended target. They had only been saved by one event.

A few days earlier, the militia protecting the two-year old capital had been notified that a large band of Cherokee and Creek warriors intended to attack. In fact, witnesses reported seeing as many as a thousand warriors heading toward the town, but at the sound of the old cannon— which was set off each morning to welcome a new day—the warriors turned and ran in the opposite direction.

When the local militia mounted their horses and rode out to the surrounding area, they saw signs of smoke in the distance. It appeared something was burning. About eight miles west of Knoxville, the group found the smoldering ruins of Cavett Station, a fortified blockhouse inhabited by thirteen members of the Cavett family. In the front yard lay the bloody

Figure 3. James White Fort in Knoxville, Tennessee.
(Courtesy of James White Fort)

Figure 4. Governor John Sevier's home at Marble Springs outside of Knoxville.
(Courtesy of Marble Springs State Historic Site)

body of the father, Alexander Cavett, his head scalped. There were seven bullets in his mouth, which told the men he had been ready to reload his gun. Next to Mr. Cavett lay his eldest son, who was also scalped and ferociously slashed. Eight of the Cavett children lay about the yard in pools of blood. Then, just before the door of the smoldering block house ruins, the men found Mrs. Cavett and her eight-year old daughter—both scalped and mutilated.[20]

Later, the tale of what occurred was told by Bob Benge, a man of mixed blood—both white and Indian—(commonly referred to in those days as a "half-breed.")[21] Benge spoke Cherokee and English, and had been present during the attack. He told the Militia that the Cavetts had defended themselves, killing two warriors and wounding three others. The Indians then called for negotiations. Benge, as interpreter, had convinced the Cavetts to come out of their fortified home, telling them they would not be harmed. The family complied, but upon their exit from the blockhouse, Double Head and his followers had fallen on them and killed them.

The one exception was the youngest child, a six year-old boy who was saved by John Watts, another man of white and Cherokee blood. The boy was taken as a prisoner to the Creek nation camp.[22] Two days later, his body was found dead with a hatchet wound in his back.

These were the conditions under which the Gums began their marriage. If Norton Gum was not a soldier by then, he, along with many others, wasted no time joining the local militia. To join the militia was a matter of honor as well as survival. A number of years later, as Sam Houston's mother sent him off to war, she told him, "I had rather all my sons should fill one honorable grave, than that one of them should turn his back to save his life."[23]

The Militia vowed vengeance on the Native Americans. There were many attacks prior to this, but none had seemed so bold or brutal. With little protection from the Federal government, the settlers had braved the wilderness to come to this land—there was no turning back. They decided they had had enough; they would destroy one or more Indian villages and set these "savages back."[24] "This must never happen again," they said, and they were true to their word.

In their anger, the Militia found and destroyed the village of Hanging Maw, an Indian who had been on speaking terms with William Blount. They also killed his wife. In October, Governor Sevier led a force of 700 men and massacred an entire village. These attacks, among others, turned the tide in the Indians' war against the white man.

Although the intensity of the previous attacks decreased after this, they did not cease completely. Murders and child-thefts would continue on and off for another decade. News of these attacks was a constant reminder that life was ever so tentative and not to be taken for granted. Meanwhile, Knoxville continued to grow. By 1796, there were about forty houses in the town.[25]

With all the difficulties of life on the frontier, many turned to religion. Faith in God brought order and comfort to the early settlers. Shortly after the founding of Knoxville, Presbyterian minister Reverend Samuel Carrack arrived in town and organized a congregation. He, like many others, traveled from fort to fort preaching the Word. It would be years before a physical church was built in Knoxville, so most fair-weather Sundays, services were held outdoors under a large tree. At other times, the congregation met in the courthouse, the barracks, or someone's home.[26]

The passion of the early Presbyterian preachers played an important role in early Knoxville. Many of the settlers, who were of Scotch-Irish descent and hated the British, connected with this denomination.[27] Although there are few church records from these early years, the Clampets were members of the Presbyterian Church at this time, and it is believed that the Gums may have been as well.

Along with religion, music was an integral part of early pioneering life. The East Tennesseans sang religious songs about God and the Almighty's glorious care for them. They also sang—as their troubadours ancestors had—songs about the latest news, love, heartbreak and moral lessons.[28] Music was a way to celebrate the good times, and to find expression and solace in the bad times.

During these early years, persons of every type came through the area. A small percentage of these persons were slaves of African descent. At the time, slaves were considered servants procured as extra hands to aid the settlers with their work. In the early pioneering years, slave and master worked side by side, each depending upon the other for survival.[29] The master of the 1700s felt fortunate if he could afford an extra pair of hands. Since there is no record of Norton Gum owning any property during this time, it is unlikely that he owned a slave. Indeed, likely much of the difficulty in finding information on Mr. Gum in Knoxville stems from the fact that he was not a property owner, or a tax payer.

Two years after the Gum marriage, a census of the territory was taken and revealed that there were 66,650 free persons and 10,600 slaves residing there. Since the number of free men now exceeded the 60,000 required for statehood, the citizens of the Southwest Territory could move toward that end.

A Constitutional Convention was announced for January 11, 1796. Representatives were elected from the various counties for that purpose, and soon began arriving in Knoxville from all parts of the territory. Among these representatives was future U.S. President Andrew Jackson. Another representative, Thomas Bedford, came from an area just outside a small town in Davidson County, called Nashville. Mr. Bedford and his dream were destined to play an important role in Norton Gum's life.

These were busy and exciting times for those living in Knoxville! Men like Norton Gum mingled on the streets and in John Chisholm's Tavern with the representatives. They listened to discussions of what their new constitution should contain and what decisions had been made. One of the decisions Norton may have been among the first to learn was Andrew Jackson's suggestion that the new state be named Tennessee—an Indian word meaning "crooked river."[30]

Representatives and Senators back in Washington, D.C. were not very eager to accept Tennessee as a new state. They feared it would tip the present balance of power. Nevertheless, on June 1, 1796, Tennessee became the 16th state of the Union.

By 1795, the County of Knox's population had increased so significantly, a commission voted to create a new county named Blount in honor of the Governor. In addition, fifty acres were laid out for a town, which they named Maryville in honor of Governor Blount's wife. Maryville was only a few miles south of Knoxville, and lay on a flat, pleasant plain in the foothills of the Smokey Mountains. In later years, this would be the site of Sam Houston's childhood home.

It appears that the Gums were living in this new county because by 1797, Norton Gum was serving in the Blount County Militia. On June 8th, 1797, he was commissioned 1st Lieutenant "for good behavior."[31]

In the midst of this amazing mingling of politics, religion, Indians, and pioneers, the Gums lived the early years of their marriage, and began a family that would remain in Tennessee for generations to come. Between 1797 and 1802, Sally Gum gave birth to at least four children. There were two girls, Hannah and Mary, a first-born son named William (as was custom for the Gums), and a second son named John.[32] In spite of the frightening Indian attacks, life was happy, with many reminders that they were blessed.

Then, on April 29, 1800, the Sheriff arrived at the Gum home without warning and hauled Norton Gum off to court. This was before "due process of law," and customary procedure at that time. It seems Alexander Coulter, a resident of Knox County, had "pled" a case against Mr. Gum, stating that he had trespassed on his property. The details of the case are unknown, but as a result of Norton's actions, Mr. Coulter was asking for "damages [of] $600."* [33]

On the second Monday of July, the judge ruled that since the Plaintiff had not filed further, the suit was dismissed. Mr. Coulter was ordered to pay the Defendant, Norton Gum, his costs in the case. It seems that there were many other cases similar to this at the time—still, it must have been very unpleasant for Norton Gum and his family.

Meanwhile, around 1803, Norton Gum learned of a newly formed county in the west called Rutherford. Rutherford County had been formed out of Davidson County, where Nashville lay. Many persons, including some of the wealthier and more educated, were moving there. Representative Thomas Bedford had plans for a new town on the river and they were looking for men with ambition and skill to help build the town. If Norton was willing to come west, there was plenty of land and unlimited opportunity. Norton Gum must have pondered this opportunity carefully. Then, he made his decision. They would go.

---

* $600 comes to approximately $13,200 in 2007. www.measuringworth.com

Chapter 2

A New Place

SOMETIME BETWEEN 1801 AND 1803, THOMAS BEDFORD AND COLONEL Robert Weakley, veterans of the Revolutionary War, formed a partnership. Together they purchased a land grant from another Revolutionary War veteran, Captain James Pearl, who had received the grant in payment for his services in the war. Captain Pearl had no intention of leaving his home to claim the land and was happy to sell it. The North Carolina grant was for 3,840 acres.[34]

Thomas Bedford and Colonel Weakley—often referred to as "the first real estate agents of Rutherford County"[35]—scouted out an area between the east and west branches of the Stones River. Both agreed this would be a prime location for a town.

The Stones River was named for Uriah Stone, who ended his journey west on its banks in 1766.[36] The river flows northeast and connects with the Cumberland River, which in turn, passes through Nashville and connects with the Mississippi River. When Bedford and Weakley realized that points as far east as Virginia and as far south as New Orleans could be reached from this spot, they envisioned it as a significant port for the central plains.

Bedford and Weakley arranged to have the new town platted and partially cleared. The town was laid out with 102 town lots and a public square. When this work was completed in the spring of 1803, the partners agreed that the town should be named after the newly elected President, Thomas Jefferson.[37]

Figure 5. East Branch of the Stones River on the shores of Old Jefferson. The river is much calmer now than in 1804, due to the creation of Percy Priest Lake.

In early June, forty lots were sold. The land was thick with woods and cane, and was not easy to clear. By selling the lots, Weakley and Bedford not only brought in some cash, they received help improving the land, for no sooner were the lots sold than the new owners cleared them and built homes and shops.[38] Some lots were given as gifts; one to William Nash, Justice of the Peace, and another to Joseph Herndon, County Trustee for Davidson County, who would soon be Rutherford County's Court Clerk.[39]

~

Most persons, traveled west by wagon train, especially those of lesser means.[40] October was the prime time to travel. During the autumn, with no rain expected, river levels were low and much safer to cross. The temperatures were also more comfortable, being neither too hot, nor cold.[41] The trip to middle Tennessee took several months.

Saying goodbye to family and friends was not easy. It was a time of excitement, but also sadness. The pioneers could not be certain they would ever see their loved ones again. It is thought that Norton's friend/

relative, John Chism, may have traveled with them. His name was listed on the Rutherford County Tax rolls during these early years.[42]

In the wagons, small children sat up front, while most often the men, and even the women, walked behind. Families could take relatively little in their wagons. The most important items were those which could not be found or manufactured in the area of their destination. Since trade routes were not yet open, items such as axes, ploughs, and other metal implements were extremely precious. Seed was also very important. The wagons were piled high with these goods, as well as quilts, pots, and pans, bags of meal, dried pork, and coffee.

The two most important things for any pioneer were a gun and a dog. By 1804, there were few Indian attacks, but one could never be too careful. Some of the natives liked to steal horses. There were also outlaws and bandits, not to mention wild beasts such as bears, wolves and cougars. Each family usually had several dogs trailing along to spot danger, as well as game for their next meal.

Prior to 1804, the pioneers had to make most of their trip west on foot, leading their horses as they climbed over boulders, and attempted to cut their way through the thick brush. By the time the Gum family left for middle Tennessee, a road the width of a wagon had been opened up, and pioneers could go straight through to Nashville, though in some cases, the road was barely wide enough to let the wagons pass.

The trip west was beautiful. It was also difficult. There were mountains to climb, valleys to cross, streams and rivers to try to wade or drive through. After a long day of travel, the pioneers formed a circle with their wagons and cooked their meals around a campfire. Then, they attempted to sleep under the chill, star-filled skies. The howling wolves and hooting owls must have made it difficult. They could only hope these sounds were what they seemed to be, and not Indians planning an attack. One or more persons always stayed up and kept watch. Then, at dawn, they packed up and continued on the trail. Dreams of a great future, and faith in God strengthened these hearty people with the resolve to move forward toward this unknown promised land.

Finally, after a journey of two to three months, the exhausted travelers passed over the final mountain, and saw the great valley beyond. Their relief was immense, for by now, they were nearly out of supplies. The Gums, like so many others, would have traveled by the little town of Nashville with its fenced-in buffalo, log courthouse, and several dirty inns. One more day of travel, and they would reach Rutherford County, the place they would call home for generations to come.

A visitor during this time described his first view of Rutherford County in this way:

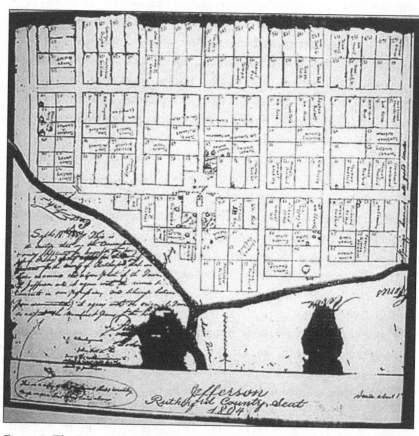

Figure 6. The Original Map of Jefferson dated 1804. The author has filled this copy in with the names of early property owners. At the top of the map, second block of lots from the left, far right of the block, are the four lots, Nos. 125–128, which Billy Norton Gum sold to Nancy Wade in 1850.

(Courtesy of the Rutherford County Property Records Office)

For hundreds of years, forests of oak, poplar, hickory, chestnut, and other trees had grown becoming giant trees. In the fertile soil, vines, wild berries, and flowers all abounded. The vines wound themselves around the trees and brush, forming thick areas that were difficult to pass through. In these forests, the animals lived in peace and multiplied. The rich lands and abundant streams were a kind of paradise to those journeying west....[43]

What joy Norton, Sally, and their four small children, Hannah, Mary, William, and John must have felt arriving in this paradise. Approaching Jefferson, they may have been surprised by the sounds of hammering and sawing. Residents of the village were busy building.

The small town lay on the hill, which rose gently between the rivers' branches. On the crest of the hill, Jefferson's founders were planning to build a town square. The town was only about eight streets deep from the river; some streets being no more than county lanes or alleys. The width of the town also grew greater as it moved away from where the river divided. A lane, running from the top of the hill down to the river, was lined with a few hastily erected shacks. Here, traders and shopkeepers kept busy, trying to sell their goods to those who passed by.

Settlers, who knew the difficulties of pioneering, welcomed the new-comers warmly. In the early days, residents often traveled for miles to bring food and other much-needed provisions to weary, and—most often by now—empty-handed travelers. In addition, the residents assisted in building cabins for the new arrivals. In this wilderness, one could not have a safe abode too soon.

Among the Gums' new neighbors was William Nash, who opened his country store just outside of Jefferson in 1803, around the same time the Gums arrived. Mr. Nash sold dry goods, groceries, gunpowder and whis-key, as well as well as deer, wolf and coon skins. These items were good export for New Orleans—a trip down river which took approximately a month to complete.[44]

In the following months, Jefferson had many new arrivals. It was a bustling place, full of energy as its new citizens worked busily to turn the barren spot into a prosperous town. Log houses were built from the rich supply of cedar trees in the area. Floorboards were made with a saw whip. Hinges for the doors were made of leather. Though glass for windows was scarce, the influx of trade from the river brought paint, and soon people began painting their log cabins in Spanish Brown, yellow ochre and red, making the place look rather "homey" and stylish. Chimneys were built of stone or wood smeared with clay. As more new residents settled, the sight and smell of smoke wafting from the chimneys turned this wilderness spot into a place of home.[45]

It did not take the Gum family long to get settled. Soon after Norton Gum's arrival, he applied to the Commissioners of Rutherford County for permission to open an ordinary in his home. An ordinary was a place, like a tavern, where one could get food, drink, and even lodging. There also might be a stable to feed and house the travelers' horses. According to Rutherford County records, Norton Gum was the first person in Jefferson to be licensed to "keep" an ordinary at "his dwelling house."[46]

At this time, the Rutherford County Commissioners set price controls for ordinaries and taverns. This was beneficial for both customer and tavern owner. With set fees, there could be no arguing over prices. The fees were set as follows, and no price could be charged above these amounts:[47]

Dinner	25 cents
Breakfast & supper	20 cents
Lodging	8 ⅓ cents
Corn or oats per gallon	8 ⅓ cents
Stabling a horse 24 hours with corn, fodder or oats	33 ½ cents
"Good Wisky" ½ pint	12 ½ cents
Peach brandy	12 ½ cents
French brandy, rum or wine	50 cents

At the time, existing currency was in silver and gold. Currency in middle Tennessee was scarce, so most goods and services were paid for by bartering—in the exchange for other goods and services. A four-year steer might be worth as much as $4.00, while a wolf scalp was worth $2.50. Rabbit skins had a value of about fifty cents a dozen.[48]

Down the road from the future square, a new shopkeeper, and future friend of the Gums, Hinchey Petaway stretched a piece of red flannel over his door, symbolizing the fact that he had opened a dry goods store.

Almost every week now, a new house or store went up. Interestingly, lawyers were the most prominent profession in town.[49]

With all the comings and goings of persons into Jefferson, the Gum family's ordinary must have been quite busy. Daughters Hannah and Mary, now between the ages of eight and twelve, helped their mother with the chores of cooking, cleaning, and serving. If the ordinary continued after September of that year, Sally Gum would certainly have needed help, for the Commissioners of Jefferson would have other duties for Norton Gum to attend to.

Chapter 3

Norton Gum in Jefferson

IN JANUARY OF 1804, PUBLIC OFFICIALS AND LOCAL CITIZENS CAME together for the purpose of organizing their new county. Since there were not yet any public buildings, Nimrod Menefee, who lived in the wilderness a little west of Jefferson, volunteered his home for the meeting.

Early on January 3rd, a large group of people, traveling from all directions on narrow cow paths and Indian trails, arrived at Nimrod's cedar log house. Seeing that his home was too small for all the people arriving and that the weather was quite cold, Nimrod built a large log fire just outside his front door where those who were waiting to do business could warm themselves.[50]

Inside the house, William Nash, Justice of the Peace, administered the oaths. Samuel W. McBride was elected Sheriff; John Howell, Ranger; James Sharp, Coroner and William Mitchell, Register.[51] As the men saw their new county take form, there was a sense of pride and excitement in the air.

Among the other items of business taken care of that day was the registration of recently purchased land, branding letters and symbols for cattle. Following this, the most important subject to be discussed was the creation of roads. Recently, many people had moved to Rutherford County, but upon arrival found the only means of travel were trails too narrow to allow a wagon to pass.

At the meeting, Thomas Bedford was appointed first overseer of roads. It was asked that a road be opened from the East–West junction of the

Stones River to the county line toward Nashville, about twenty miles away.[52] After the commissioners met with many citizens, the meeting was adjourned.

Eight months later, in October of 1804, Norton Gum was ordered to appear in Jefferson at the two-story log building just off the square, then being used as a courthouse. Standing before the court with a few other men, Norton received the following commission:

> Ordered by the Court that James Cochran, Andrew McMekin, William Hanna, William Edwards and Norton Gum to lay out a road from Cummins Mill to the Wilson County line near Solomon George's so as to meet the road from Lancaster's Mill at said line and make report thereof to our next County Court.[53]

Upon receiving this assignment, the men were required to take the following oath:

> I, ___, do solemnly swear or affirm that I will lay out the road now directed to be laid out by the court of pleas and quarter session to the greatest advantage of the inhabitants; and with little prejudice to enclosures as may be, without favor, affection, malice or prejudice, and to the best of my skill and knowledge.[54]

In August of that year, Jefferson had been named the seat of justice for Rutherford County. This designation had increased the town's traffic greatly. Sadly, Thomas Bedford died shortly before this and never knew how far Jefferson had come. His widow, Ann, and son, John R. Bedford, became administrators of his estate. Jefferson's land holdings at this point were divided equally between the Bedford and Weakly families.[55]

Meanwhile, Rutherford County's population as a whole was growing rapidly and it soon became evident that even more roads were needed. A few roads led to Jefferson, but for the most part these were trails created by buffalo and Indians. There were also a few paths cut through by early settlers.

That year, 1804, the state of Tennessee passed new legislation regulating the creation of roads. The General Assembly now considered any road previously laid out by a private individual to be a public road. The legislation further stated the newly proposed roads were to be laid out by a jury of five to twelve men.

Norton Gum and the other men were required to "lay out" a road twenty feet wide. To do this, they would have to figure the most direct route and the best lay of the land. The men were to "completely cut and clear all stumps, rocks, brush and obstructions so far as practicable for the width of sixteen feet in the center of the road under their care."[56] Bridges had to be at least sixteen feet across. Money for the construction of roads would come from county taxes.

The legislation further stipulated that the court might call upon any man between the age of eighteen and fifty years of age for the creation of these roads. Generally, men were called to work upon roads within two miles of their homes. They should not by law, be called to work on more than one road.[57] Slave owners could send their male slaves of the same age to work in their stead. (To our knowledge, Norton Gum did not own any slaves at this time.) Other men exempted from this work included ministers, judges, justices of the peace, and other government officials. Anyone refusing to work would be fined 75 cents a day,* which could add up to a significant amount for persons at that time.[58]

In an area that was basically a wilderness of forest and rock, the work was heavy labor. However, with autumn upon them, the men were glad the terrible heat of the Tennessee summer was gone. The morning chill of early autumn turned to comfortably warm weather in the afternoons. Many trees soon would be without leaves, and the rattlesnakes, which were plentiful in this area, would—for the most part—be below ground. Even so, they would have to watch for them.

The men made good progress between October and December, and on January 8th, 1805, Norton Gum received a new job. He was to oversee a road being built from William Edwards's property to the Wilson County line. The commission read further:

> … all hands within three miles of said road on each side, on the north of the East Fork of the Stones River, to work thereon under him.[59]

With winter upon them, a new set of difficulties beset the men. Although Rutherford County receives less snow in winter than many

---

* Approximately $13.59 in 2007.

other areas, the winter months can be quite cold. The building of a road during January and February must have been difficult work.

This time things did not go as smoothly as before. Only a few days after receiving this commission, Norton was hauled into court to answer a charge by John H. Jones. It is not known whether the charges occurred because of the road building, or a more personal matter, but both men hired attorneys. A jury was seated, which included William Edwards, one of the owners of the land where Norton was building the road. The jury found Norton not guilty. John Jones was not satisfied with the verdict and asked for a second trial, which was granted. In April 1805, Norton Gum was exonerated of all charges in this case, which must have been a great relief to him.[60] Generally, he seems to have been a hard worker and well-liked.

Within a few days of exoneration, Mr. Gum was appointed constable of Jefferson. As was customary, William Gilliam and John Hoover placed a bond of $625.00 for him.* This appointment must have been wonderful news for the Gum household.

Life in Jefferson at this time was extremely busy. In April, the commissioners of Rutherford County levied a tax for the purpose of raising money to erect public buildings—including a brick courthouse in the center of the square. Meanwhile, the County Court held its sessions in various locations, making it easier for citizens conduct their business.

At the same time the courthouse was being built, warehouses and wharves were being erected along the river to accommodate the load of goods arriving and departing from Jefferson's port. William P. Anderson "petitioned the court to build a mill on the East fork of the Stones River, about 600 yards from the town of Jefferson." More small shops were springing up along the road running from the river to the square, showing that the town had indeed become a bustling and prosperous place.

July saw the county's first elections, with Jefferson as the polling place. Constant Hardeman, an early resident and owner of several lots in town, and Joseph Herndon were among the court appointed inspectors and judges of the election.

---

* $11, 327 CPI according to measuringworth.com.

Before the end of the month, Norton was busy marking a new road with six other men. The road was to go from Jefferson to Howells Mill, and the men were to make sure the road passed Joseph Herndon's western enclosures, William Gilliam's property on the South, and finally went east to Howells Mill. All of this was to be done "in the nighest [nearest] and best way."[61]

However, July of 1805 would be an important month for Norton Gum, personally and professionally, for other reasons. In this month, the court appointed him "overseer of the streets and Publick Square in the Town of Jefferson." The appointment further stated that "all hands within the limits of the Town to work under him as such."[62]

Norton Gum, who had only lived in Jefferson for a little over a year, had gone from owning an ordinary to being appointed constable, and now overseeing all hands within the limits of the Town of Jefferson. This was quite amazing! One can imagine the sense of importance Mister Gum felt as he walked around the square greeting and being greeted by the locals.

At home, Sally and the children were a lively group. This year saw the Gum brood go from four to five. They called the new baby Robert E. Gum. Although what the "E" stood for is unknown, it is very possible that he was named for Irish Revolutionary, Robert Emmet. If this is so, it would tell us even more about the Gums.* Sally, a strong lady, kept everyone in line, as Norton was a busy man. Along with his other duties, he was often called to court—sometimes as a witness, and other times as a juror.

During this period, John Chism also appeared on several jury lists.[63] In 1806, his name was on a list of petitioners requesting that bridges be built over the East and West forks of the Stones River into Jefferson.[64] Chism appeared on the tax rolls, as John Chism, Esq. signifying that he was an attorney. His financial status and education level were doubtless greater than that of Norton. To the best of knowledge, Norton Gum did not appear on any of the tax rolls.

---

* Robert Emmet (1778-1803) was an Irish patriot who wished to see his homeland out from under British control. He was tried for treason and hanged in 1803.

In October, Norton Gum was called to court in response to a complaint against him by Miles Gibbs. Although court records do not state the content of the case, John Chism appeared as witness on Norton's behalf. In the end, a jury of "goodly men" declared the defendant not guilty.

The year ended on a happier note, when on November 30th, Norton posted a surety bond for the marriage of Timothy Davis and Frances Ross. Timothy was likely a friend of his. The New Year—1806—also began happily because Norton Gum had finished his one-year term as overseer of the roads, and was relieved of his duties.

By the beginning of 1806, Jefferson had grown from a tiny hamlet into a real town. Residents watched with pride as the two-story red brick courthouse, 40 feet square, rose in the public square. The soil of the area had much red clay, so bricks were easily manufactured. In addition to the courthouse, a whipping post, stocks and a pillory were also erected.[65]

Not all those who passed through Jefferson were of good character. In fact, there were many passing through who wished to escape the law. Because of this, the commissioners of the town found it necessary to erect these articles of punishment, hopefully as a deterrent. John Spence explained in his *Annals of Rutherford County* that besides the whipping and branding posts for the punishment of criminals, there were also stocks:

> "In one, the performer stands for hours, head and hands through holes in a half bent position. The other, the preference, in a sitting position, a little reversed, feet and hands through holes...."[66]

In early April 1806, the new Rutherford County Courthouse opened to the public. County Clerk, Joseph Herndon was given an office on the upper floor of the courthouse at the head of the staircase. A small jailhouse made of logs two-stories high also was constructed on the northwest corner of the square. Due to the increase in local crime, the first two patrollers of Jefferson, John Spence[67] and William Gilliam, were appointed.[68] Other patrollers were assigned for various parts of the county.

As a thriving town, Jefferson saw many types of people pass along her streets. There were farmers, politicians, slave traders, manufacturers, and every other kind of person imaginable. Many illustrious guests also found their way to Jefferson. Men like Indian War hero and future president, Andrew Jackson could often be seen about town. Another frequent visitor was Felix Grundy, former Chief Justice of Kentucky's Supreme Court. Grundy moved to area around 1807, and by 1811 was serving as a member of the U.S. House of Representatives. Eventually, Mr. Grundy became Attorney General of the United States.

Jefferson seems to have been an interesting place to live. In the *Annals of Rutherford County*, John Spence notes several places of entertainment in Jefferson. Outside, these taverns were swinging signs and horse posts for travelers. Inside, one could find a gallon bowl with hot apple toddy, and large barrels marked "Brandy," "Rum" and "Whiskey." The rooms usually had immense stone fireplaces, where—in the early days—old Revolutionary War soldiers gathered to recall and fight the old battles again, while the younger men gathered around, listening for hours to their tales.[69]

Traditionally, taverns were places of information. Hunters, explorers, scholars, and politicians gathered there to tell tales and discuss ideas. The ideas often included how the government should be run and the future of America. It was a very stimulating time, but the effects of strong whiskey had varying results for different people, and as previously mentioned, not all persons traveling through Jefferson were of good character. Along with the pleasant moments of socializing, tempers could be short.

Among Jefferson's visitors, there were men who after a drink of whisky might easily turn a hand on the shoulder into a brawl. In Rutherford County, guns were seldom used for any purpose but hunting. Most often fists, and sometimes knives, found their way into the tavern brawls. As time went on, these brawls became increasingly common, causing the small log jail—with its upper loft for sleeping—to be full.

During this period, it seems there was some extremely good, or potent whiskey being sold in the area. Liquor was known as "spirits," and no election was conducted without it. The whiskey available in Jefferson was made from corn juice, which seemed innocent enough, but its effects were powerful. It not only "exhilarated" the drinker, it blunted the mind, making those who drank it more combative than usual.

John Spence describes the use of these "spirits" as a kind of disease taking over the population. "The spirits," he wrote, created a "long worm ... emitting a slow poison exhilarating in the first stages, in the second, find the patient ... inclined to be quarrelsome, fighting, stealing and often murdering ... [and finally], in the third and last stages, having lost all respect for himself ... becomes lean and abandoned to the lowest depths. A disposition to drink all he can get, loss of appetite being reduced, delirium tremors come on, Death finishes his career."[70]

According to Spence, this addiction to whiskey had become an epidemic in the area of Jefferson, and it appears Norton Gum was no stranger to it.

In April of 1806, three men were called to appear before a Grand Jury. Bills of indictment for assault and battery were presented against them. One of the three men was Norton Gum; the others were Thomas Mitchell and Patton Anderson. The men had caused a huge brawl, and the charges were serious.

A short time after this, the court recorded another case: *The State vs. Norton Gum*. In this trial, Norton pleaded guilty. As was the custom, Crozier Craig, Mathew Haley and Hiram Kile were paid to appear as witnesses for three days.[71] At the trial's conclusion, Norton was charged and fined $10.*

While business boomed in Jefferson at the offset, there were those who fell into trouble over time. As with any group of people in business, some succeeded and some failed. As constable, it was Norton Gum's sad duty to collect fines from residents who could not pay their bills, and ultimately, conduct a sale of their property.

In the same month of his great trouble, Norton ordered that Mr. John Murell's lot, No. 53, be sold to pay his debts. Norton was required to oversee the sale and sign the documents. Later that month, he was required to levy fines on two lots belonging to the business of Dederick and Petway. The court then ordered that two lots owned by the men—Nos. 118 and 140—be sold to pay their debts. Since Norton was friends with Mr. Petway, this could not have been an easy task.

Toward the end of 1806, the court received and accepted two more requests for ordinaries in Jefferson. One request was by Thomas Mitchell— the very same man who had been indicted with Norton Gum for assault

---

* $10 equaling approximately $157.00 in 2006.

and battery. Mr. Mitchell was requesting to have an ordinary in his dwelling place. The other request came from John Nash Reade. Reade's Tavern would be the largest in Jefferson, with stables on East Main Street.[72] It was a place Andrew Jackson often spent the night when he was in town. Whether or not the Gums still had their ordinary at this time is unknown.

Financially, the Gum family seemed to be doing well. On October 23rd, Norton Gum attended John Miller's estate sale and purchased several items. Around the same time, he and his friend, Hinchey Petway attended another auction where they each purchased a horse. Norton's was a fine black stallion for which he paid around $35 (approximately $566 in 2007).[73]

Despite the growth of Jefferson, the surrounding woods held plenty of game. Most residents had dogs and went hunting as needed. Others were regular hunters and dressed in buckskin (like Davy Crocket), traveling with two or more "bear dogs." These hunters shared their bear and deer meat with others in the settlement.[74]

The settlers who kept hogs, allowed them to run wild; to feed and fatten on the plentiful foliage in the woods. In October—after the first chill—the men of Jefferson gathered together and hunted down the hogs. A hole was dug in the ground and a fire built there. Then, a large pot was placed in the hole over the fire and filled with water. To heat the water quickly, large, red-hot stones were dropped into it. Once the water had reached boiling point, the bodies of the slain hogs were dropped into the pot to help remove their bristles. This was the first step toward getting them ready for the smoke house.

Of all the dogs living in the area, one of the town favorites was a shaggy eighteen-pound dog named Sampson. He knew his place, and because of this at hog-killing time each year he was allowed in the preparation area, where the settlers enjoyed giving him a few scraps of meat for a treat.

This particular year, a new resident had moved into town, bringing with him a large, rather hostile dog. At hog-killing time, this cur showed up, greedy for whatever he could find, and began chomping into the loose pieces of meat lying around the camp.

Sampson, on seeing this, rushed in, and attempted to scare the intruder off. He knew it was not right for the dog to take the meat. The other dog however, weighed nearly sixty pounds, and lunged at little Sampson.

Grabbing him, the cur shook him like prey, and tossed him into the pot of boiling water. The men yelled. One grabbed a rake and lifted Sampson out. It was not quick enough. Sampson came out of the pot steaming, but he was not licked yet. Snarling, yelping, and growling, he flew at the other dog, his fur flying off of him, as the steam rose from his body. The large dog took one look at him and ran away, yelping in terror.

Sampson never did get his fur back. He remained hairless, but according to legend, lived to a ripe old age—"a true example of the fearless and vanity-free pioneering spirit."[75] This too, was life in Jefferson.

By early 1807, there had been some robberies and other crimes around town, causing the citizens to fear for their safety. The Court appraised the situation and decided there should be night patrollers on the streets.

Figure 7. The logs in this building are said to have been part of the jail in Old Jefferson— the very place Norton Gum was imprisoned on more than one occasion. The building now stands on private property.

Beginning in January, Norton Gum and William Locke were assigned the night-time job of patrolling the streets, docks and shoreline.

After six months of carrying a torch to light his way on the dark streets and docks, Norton was once again appointed Constable. He took over this appointment in July of 1807. William Locke and John Bradley signed a bond for him in the sum of $620.

At this time, most people let their cows and other livestock roam wherever they pleased. To keep track of which livestock was theirs, they would either brand them, or cut their ears. Some put bells on their animals to mark them. In addition to the larger beasts, there were also a multitude of dogs, cats, and other small animals running free. Residents had come and gone with little care for these animals, and in time, the situation was out of hand. In the late summer of 1807, the Commissioners gave Norton Gum $47 to build the first animal pound in Jefferson.[76]

Like many other men of the area, Norton spent some of his free time having a drink or two at the tavern, and as stated before, brawls were a way of life in these taverns. So it was, in October of 1807 after taking part in a brawl, Norton found himself in jail for four days.[77]

~

By early 1808, Norton Gum was in more trouble than before. John R. Bedford, son of the late Thomas Bedford, had won a case against James Locke. The security money—deposited before the trial—was to be held by the constable—in this case Norton—and at the close of the case, was legally to be turned over to Mr. Bedford.

In January, John Bedford went to court against Norton Gum demanding that his securities be turned over to him. Whether Norton refused for personal reasons, or had borrowed public money and did not have it, is unknown. At the time, few persons carried money—which would have been in silver or gold. In any case, Norton Gum was ruled against and ordered to pay John Bedford his $15,* along with the costs of the warrant and motion.[78] What occurred between Norton Gum and John Bedford is unknown however, the case seems to have been settled shortly thereafter.

---

* $15 would be approximately $255.56 in 2007.

Despite the aforementioned events, the Gum family was still doing fairly well. Early that year, Norton acquired two properties which were recorded by the court. The first was the acquisition of a female slave; a "Negro woman" named Hannah, who was sold to Norton Gum by Micajah Peacock on February 9, 1808 for $400.00.* [79]

Hannah may have been a gift to Norton's wife, Sally, to help around the house. There were few persons in middle Tennessee who did not own at least one slave at this time. Pioneering life was difficult, and slavery was often seen as a necessity, as well as a symbol of prosperity. Slaveholders were looked up to as persons of means. According to record, Hannah was the only slave Norton and Sally Gum ever owned.

The second property transaction made by Norton Gum at this time remains a mystery. When the Gum family arrived in Jefferson in 1804, no deed was recorded showing the purchase of land. Possibly, the family acquired property without recording it—which was sometimes done. The Rutherford County Property Index indicates Norton Gum purchased one or more lots from the Commissioners of Jefferson in 1808. The exact information regarding this transaction no longer exits. The book containing the handwritten copy of the deed, "Book G," is one of the few missing from the Rutherford County Records Office. Book "G" was either lost when the Jefferson Courthouse was abandoned, or was one of those burnt in 1861 during Union occupation. (An attempt to trace the property backwards did not succeed.)

In April of 1809, after a short period of peace, Norton Gum received more bad news. He was called into court for a case titled *The State vs. Norton Gum*. The details of this case are unknown. The record simply states Norton Gum was "charged and pleaded guilty, fined one cent beside costs in this behalf expended."[80]

Three months later, when merchants Dederick & Petway brought a case to court against Norton Gum and Jackob Fowler, the two defendants did not even bother to appear. As a result, the judge entered a judgment in favor of Dederick and Petway. The costs of the suit to be

---

* $400 would be approximately $6,626.00 in 2006.

collected from Gum and Fowler included a fee of $62.82* plus interest from October 1807.[81]

Norton's situation was not getting any better. For a man who had come early to Rutherford County and risen quickly, his star was sinking. Whether he was drinking, tired or otherwise affected, the instances of being called to court did not end here. In October 1809, the *State vs. Norton Gum* came to trial. The court record states: "Defendant submits, fined $50 and costs."[82]

In April of that same year, another case appeared on the record books against Norton Gum titled, *Thomas Williamson vs. Norton Gum. Debt.*[83] The jury decided in favor of plaintiff Williamson. Norton Gum owed him, and the jury's decision was to "assess his damages by reason of the detention of his said debt..." The total amount awarded Mr. Williamson came to $104.72, a hefty sum at the time. (Approximately $1,373.33 in 2007.)[84]

Shortly after this, another case was called against Norton by one Alexander McMillen. The case was serious; one of assault and battery.[85] The jury consisted of men Norton had known and worked with, including Hiram Jenkins, John Bradley and William Locke. There is little doubt Norton's temper was short, and his situation dire. We can picture Norton Gum's unhappy face as he sat in the same courthouse he had watched being built, on the very square where he had been in charge of all hands, now charged with a serious offence of assault and battery.

The jury found in favor of Alexander McMillan. Norton Gum was to pay damages in the amount of $250 ($3,774 in 2006 values.)[86] The damage to Mr. McMillen must have been quite severe, and the jury obviously felt he was innocent of Norton Gum's response to him.

Norton, with his many offences and fines, was sinking. Folks in Jefferson no doubt viewed him with contempt, and questioned his ability to keep his job, or behave in a responsible manner. The depression and sadness of the entire Gum family must have been intense. If they were unable to pay the fines, Norton would likely be imprisoned, and they would be forced into the poorhouse.

---

* $62.82 would be approximately $948.28, and $50 = $754.86 in 2006. http://www.measuringworth.com

Poor Sally. The Gum daughters, Mary and Hannah were young ladies now, between twelve and fifteen years of age. The sons, William, John, and Robert were old enough to hear their father called names and be teased by their playmates, in the way children do. What an unhappy place the once bustling and prosperous home had become.

In July of 1809, Norton Gum was still working as constable for Rutherford County. In the case of *Micajah Peacock* (the man who sold him Hannah) *vs. Samuel McBride & Norton Gum*, Norton was sent to jail. John Orr, a man who owned over three hundred acres of land in the area, bailed him out, and delivered him to court.[87]

In the court records, there is an additional note on Obediah M. Benge, a forty-five year old Revolutionary War veteran from Virginia, who was rumored to have married a Cherokee woman and had children with her.[88] The note regarding Norton Gum states that Benge "acknowledges himself special bail."[89] It seems Norton had some interesting friends and acquaintances, who were willing to help him in his time of need.

The trial was not settled in July. Possibly Norton called for a retrial. The final decision came in October. In the case of *Micajah Peacock vs. N. Gum & S. McBride*, the jury found for the plaintiff. Gum and McBride owed a debt of $150 with damages of $6.98.[90] This is the last official record of Norton Gum.

What happened to Norton Gum after this last trial? Perhaps he retired from public life, and settled down to farm his land. He had had a full career in both Knox and Rutherford Counties. Some have also suggested Norton Gum went to prison to pay for his crimes and debts. With his temper, he also may have found himself challenged to a duel. Life in Jefferson was not the Wild West, but it was a rough place. Men who were tough enough to withstand the cold, rough land, Indian attacks and wild beasts, also had high tempers and quick hands. Many, like neighboring Andrew Jackson, fought duels.

We will likely never know what happened to Norton Gum. What we do know is that after his rise on the square of Jefferson, he had much trouble. Then, some time after 1809, he disappeared from public life forever.

Chapter 4

Murfreesborough

I N THE FIRST YEARS OF ITS EXISTENCE, LIFE FOR THE RESIDENTS OF JEF-
ferson was fairly prosperous. Then, with each succeeding year, more
and more people became unhappy with the town's position as county
seat. To begin with, Jefferson was no where near the center of Rutherford
County. It took some residents almost a full day of travel to get there.

Geographically, there was another problem. Each year during the rainy
season, the Stones River flooded the surrounding area, often turning
Jefferson into an island. Then, as time went on, the situation began to
reverse. During the summer, river levels became so low that even the
flat-bottom and keel boats—popular for delivering goods—could not get
through.

In 1811, the General Assembly concurred with the citizens' opinion
and passed an Act to establish a new county seat.[91] Those living in Jefferson were naturally upset. The removal of the courts from the town
would mean a great loss of traffic, and thus business. Jefferson's residents
even took up a petition to protest the change, asking remuneration for
their losses, but to no avail.[92]

The Act changing the county seat was passed on October 17th, 1811. It
stated that sixty acres of land in an area all approved of would be donated
for a town which would serve as the new county seat. The town was to
be called Cannonsburgh.[93]

Captain William Lytle offered sixty acres of his land for the new town.
All agreed that this was an excellent location. It was suggested that

rather than Cannonsburgh, the town be named in honor of Captain Lytle. Mr. Lytle—who was grieving the passing of his dear friend, Revolutionary War hero, Colonel Hardee Murfree—asked that the town be named after Murfree instead. Col. Murfree's son then donated some of his father's land, which was in the same area as the Lytle property. So it was that the town of Murfreesborough was established.

The land for the town lay on a slightly inclined plateau just across from Lytle Creek. This land, sat above most of the surrounding area, which meant that when the courthouse was built, it would be seen in the distance for many miles.

In 1812, the Commissioners of the County agreed to meet on Captain Lytle's property to discuss the formation of the new town. Interest in the subject was great, and many of the county residents attended. The meeting took place in a grove of trees near William Lytle's house. A table was laid with food and "good liquor." The day passed quickly and many expressed their opinions on the founding of the new county seat. As the hours passed, many persons lay in the grass, and spoke of other matters such as deer hunting.[94] This, too, was life in Rutherford County then.

When the vote was taken, the Lytle land was chosen four to three. In June, the town was surveyed and platted, and the streets were named. By August, town lots were being sold. The land—which was covered with heavy timber, brush, cane, and grapevines—was no small job to clear, but the town rose quickly.

A log courthouse, stocks and prison soon were built. On the square surrounding these buildings, some put up temporary stores and homes to get their businesses started. Eventually, many of the stores made of logs were covered with boards, and then painted yellow ochre, or Venetian red. A good portion of the stores on the new Murfreesborough square were owned by merchants who had moved there from Jefferson.

In a few years, Murfreesborough would serve as Tennessee's state capital, and her courthouse as the capitol building. Men like Andrew Jackson, James K. Polk, David Crockett and Sam Houston would all be familiar figures around the square. It would not be unusual to see Andrew Jackson in town to have a new suit fitted, or Davy Crockett meeting with his local kin folks.

A good number of Jefferson's one hundred and fifteen residents moved to Murfreesborough. As a result, some of the town's originally platted lots were bought up by residents and turned into small farms. Though river trade and the inspection of goods continued, the old brick court building sat in the middle of the square, vacant and unused. Slowly, Jefferson would change; never again to be the bustling place it once was.

Chapter 5

The Marable Family

NOW THAT RUTHERFORD COUNTY WAS WELL-ESTABLISHED, MANY respected and interesting families began to arrive. One of these was the Marable Family (pronounced mahr-ble). The Marables, who originated in England, were considered a fine old American family, having resided in the Jamestown Colony as early as 1663.[95]

In 1800, a Marable descendant, Henry Hartwell Marable was listed on the Brunswick County, Virginia census as a farmer owning 300 acres of land. Marable had married in 1775, at the age of twenty-two. His bride, the lovely Elizabeth Mason was eighteen. Two years later, around the time their first child was born, Henry Hartwell converted to Methodism. Five years later, Mr. Marable became a Methodist preacher.

Methodism had begun as a movement in England around 1729, however, it did not become a separate church until 1791. Three years later, the Methodist Church was founded in the United States. Based on John Wesley's belief that the study of the Bible would lead to the perfection desired by God, many itinerant preachers were inspired to travel, spreading the Word. Their work was done without hope of recompense. It was a passion of the soul.

Sometime around 1807, Mr. Marable and his wife, Elizabeth, decided to leave Brunswick Country, Virginia and move to the wilds of Tennessee. What role Reverend Marable's calling as a Methodist minister played in this decision is unknown, but it seems likely that his vocation to spread the word of Christ played some part in the family's move. In 1807, it was not so usual for a man of fifty-four years to give up his home, and move his entire family to the "wild west."

After selling the family's 350-acre farm in Pea Hill Creek, Sussex County for $1300, the Marable family packed up their home of thirty years, and set off to begin a new life.[96] The traveling party included Rev. Marable, his wife, Elizabeth, and six of their children. There was Braxton in his late 20s, who was married with two children, John, 21, who had just completed medical school at the University of Pennsylvania, Travis, 17, Henry Jr., 14, their only daughter, Elizabeth, 11, and the youngest, Isaac, 10. (It should be noted that prior to attending medical school in Philadelphia, John was educated privately by a tutor.[97] This may have been true for the other children as well.) Also traveling with the Marables were nine slaves and their children.

Staying behind in Virginia was the Marable's second son, thirty year-old Benjamin. Benjamin was a farmer, and had been married to Lucy Barner for eight years. The couple had three small sons, and apparently were not ready to make a move of this kind, nor perhaps, did they have the desire.

The Marables were a handsome family. The men were tall with dark hair and tended to be "barrel-chested." The women, in their own way, passed on this trait, having broader shoulders, and smaller hips—something that often was accentuated in later life.[98]

To journey west, most likely the Marables traveled by river. This was the preferred route for persons of means in the early 1800s. It was the easiest and quickest way to travel. Traveling by river allowed the settlers to carry a large amount of goods, including furniture and farming equipment.

The pioneers took their belongings in horse-drawn wagons to the Ohio River. Here, they boarded boats which brought them to the Cumberland River and Nashville. The trip to middle Tennessee was approximately 300 miles by river and took about a month to complete.

Immediately after arriving in Rutherford County, the Marables may have stayed with friends from Virginia. There were also quite a few inns around Jefferson which could have accommodated them. Since no record of early land holdings by the Marables exist, we can only guess how they lived during their first years in middle Tennessee.

In Jefferson—as in many Southern cities—Saturday was market day. Along with the sale of crops and cattle, there were auctions for the sale of black men, women and children held on the courthouse steps. Slave traders came from as far as North Carolina and Virginia to sell their human goods. The traders knew that the new landowners had need of laborers to clear and farm the land, and that they would be willing to pay good prices for these able-bodied persons of African descent.

In some cases, the slaves had been taken from local citizens who were in debt. All were sold at auction to the highest bidder with little thought or concern about breaking up families. At one auction in 1807, Jefferson resident, Hinchey Petway, bought an eleven year-old boy named Morgan, and an eighteen month-old baby named Isaac. These sales were recorded in the Rutherford County Property Record Books along with other property sales.

The first publicly recorded transactions by a Marable in Rutherford County took place in late 1807 and pertained to the buying and selling of three slaves. The sale—as recorded in Rutherford County Property Records, Book M, page 179—states as follows:

> "Know all men by these present that I, Henry H. Marable of Rutherford County & State of Tennessee have this day bargained, sold and delivered unto Edmund Jones of Halifax County & State of North Carolina all my right title and interest & claims to three Negroes, viz Bob & Peter; two Negro men, and Dorcas, one Negro woman, this day bought at public sale for and in consideration of the sum of nine hundred and six dollars* to me in hand paid by the said Edmund Jones as witness my hand and seal this, the 8th day of October 1807.

What is odd about this sale is that after selling these three persons of color, Henry H. Marable—almost immediately—bought them back. This seems to have been a frequent occurrence with both slaves and property. Possibly these transactions were the means by which owners could gain collateral, or cash, to purchase land, without the loss of their slaves.

The following year, 1808, saw the marriage of the Marables' son, Dr. John Hartwell Marable. After his marriage, Dr. Marable moved north

---

* $15,887.00 in 2007 terms per http://www.measuringworth.com

Figure 8. Dr. John Hartwell Marable, son of Rev. Henry Hartwell Marable and brother of Benjamin.

to Davidson County. His new wife, Anne Watson was the daughter of Thomas Watson, a former business partner of Andrew Jackson.

John Marable's marriage would lead him to a new and exciting life; one that involved not only medicine, but politics. In Davidson County, John Marable would come to know some of the most important men of his day, including Andrew Jackson and Sam Houston, both with whom he corresponded over time.[99]

The other Marable sons; Braxton, Travis and Isaac bought property in the area surrounding Jefferson. This area is now in the town of Smyrna. These Marables also owned slaves, which property records show—they both sold and gave to one another—in order to keep them in the family. In 1817, Braxton Marable had trouble with one of his slaves as noted in the Rutherford County Court Records. The "Negro" (as he was referred to) had been jailed and was being kept on the property of the jailor. During this time, he apparently did some damage to the jailor's property for which Braxton was fined. Later, this same man was charged with burning the property of Constant Hardeman.

Considering the treatment of slaves at this time, it seems difficult to imagine that any slave would misbehave. It was noted at the time that while a white man convicted of murder might be let off with a fine, a black man convicted of a minor offense would often be hung.

~

Rutherford County Property Records show that on January 1, 1817, Henry H. Marable bought 100 acres of land by Harts Spring from John Moseby. The following year, Marable bought another 115 aces adjoining that property from Cary James. The property lay on the west side of Stewart's Creek, a branch of the Stones River.[100] The land here is flat, with rich soil for farming, and plenty of water from streams and creeks. It was a huge job to clear the land, much of which was still full of wild vegetation and rock. This was the slaves' job. During these years, Rev. Marable's ownership of slaves increased from nine to thirty.[101]

A portion of Rev. Marable's newly acquired land included a gently sloping hill where wildflowers bloomed. Here the Marable home was built; a two-story log house with a tall stone chimney at one end. At

Figure 9. Rev. Henry Hartwell Marable's log home now resides at the Sam Davis Home in Smyrna, TN, and is preserved as the birthplace of Sam Davis, a Southern hero. (Courtesy of the Sam Davis Foundation)

the other end, was a smaller one-story log cabin. It was here that the meals were prepared. Fires occurred so frequently, it was thought best to keep the kitchen separate from the home. The kitchen was connected to the house by a roof-covered walkway known as a "dogtrot"—so-called because of the way the dogs ran between the house and the kitchen to see what treats they might get. With few homes in the area at this time, the two-story Marable home, sitting north of Almaville Road and west of the Old Nashville Highway, could be seen from miles away.

There were four windows on both the front and back of the home, with a door in the center. The entrance faced away from Almaville Road, and had an upstairs and downstairs veranda the full length of the house. Here the family could rest on the hot summer days, and view the lands beyond. Not far from the Marable home were many small log cabins where the servants lived.

The Marables came to love Rutherford County. The beautiful rolling hills, the rich crops, the distant trees against the blue and cloudless sky—all these touched the heart. The wildlife, now less abundant than once, was still rich with songbirds, rabbits and deer. Cattle grazed along the streams and creeks, which sang as the waters rippled and flowed on their way. In this land, the Marables felt the abundance of God's grace.

Along with country living, Rutherford County was quite a social place. There were house parties, balls, horse races, and in the town of Murfreesboro, a theater where touring actors performed. From various writers' descriptions, Rutherford County during this period seems to have been like something out of Jane Austin's England. In fact, many of the local residents were of Scotch, Irish and English descent.

In October of 1815, a young man in his early twenties, Samuel Hervey McLaughlin, moved to Murfreesboro to begin his practice of law. In later years, McLaughlin wrote about his "sojourn" in the town and of a visit with the Marables. During his stay, Mr. McLaughlin lived in Mitchell's Tavern on the east side of the Murfreesboro public square. It was here that he first met future President James K. Polk, who was attending Bradley Academy. During this time, Polk met his future wife, Sarah Childress. Sarah was the daughter of Joel Childress, a merchant and local tavern owner. His tavern house—where the family also lived—was on the west side of the square.[102]

In his story, Mr. McLaughlin says that the "most prevailing and fashionable vice" at that time was gaming.[103] Cards games and billiards were played for money out in the open, and even the most respected businessmen took part in them.

One day, Samuel McLaughlin agreed to go out riding with Dr. Clarke, a well-respected physician in the area. It seems, on occasion the doctor had a problem with alcohol. His friends suggested that some exercise in the form of a ride in the country might help him overcome his desire.

Dr. Clarke was a former resident of Virginia, and apparently an old friend of Reverend Henry Hartwell Marable, so after "a glass of toddy" he led the way out the old Nashville Road to the Marable home. Mr. McLaughlin writes,

"We dashed on until we got to old Mr. Hartwell Marable's.... We stopped and went into the house, he introducing me to the old people." (Rev. and Mrs. Marable were in their mid-sixties.)

McLaughlin comments that when they arrived, Dr. Clarke was nearly sober, and did not ask for anything to drink.[104] It might be assumed from this that the Marables did not believe in the imbibing of alcohol. Apparently, Dr. Clarke really wanted a drink, so he left the house and went to a blacksmith's shop they had passed earlier. Here, he was able to get some whiskey.

The men returned to the Marable home briefly. By now, Dr. Clarke was quite intoxicated and talking more than he would ordinarily. Rev. Marable invited them to dinner, but Dr. Clarke said they had to go on to Captain Bass' home, so the two men left.

Mr. McLaughlin says that on leaving the home, they traveled down the Shelbyville Road, and "turned off at the corner of Mr. Marable's fence to the south." There, they crossed Stewart's Creek (also part of the Marable property border), and went through Searcy's, or White's Mill Dam, to visit the Bass and Howse families in the Blackman area.[105] All this is a fascinating glimpse into the past life of Rutherford County.

While the Marable slaves farmed the land—a business which apparently did quite well—Rev. Marable's main concern was preaching the Word of God. In this central location, he was able to reach many surrounding areas. As an older gentlemen, he had not the endurance to be circuit rider (a preacher who rode from location to location on horseback), but held church services in his own home, and possibly neighboring homes.

Early Rutherford County was not a God-fearing, Bible worshipping area. As mentioned before, some of the men who came through these parts were criminals escaping the law. Others wished to live by no set rules; however Sunday services were the one time in the week when people could get together. Through the hard work, even life-risking work of the early preachers whose belief in God was strong, the people of Tennessee became a religious Christian people.

Beginning in 1810, during the height of the summer, tent meetings were held. At that time, stores closed and business of all kind ceased as people came from miles away to camp and listen to many different preachers –all for the good of their souls. Rev. Marable, with his powerful voice, likely preached at some of these tent meetings where singing, shouting and praying took place without restraint.[106] It is said that if a preacher preached "fire and brimstone," there was little doubt that intense religious feeling would follow. In the midst of singing hymns, men and women would shout and be filled with joy. There was no need to be proper or restrained at these spiritual events.[107]

Reverend Marable's obituary would later state that he preached "the doctrine" for fifty years. From this we may assume that although he did not have a church, he kept very busy between 1783 and 1833.

While living in Rutherford County, Rev. Marable sold both land and slaves to his children. He also made gifts of these to his children. Most notable of his gifts were the 100 acres he gave to his son Travis in 1819. Even with this, by 1830 the estate of Henry Hartwell Marable was of good size. It included 37 slaves, 33 head of cattle, 50 hogs, 24 sheep, 9 horses, 6 ploughs, 16 hoes, one ox cart, 4 ovens and 7 axes.[108]

Hartwell and Elizabeth Marable had much success and happiness during their years in Tennessee, but there was also great sorrow. In 1819, their youngest son, Isaac died at the age of twenty-two. Left behind were his wife, Elizabeth, and three small children.

The following year was much happier for the Marables as they learned their son Benjamin had finally decided to join them in Tennessee. It seems that quite a few families from Brunswick County, Virginia, including the Howse family, had recently moved to Rutherford County. Benjamin's brother, Dr. John was doing quite well, and was serving as a Tennessee State Senator. All these events may have helped convince Benjamin that a move to Tennessee would be wise.

Since his parents had moved west, Benjamin Marable's family had grown by two. In October of 1808, his son and namesake, Benjamin jr. was born. Then on August 6, 1812, a little girl, whom they named Mary Ann was born. Now that Mary Ann was eight years old, the family was ready to make the journey.

Benjamin, like his father, farmed the land and owned a number of slaves. It is believed that Mary Ann had her own servant and companion at this time—a little black girl about her own age named Miranda, or "Miranday" (as it was pronounced). In the south, it was common for children to be raised by their black "Mammy." They also spent time playing with the young black children. Often,—whether then, or later—one of these young children would become their personal servants. Thus, the bond was very close. In general, it was not unusual for there to be more affection and intimacy between the white children and black men and women who cared for them, than with their own white parents. That relationship was one of proper behavior and custom.[109]

As the youngest child in a large family, Mary Ann grew up in a very social atmosphere and was not shy. She was a bright young girl, who enjoyed people and new adventures.

On their arrival in Rutherford, Benjamin and his family probably stayed with Rev. and Mrs. Marable. Their household was one of Christian charity, with a great deal of thought and care for others. During these early years, Mary Ann learned from her grandparents—as well as her parents—how to be polite, kind, and concerned about the welfare of others.[110]

Once the family had recovered from their journey, Benjamin Marable began to look for land to purchase. He rode his horse south along Shelbyville Road—the same path which Samuel McLaughlin had taken with Dr. Clarke on their visit. Traveling this way, Benjamin came to a wide expanse of farmland which would later be known as the "Blackman Community." The farmland here was flat and free of stone with some of the richest soil in the county. Most of the people living in this area had been there for ten to twenty years. They were hardworking, cultured and religious people, and they were doing quite well financially.

Ben Marable met a gentleman named John Burlason, who agreed to sell 100 acres of good farmland for $1,000. The land had come from General James Armstrong's original claim—a payment for his years of service in the Revolutionary War. The purchase, which took place on the 6th of February 1821, stated that the land began at "two dogwood trees" going "one hundred and sixty poles" south, "sixty-two and half poles" west, then south, "sixty-two poles to a walnut tree, west sixty-two and one half poles to a dogwood and ironwood, then south ninety-eight poles to a post oak," and east "one hundred and twenty-five poles to the beginning." There was a barn and some other "appurtenances" included with the land.[111]

In December, Benjamin Marable bought a seventy-five acre plot next to the land he had just purchased. For this purchase from Jesse Bethshears, he paid $750.00—about $10 an acre. The property contained some buildings and also woods, mainly consisting of cedar trees.[112] From these woods, Benjamin Marable had his slaves build a house.

On their arrival, the early settlers had built one and two room log cabins to live in. The style was quickly changing, however. Now people wanted homes that looked more elegant. To do this, they were covering the logs with boards. Dr. Manson, who lived down the road from Benjamin Marable, near the Wilkinson's crossroads, had done this to his home. Many other homes in the area, such as the Oaklands Mansion in Murfreesboro, had begun with a log cabin that over the years was added to and covered over.

In time, Mr. Marable's home probably looked very similar to his neighbors' with upstairs and downstairs porticos to sit on during the hot summer days. The interior of the homes had painted walls, or wallpaper, elegant mantles, and framed windows. Benjamin Marable would have followed in the style of his neighbors, the Smith, Howse and Manson families down the road, and that of his brother, Dr. John Marable.

The Marables were now Tennesseans; firmly entrenched in her customs and styles. While Travis and Isaac had trouble keeping their money, Benjamin lived quietly and securely. He was an educated man; a man of means who was happy to live in peace with his wife, a kind and devout woman, and his children.

Chapter 6

The Crosthwaits

SOMETIME AROUND 1810, ANOTHER INTERESTING IMMIGRANT ARRIVED in Rutherford County. Shelton Crosthwait came to town with a three-hundred acre land grant and settled just above the town of Jefferson, on the northeast side of the Stones River fork. Within a short amount of time, these three hundred acres would become three thousand.

Shelton Crosthwait was a member of the very cultured Crosthwait family of Virginia. The Crosthwaits, like the Marables, were from England, and had settled in the colonies early. By the early 1700s, they were living in Pennsylvania. It is said that Shelton's father, was the same William Crosthwait who helped Benjamin Franklin set up the library in Philadelphia.[113] Shortly after this period, William moved to Spotsylvania, Virginia and then to Orange County, where Shelton was born in 1775.

As a young man, Shelton worked as a bookkeeper.[114] He married Elizabeth Thompson, a native Virginian, born in 1785. Together they had three children: Mary, George Divers and Rebecca. Photos of Shelton and Elizabeth's grandchildren reveal a very handsome family of finely proportioned features and wavy, golden hair.

The Crosthwait mansion sat on a hill overlooking the Stones River. It was built in the style of many early 1800s homes, with one long hallway running down the center of the home, and entrance doors at either end. When opened on hot summer days, these doors allowed a breeze to pass down the long hallway and throughout the entire house.

Down the hill and away from the house were slave cabins where forty black men and women, and their children lived. Beyond this were the acres of cotton, corn and other crops which the slaves labored over. The Crosthwait plantation was a beautiful place, and must have seemed idyllic to those who did not face the harshness of slavery. An overseer took care of the property and the slaves, so Mr. Crosthwait did not have to concern himself with the day to day difficulties of running such a large plantation. Instead, he concentrated on increasing his holdings, and political matters in the town which were of interest to him.

On arriving in Rutherford County, Shelton Crosthwait quickly became involved in county life. Not one to sit quietly by, one of his first ventures was to work with several other men of the Jefferson community to turn the abandoned Jefferson Courthouse into a school for boys. Shelton believed strongly in education.

Although civic-minded, Shelton Crosthwait was a tough businessman. He would not allow a debt to go unpaid. If a man owed him money, he did not hesitate to take him to court in order to get his due. Many court cases will attest to this fact, including one case against the Braxton Marable, the son of Rev. Henry H. Marable, who owed Mr. Crosthwait $135.00 (approximately $2,348 in 2007 terms).[115]

Over time, many of the Crosthwait relatives settled further north in Kentucky. Only his brother, Thomas, chose to join him in the area of Jefferson. There are mentions of the fact that Thomas had other sons, but according to available information, the only members of his family residing in Rutherford County were his wife, Elizabeth, and his youngest son, William.

In 1815, Thomas Crosthwait, realizing that he was not well, wrote his will. It read as follows:

In the name of God, Amen, I, Thomas Crosthwait of the County of Rutherford in the state of Tennessee, being of sound mind and memory, do make this my last will and testament—First, confiding in the justice and mercy of the creator of the Universe, I resign to him my soul and at the discretion of my executrix and executor my body to the earth from where it was taken—Secondly, I hereby constitute and appoint my beloved wife, Elizabeth Crosthwait and my beloved brother Shelton Crosthwait, executrix and executor of this my last will and testament.—Thirdly, I require that all my just debts be paid immediately out of the sales of as much of my perishable property as will be sufficient there from, Fourthly, I give and bequeath to my beloved wife, Elizabeth R. Crosthwait, all my property remaining after my debts shall be paid, during her life to be disposed of after her death as she shall think property, among my children.—Fifthly I desire and hereby empower my executor and executrix to do that as much of my property as will be sufficient therefore be sold for the purpose of education my children—Sixthly, I do hereby constitute and appoint my beloved brother, Shelton Crosthwait, the guardian of my son William Crosthwait until he shall arrive at the age of twenty one years, and I do desire that my said brother bind him to serve an apprenticeship to such a trade as my brother shall think proper and that the expenses of his education until such time as he shall be bound aforesaid, shall be paid to my brother out of my property if he shall think proper—In testimony whereof, I have hereunto set my hand and affixed my seal this twenty-second day of November in the year of our Lord one thousand eight hundred fifteen, in presence of the subscribing witnesses who witness this will in my presence and in presence of each other: W. Keeble, Jr. & George Simpson

Signed   Thomas Crosthwait

A short time after the will was completed the Nashville paper announced that Thomas Crosthwait had died near Jefferson on the plantation of his brother.[116] The Nashville Wig said that Thomas was eighty-eight years old. This was obviously a misprint, though there is some question about the Crosthwait family dates. According to record, Thomas was around forty years old. William was merely fifteen.

So, William Crosthwait was raised by his Uncle Shelton, one of the richest and most cultured men of Rutherford County. William's cousins were all younger than he: Mary, four years, George, six years and Rebecca, ten years. (See the *Crosthwait Family Tree, page 129.*) It is possible that before William was apprenticed to a trade, he attended the Jefferson school his Uncle Shelton helped to found.

As time went on, Shelton Crosthwait continued to be an important and respected part of the community. In July of 1817, he was appointed to serve in Jefferson—along with Samuel Bowman and William H. Davis—as a judge of the election for governor.[117]

Then in 1826, forty-three year old Shelton Crosthwait died without warning. He had not yet written his will. His wife, Elizabeth, was named administratix of his estate and the Court ordered an inventory of his goods.

The Inventory List in the Rutherford County Record Book, (Book No. 7, page 27), is written in careful, tiny handwriting that goes on for seven pages. The items listed included 10,800 lbs. of salted pork, 50 gallons of cordial, 546 barrels of corn, silver ladles, china, and fine furniture. His books included *Nicholson's Encyclopedia*, Begland's *View of the World*, and Ramsey's *History of America*.

The inventory of Shelton Crosthwait's goods was perhaps the longest of any person living in Rutherford County at that time, and showed him to be a man of rare education and culture. He had come a long way from being a bookkeeper, and he left his wife well-situated. For the rest of her life, Elizabeth Thompson Crosthwait would live in their plantation home, near the banks of the Stones River.

At the time of his passing, Shelton Crosthwait had acquired 3,000 acres of land, which lay "on both sides of the East fork of the Stones River."[118] Most of this land was above the fork of the Stones River, just opposite Jefferson. The rest of the land ran alongside Jefferson all the way to the southern lands along the river on the East fork. (*See* maps, pages 122 & 204.)

In coming years, the Crosthwait children would go on to new lives. Mary would wed Mr. Richardson, George would attend college in Virginia, and medical school in Kentucky, and Rebecca would wed the promising attorney, Bromfield Ridley.

As for Cousin William, he was educated as promised—taking on the trade of stone-cutter. One thing William appears to have learned from these years was compassion, for in the future, he would welcome into his home three children who had lost their father.

Chapter 7

The Gums Spread Out

Although Norton Gum disappeared from public life in 1809 and does not appear in the 1810 census, there is evidence that he was still in the area. To begin with, in 1811 a baby was born to Norton and Sally. They named him Hinchey Petway Gum, after the businessman with whom Norton had had so many dealings over the years.[119] Hinchey Petway, who opened his Jefferson trade store in 1804, was appointed commissioner in 1808.[120] If not a friend of Norton's, at the very least he was someone the family looked up to.

Following Hinchey Petway Gum's birth, the next publicly recorded events in the Gum family were their marriages. On December 9th, 1815, Hannah Gum married Benjamin Fuller, who came from one of the earliest pioneering families in the area. Travis Marable, who was likely a friend of Ben Fuller's, posted the bond. Then, three years later on May 17th, 1818, Hannah's sister, Mary Gum married Thomas Stroud. Both of these marriages took place in Rutherford County.[121]

Now, in quick succession, the Gum children were leaving the nest. Less than a year after Mary's marriage, John Gum married Malinda Bryant in Wilson County on March 20, 1819.[122] Ten days later, on March 30th, young William Norton Gum was married to eighteen year-old Melinda Nugent in Rutherford County by Justice of the Peace, John Jetton. Melinda was the daughter of long-time Jefferson resident, John Nugent (sometimes spelled Newgent).[123] William Gum worked as a brick mason, and would have found plenty of work in the Murfreesborough area, which was growing rapidly.[124]

Some records point to evidence that Norton may have been present for at least a couple of these marriages.[125] If this is true, then perhaps he had mended his ways significantly by 1811, and was living quietly as a farmer. It does seem almost certain though, that sometime between 1811 and 1820, Norton Gum, founder of the Gum family of Tennessee, was deceased.

~

Searching for the family which had been prominent in the beginnings of Old Jefferson, and then so suddenly disappeared, we travel east—perhaps on the very roads Norton Gum helped to build. These roads wind through hills where old houses made of slim logs are built into the sides of the hills. This is Wilson County, and it is here, in 1820, that we find the Gums.

Nestled between the hills of Wilson County, just southeast of Jefferson, a tiny village known as Maryville had long existed. Then, in 1812, Mr. Bumpas donated land so that a town could be built. Soon after his donation, a two-story hotel, four saloons, a general store, cotton gins and a doctor's office sprang up along the single street of the town. The residents renamed the place Statesville, after Statesville, North Carolina.[126]

Statesville soon became a bustling area, with scores of people coming through daily by horse, carriage and stagecoach. The biggest cause for all this business was cotton. It is said there were more cotton gins in the area of Statesville than any other place in Middle Tennessee.

Since you couldn't get too far in a day with a horse and wagon (especially in this hilly region) many travelers stayed over night. Peddlers came to stay, knowing that hotel visitors would be eager to purchase items from their wagonload of goods. Along with all the business, there were bar room brawls like something out of the Wild West. Still, Statesville was a nice place to live.

The town was surrounded by farmland. The 1820 Federal Census of Wilson County, Tennessee shows that one of these farms was owned by John Gum. Living with him were his wife, Malinda, and young daughter. Both adults were between the ages of 16 and 25. Next door lived John Bryant, Malinda's brother.[127] Down the road, lived an older woman named Sarah Gum, who was listed as head of household. Residing with her were three children, two boys between eleven and sixteen, and a girl between sixteen and twenty-six. The ages of the boys would match Hinchey Petway and Robert E. The girl could have been Hannah or Mary, possibly widowed by now, or another sister. Living on nearby farms, there were also two Clampets—William and James.[128]

We cannot verify that these persons are the same Gum family from Jefferson. All census records prior to 1850 contain only the name of the head of household, along with the sex and age range of the other occupants. It does seem, however, there is a good possibility that this is the family of Norton and Sally Gum.

By 1830, John Gum was living in Rutherford County near Robert Gum, but the other Gums had disappeared. During the 1820s, Hinchey Petway Gum lived in the area of Jefferson for a while.[129] By then, Sally Gum was likely deceased, and H.P. or "Petie"—as he was later called—was left with the responsibility of his own care. In the 1800s, even six years of education was considered a lot. Most children only went to school seasonally, and worked on farms the rest of the time.

As previously stated, it seems that Norton Gum lost much of his estate and likely was deceased prior to 1820. Sally Gum had little means to support her children, so it would have been natural for them to be on their own at a very early age.

On April 11, 1821, two years after William Gum's marriage to Malinda, sixteen year-old Robert E. Gum wed fourteen-year old Mary Ann Fulks.[130] It is not known how Robert and Mary Ann met, but at the time country dances were a popular way for young folks to become acquainted. However they met, it appears to have been love at first sight. Apparently, Mary Ann's parents thought well of the young man, because they had no problem allowing the pair to marry.

Mary Ann's parents, John and Elizabeth Fulks, had moved to Tennessee from Pennsylvania around the same time the Gum family settled there. John Fulks was a veteran of the Revolutionary War, and had received a land grant for his war services. The Fulks first settled south of Jefferson on land that would later become the site for the county poor house.[131] Here the couple opened a small trade store. Like Norton Gum, Mr. Fulks was also in charge of supervising the building of at least two roads.[132]

Several years later, John Fulks—while scouting for better farm land— discovered an area about eight miles southeast of Murfreesboro, just off the Bradyville Pike. In 1815, he and Elizabeth purchased this land, totaling approximately 800 acres. It was good flat land on the edge of Cripple Creek, though at the time this area was still a wilderness.[133]

John Fulks owned many slaves. They cleared the land and built a small two-story log cabin with a rock chimney for John and his wife, as well as a row of smaller cabins for themselves. Grandson John Anderson Gum built a new home sometime after 1913, and tore the old Fulks home down. When the Fulks cabin was torn down, it was said to be 106 years old.[134]

The soil in southern Rutherford County, though rich, was often rocky. Besides clearing the brush, much of the slaves' work involved taking large pieces of limestone out of the ground. The stones were then piled carefully on top of one another to create walls around the property. There were many hickory trees on the Fulks land, which supplied the family with loads of nuts for eating. The wood from the hickory trees is hard, and excellent for making tools. On this land, the Fulks would live peacefully for many years.

When Robert E. Gum married Mary Ann, her parents allowed him to build his home across the way from theirs. John and Elizabeth wanted their daughter to stay nearby, and it was a good situation for Robert, who does not seem to have had much in the way of money or property.

Of all Norton Gum's sons, Robert E. seems have been the one who took most after his father. He was a man full of energy and ambition. He was also somewhat hot-tempered and knew how to make a commotion around town.

In 1820, Robert Gum became involved in his first court case when he pressed charges against William Woodson. At the conclusion of the case, Mr. Woodson agreed to pay all the court costs.[135] The following day, however, Robert decided he was not going to prosecute Mr. Woodson any further. Mr. Woodson paid half the court costs, and Robert E. paid the other half.

Robert Gum was not the only person with a complaint against Mr. Woodson, however, because around the same time at least four other citizens (and businesses) pressed charges against him. One of these persons was James Maney, a well respected doctor who was married to Hardee Murfree's daughter, Sallie. The couple built the Oakland's plantation in Murfreesboro—a place which will later play into this story.[136]

Robert Gum was very much in love with Mary Ann, but it seems he spent quite a bit of time in Murfreesboro. The Gum home was approximately eight miles out of town—at least two hours or more in a horse-pulled wagon. Besides his business transactions, the many court cases he was involved in were enough to bring him to town quite often.

In 1823, Robert E. Gum, brought charges against Emmit & Porter, a store in Murfreesboro. They, in turn, brought charges against Anderson Childress, a lawyer and alderman of the city.[137] Interestingly, once the case had gone to court, Robert E. again decided not to continue the suit. Following this, Anderson Childress came into court and paid all the court costs. Around this same time (July), Robert E. bought a twelve year-old African-American boy named Mack.[138]

In September of 1823, Robert E. Gum was commissioned Captain of the 9th Brigade Cavalry Regiment of the Rutherford County Militia.[139] Joining the Militia and carrying a title was part of the duty and pride of most men in Tennessee.

Toward the end of the year, Robert E. Gum followed in his father's footsteps when he was appointed constable in Rutherford County—along with Benjamin Ransom, Henry Vincent, Michael Finneky, Benjamin McFarlin and Edmund Tennison. The appointment was for two years-with bonds and security given.[140]

Meanwhile, more little Gums were being born. Robert and Mary Ann's first child was born on January 9, 1822. They named him John after his Fulks grandfather. Six months later, in the town of Jefferson, Robert E.'s brother, William N. and wife, Malinda had their first son whom they named William Norton Gum. Billy, as he would later be known, was born June 2, 1822.

Robert E. Gum was a very high-spirited young man; a trait that seemed to run in the Gum family. On July 19th, 1824, this trait got him into some trouble. Robert may have been angry at a court decision, and perhaps he'd had a nip or two. Whatever the case, early one morning he got on his horse and rode to the Murfreesboro Square. He did not stop at the doors of the courthouse, but rode directly inside, where the court was in full session.

Imagine the sound of galloping hooves, and people in the courtroom rising from their seats as a horse with Robert Gum astride entered the room at full gallop. Imagine too, the judge pounding the gavel, his face turning red with anger as he commanded the guards to seize Mr. Gum. The judge was incensed with Robert Gum's actions, and declared him "in contempt" of court. He ordered that he "be committed to the jail ..." and "...kept in close confinement until tomorrow morning at nine o'clock."[141]

Mary Ann must have looked for Robert that evening. She had no way of knowing what had happened to him. It would have been necessary for someone to ride down Bradyville Pike to inform the family.

After cooling off in jail at least twenty-four hours, Robert E. was fined $10.00 for this offense.* Once the fine was paid—possibly by his father-in-law—Robert was released and allowed to return home. As the people of Murfreesboro would soon learn, this would not be the last of Robert E.'s lively antics.

A few months later, Bobbie Gum—as he came to be known—was back in court with a case against James Richardson. It was a large case, and a jury of twelve men, including Dr. William Maney, was called. The trial went on for two days, at which time the jury decided in favor of the defendant, Mr. Richardson. Robert Gum was ordered to pay the court costs without delay.[142]

Not long after this, on January 27, 1825 to be exact, Robert Gum returned to the courthouse stating that he was dissatisfied with the judgment against him. The judge allowed him to appeal, but it is unknown what the results were.

During 1825–1826, it appears Robert Gum did quite well with farming and whatever other business he was doing. In 1826, he brought a land grant of fifty acres for $4,412,† no small amount at that time.[143] In 1827, there is also record of Robert buying a twenty-two year old

---

* About $204.00 in 2007 per measuringworth.com

† About $95,390 in 2007.

African-American woman named Letty from his father-in-law. For this sale, Robert E. paid $300.* [144]

Childbearing in the country, or the woods—where Robert and Mary Ann lived—must have been quite difficult. Summers in Tennessee are swelteringly hot, and winters intensely cold. A small log cabin, of the kind the Gums resided in could be quite drafty. Although it is possible the couple lost a child during these years, the next recorded birth for Robert and Mary Ann Gum was on October 27, 1826. The baby was a girl, and they named her Cinthia. [145]

Meanwhile in Jefferson, William and Malinda Gum had seen the birth of two more children. Little Sarah—doubtless named for her grandmother Sally Clampet Gum—was born in 1825. She was followed two years later by a boy, John Alexander Gum born November 3, 1827. The baby was named for an attorney in town, John Alexander.

For a while, all seemed peaceful and happy in the Gum family. Then, a few years after John Alexander Gum's birth, events occurred which would confuse Gum genealogists for years to come.

---

* About $6,486 CPI in 2007.

The Gum Family Tree

Norton Gum   m.   Sally Clampet

Hannah 1795? (Fuller)	Mary 1797? (Stroud)	John 1798? (Bryant)	William 1800?–1830? (Nugent)	Robert E. 1805–1847 (Fulks)	Hinchey Petway 1811–1895 (Welch)
		Girl (1817)	William (1822)	John (1822)	Sarah (1835)
			Sarah (1825)	Cinthia (1826)	Mary (1837)
			John (1827)	Sara (1830)	Sydney (1840)
				Wilson (1832)	Payton (1842)
				Malinda (1836)	Catherine (1844)
				Mary Ann (1838)	William (1846)
				William T (1840)	Elizabeth (1854)

The Marable Family Tree

Henry Hartwell Marable (1753–1833) m. Elizabeth Mason (1757–1861)

- **Braxton** (177?–1840) (?)
  - James
  - William

- **Benjamin** (1777–1863) (Barner)
  - John (?)
  - Elizabeth (1800)
  - Henry H. (1802)
  - Benjamin (1808)
  - Mary Ann (1812)

- **John H.** (1774–1844) (Watson)
  - Fredonia (1809)
  - Arcadia (1811)
  - Sarah (1813)
  - John H. (1813)
  - Ann J. (1817)
  - Elizabeth (1819)

- **Travis** (1790–1824) (?)
  - Mary
  - Martha
  - James (1819)
  - John (1820)
  - Isaac (1821)

- **Henry H.** (1793–1841) (Richardson)
  - Mary & Cora (unable to fit complete list of children here.)

- **Elizabeth** (1796–1835) (Jones)
  - George
  - Henry (1815)
  - Eliza (1819)

- **Isaac** (1797–1819) (Williamson)
  - Elizabeth
  - Martha
  - Isaac

Endnotes
Book 1—The Pioneers

Note: RCHS = Rutherford County Historical Society

1. The area referred to is the future Rutherford County, 220 miles west of No. Carolina; midway between NC & the Mississippi River.

2. *Rutherford County*, Mabel Pittard, Memphis State University Press, Memphis, TN, p. 7; *A History of Rutherford County*, Carlton C. Sims, p. 4

3. *A History of Rutherford County*, Carlton C. Sims, p. 7

4. *The Life of George Washington*, David Ramsey, NY, 1807, http://www.early america.com/lives/gwlife/chapt11/

5. *Tennesseans and Their History*, Paul H. Bergeron, Stephen V. Ash, Jeanette Keith, The University of Tennessee Press, 1999, p. 47-48

6. *The Life of George Washington*, David Ramsey, NY, 1807, http://www.early america.com/lives/gwlife/chapt11/

7. *Incidents in the Early Settlement of East Tennessee and Knoxville, Early History of East Tennessee*, Prof. G.H. Stueckrath, *De Bow's Review*, October 1859. Vol. XXVII, p. 407; also book on Knoxville, TN history, Linebaugh (misplaced), p. 17

8. *Goodspeed's History of Tennessee*, C. & R. Elder Booksellers, 1972, p. 926

9. *Charles McClung*, Fred Brown, The Knoxville News-Sentinel, July 25, 1999

10. *Incidents in the Early Settlement of East Tennessee and Knoxville, Early History of East Tennessee*, by Prof. G.H. Stueckrath, *De Bow's Review*, October 1859. Vol. XXVII, p. 407 All info in this paragraph from same source. Author quotes liberally from Ramsey's "History of Tennessee."

11. Information taken from the U.S. Census and other local TN records.

12. *Early Tennessee Marriages*, preface. Tennessee Historical Society.

13. http://genforum.genealogy.com/cgi-bin/pageload.cgi?ann,carter::chism:
112.html *John L. Chism married Mary Gum in Kentucky between 1740–1750.
No further information as of now.

14. Originally, the bond was 500 pounds but was reduced, with only a percentage of it required—so that people could afford to be married.

15. *Goodspeed's History of Tennessee*, C. & R. Elder Booksellers, 1972, p. 926

16. *Ulster-Scot Who Designed Knoxville*, by Fred Brown, The Ulster Scott,
Knoxville News/Sentinal Tennessee, February 2003

17. This information is assumed by the author. Very few persons lived outside
of forts. It was not safe to do so.

18. *Incidents in the Early Settlement of East Tennessee and Knoxville*, Prof. G.H.
Stueckrath, (see above) *De Bow's Review*, Oct. 1859, p. 408

19. Robert McGinnis, historian and descendent of James White—who gave
me a tour of the James White Fort, 2007.

20. *Incidents in the Early Settlement of East Tennessee and Knoxville*, Prof. G.H.
Stueckrath, published in *De Bow's Review*. Oct. 1859. p. 407–419 http://www
.knoxcotn.org/history/debow.html

21. Ibid pgs 407–419

22. Ibid pgs 407–419

23. *The Autobiography of Sam Houston*, Ed. Donald Day & Harry Herbert
Ullom, University of Oklahoma Press, 1954, p. 9

24. *Incidents in the Early Settlement of East Tennessee and Knoxville*, Prof. G.H.
Stueckrath, *De Bow's Review*, Oct. 1859. pgs. 407–419

25. *A History of Tn from 1663 to 1924*, Gentry Richard McGee, 1924, p. 927

26. Tour of James White Fort & librarians at the East TN Historical Society.

27. *Religion in Tennessee 1777–1945*, by Herman A. Norton, The Tennessee
Historical Commission, The University of Tennessee Press, 1997, p. 9

28. *Tennessee Strings*, C.K. Wolfe, University of Tennessee Press, 1977, p. 6–8

29. Information learned on tour at James White Fort 2007

30. *Flowers for Grace* by Elisabeth O. Howse, 1972, p.3

31. http://tsla-teva.state.tn.us/landmarkdocs/transcripts/140.transcript.pdf
TN Civil and Military Commission Book, Vol. 1, Blount County, p. 27

32. Some of these family associations are guesses, but after researching time,
location, age, etc., we believe they are accurate.

33. *Records of Knox County Minutes Book*, No. 2, 1799–1800 (typed book at
Tennessee State Archives, p. 202–203) Original records, #1197 & #1238

34. RCHS, No. 17, Summer 1981, *History of Jefferson*, Kevin Markuson, p. 1

35. *Rutherford County*, Mabel Pittard, Memphis State University Press, 1984, p. 25

36. *Annals of Rutherford County*, Vol. 1, by John C. Spence, RCHS, 1991, p. 25

37. Ibid, p. 30

38. *Annals of Rutherford County*, Vol. 1, John C. Spence, RCHS, p. 30

39. Rutherford County Historical Society Pub. No. 17, Summer 1981, p. 1

40. Ibid, p. 26

41. *Annals of Rutherford County*, John C. Spence, p. 28

42. 1807–1810 Rutherford County Tax Rolls.

43. *FROW CHIPS*—date?

44. RCHS No. 18, p. 113

45. *Annals of Rutherford County*, Vol. 1, John C. Spence, RCHS, p. 34–35

46. RCHS, Pub. No. 17, *Jefferson—The County Seat*, Kevin Markuson, p. 19; RC Court Clerk Minute Book A, p. 80

47. RCHS, Pub. No. 17, p.24

48. *Annals of Rutherford County*, Vol. 1, p. 39

49. Ibid p. 36—this citation includes source for the entire paragraph.

50. Ibid, p.32

51. Ibid, p. 33

52. Ibid, p. 33

53. *Pioneers of Rutherford County, Tennessee, Abstract of County Court Minutes 1804–1810*, by Carol Wells, Ericson Books, Nacogdoches, TX, p. 17

54. Public Acts (1804) p. 4; RU County Historical Society Pub. No. 20, p. 18

55. RCHS, No. 17, 1981, *Thomas Bedford* by Kevin Markuson, p. 15–16

56. Ibid, p. 4; Ibid, p. 19

57. Ibid Public Acts (1804) p. 5–6, 9; RU County Historical Society #20, p. 20

58. Ibid, p. 5–6, Ibid, p. 20

59. *Pioneers of RC, TN, Abstracts of Court Minutes 1804–1810*, by Carol Wells, Ericsons Books, p. 26; RU County Court Minutes, Book A, p. 50

60. *Pioneers of Rutherford County, TN*, Ibid, p. 26

61. County Court Minutes, p. 55

62. *Pioneers of Rutherford County, Tennessee*, by Carol Wells, p. 41

63. Ibid, p. 45, 46 & 55

64. *Frow Chips*, RCHS, Volume 35, Issue No. 3, p. 9

65. Ibid, p. 35

66. *Annals of Rutherford County*, Vol. I, John C. Spence, p. 35

67. This John Spence may be the father of the author, John C. Spence, mentioned in this book. He was Irish born, but it is said he came to Rutherford in 1809. His mother, Mary Chism, was born in Virginia.

68. *Pioneers of Rutherford County, Tennessee*, Carol Wells, p. 103

69. *Annals of Rutherford County*, Vol. I, John C. Spence, p. 50–51

70. *Annals of Rutherford County*, Vol. I, John C. Spence, p. 57–58

71. *Pioneers of Rutherford County, Tennessee*, by Carol Wells, p. 72

72. RCHS Pub. No. 17, p.22

73. Rutherford County Record Book 2, p. 25

74. *Annals of Rutherford County*, Vol. I, by John C. Spence, p. 41

75. *Old Jefferson, Ghost Town*, Ed Bell, *The Nashville Tennessean*, March 26, 1950, p. 4

76. *Pioneers of Rutherford County*, by Carol Wells, p. 142

77. Ibid, p. 135

78. Ibid, p. 149–165; Rutherford County Court Records for 1808

79. Rutherford County Court Records, Book F, p. 472, 557

80. *The Pioneers of Rutherford County, TN*, by Carol Wells, p. 156

81. Ibid, p. 209, p. 7

82. Ibid, p. 182

83. Ibid, 199; Original Court p. 115

84. http://www.westegg.com/inflation/

85. *Pioneers of Rutherford County*, Carol Wells, p. 201

86. How much is it? http://www.measuringworth.com/calculator/uscompare/

87. *Pioneers of Rutherford County*, TN, p. 209; (RC Court Minutes p. 151)

88. *Rutherford County, Tennessee Pioneers Born Before 1800*, Compiled by Susan G. Daniel, Rutherford County Historical Society, p. 22–23

89. Ibid, p. 209

90. *Pioneers of Rutherford County, TN*, Carol Wells, p. 209

91. *Annals of Rutherford County*, Vol. 1, by John C. Spence, p. 71

92. *Rutherford County Historical Society*, Pub. No.17 p. 36

93. *Annals of Rutherford County*, Vol. 1, John C. Spence, p. 72

94. Ibid, p. 85

95. *Notes on the Marable Family of Virginia*, Charlotte Wilcoxen, Paper housed at the TN State Archives—Marable file; Archaeological Excavations at Jamestown, Virginia, Archaeological Research Series No. 4, John L. Cotter, National Park Service, US Dept of the Interior, Washington, DC, 1958, p. 51

96. Brunswick Co., Virginia, Deed Book 20, p. 17, *Curry Wolfe Research*. It appears that while Rev. Marable had a farm in Brunswick Co., he also inherited this farm in Sussex County from his Uncle H.H. Marable, Sussex Co., Virginia, Will Book C, p. 194–195.

97. From John Marable's descendent, Grace Paine Terzian

98. Per Curry Wolfe

99. http://www.marable-family.net/jlmarable/jhm-coorespondence.html

100. This area lies in present day Smyrna between Old Nashville Highway & I-24.

101. Rutherford County Tax Records, *Curry Wolfe Research*

102. Ibid, p. 17

103. RCHS Pub. No. 1, *"Sojourn in Murfreesboro"* from the diary of Samuel Hervey McLaughlin (1796–1850), p. 18

104. Ibid, p. 21

105. Ibid, p. 21

106. *Religion in Tennessee 1777–1945*, Herman A. Norton, University of Tennessee Press, 1981, p. 26

107. *Annals of Rutherford County*, Vol. 1 by John C. Spence, p. 184

108. Inventory at the time of Henry H. Marable's death 1833. RU Cty Records

109. Suggested by several interviews with local descendents.

110. This was shown to be true in later court records where persons recall even on her deathbed, she inquired as to their family's health.

111. *Curry Wolfe Research*, RC Property Records Book #?, Record No. 83

112. *Curry Wolfe Research*, RC Property Records Book #?, Record No. 203

113. *Pennsylvania Magazine*, Vol 23, p.107

114. Albemarle County Deeds 10, 1789–1793, 1–2

115. Rutherford County Record Book of 1819, p. 253 (typed notes p. 88)

116. The Nashville Wig, December 20, 1815; Obituaries from Early Tennessee Newspapers

117. Rutherford County Court Minutes, 1817–1818, p. 32

118. Rutherford County Court Minutes, Book T, 1824–1825, p. 71

119. This fact has been gained via Gum family letters written by H.P. Gum.

120. RC TN Pioneers Born Before 1800, Susan G. Daniel, RCHS, 2003, p. 204

121. All marriage dates in this chapter taken from the Rutherford County Marriage Records in books at the Linebaugh Library, Murfreesboro, TN

122. The fact that John Gum was Norton and Sally Gum's son is only conjecture, but the pieces seem to fit. His descendants are unknown.

123. RC TN Pioneers Born Before 1800, Susan G. Daniel, RCHS, 2003, p. 192

124. 1820 U.S. Federal Census, Wilson Co. Tennessee; & Goodspeed's History of Southeast Missouri, Dunklin County, 1882—"Billy" Gum on father.

125. Some Marriage Record books list his name—but no evidence in the records or bonds, to prove Norton Gum was still alive at the time.

126. Sue Corley, Statesville historian—all information on Statesville

127. John Bryant's name appears on the marriage bond for John Gum and Malinda Bryant.

128. 1820 U.S. Federal Census, Wilson County, TN

129. 1867 letter of H.P. Gum to his nephew, John Gum. (Ralph Puckett)

130. From the Gum Family Bible owned by Ralph Puckett. Also June 30, 1980, letter from Mattie Gum Puckett, great, granddaughter of Robert E. Gum.

131. Elizabeth Fulks obituary, Murfreesboro newspaper of May 1875

132. RC Pioneers Born Before 1800, Susan G. Daniel, RCHS, 2003, p. 91

133. Research of Ralph Puckett, Guy Wilson and Curry Wolfe

134. Per Ralph Puckett and others.

135. Rutherford County Court Minutes, Book P, 1820–21, p. 169.

136. Ibid, p. 170

137. RC Court Minutes 1823–1824, Book S, p. 123; Appeal No.15, Case No. 16

138. Rutherford County Property Records, Book Q, p. 81

139. RCHS Pub. No. 3, Summer 1927, p. 61

140. Rutherford County Court Minutes, 1823–1824, p. 278

141. Rutherford County Court Minutes, Book T, 1824–1825, p. 1

142. Rutherford County Court Minutes, 1824–25, p. 219

143. Curry Wolfe research, TN, Rutherford Co. Land Deed Book 27, p. 298

144. Rutherford County Property Record, Book R, p. 153

145. Taken from the Gum Family Bible.

Peace and Prosperity

Chapter 8

John Aldridge Baugh

IT WAS LIKELY A BEAUTIFUL MORNING IN THE AUTUMN OF 1828 THAT John Aldridge Baugh set off to visit his relatives in Rutherford County, Tennessee. The harvest time in Waterloo, Alabama was over, and the hot, sometimes stormy weather of early autumn had passed. Now, as the stagecoach bounced over the deeply rutted roads, twenty-two year old John Baugh was eager to begin a new adventure.

Although no pictures of John Baugh have been found, we can guess from the features of his relatives that he was tall and thin with curly, blonde hair and deep blue, wide-set eyes.

Some say John Aldridge Baugh came to Murfreesboro to attend school—or even to teach. The truth is he had several relatives in Rutherford County who would have been eager to see him.[1] There was his cousin Thomas Harwell, his Aunt Frances MacGowan, and his Great-Aunt Lucy Marable. Of these three, Aunt Frances was perhaps the nearest and dearest, being his father, Richard Baugh's sister.

In 1797, nine years prior to John's birth, sixteen year-old Frances Baugh had married thirty-one year old Ebenezer MacGowan, a widower with two children, John, 10 and James, 7.[2] The couple settled down in Mecklenburg County, Virginia where a large portion of the Baugh family lived. To support his family, Mr. MacGowan worked in the mercantile business. On March 10, 1798, Ebenezer MacGowan was ordained a deacon in the Methodist Church.[3]

When John was six years old, Uncle Ebenezer and Aunt Frances moved to St. Tammony in hopes of starting a Christian community.[4] Four years later, Reverend Ebenezer once again felt God calling him to move onward. So, with twenty-two family members traveling in ox carts, the Mac-Gowans crossed the mountains to settle in Rutherford County. The year was 1816. Those traveling west included Frances and Ebenezer's seven children (ranging in ages from one to fifteen,) James, (Ebenezer's son from his first marriage) and his 3 children, and nine African-American slaves.[5]

Shortly before the MacGowan exodus west, the Baugh family joined the many pioneering families leaving Virginia for Tennessee. Their destination was Giles County in middle Tennessee, where many of Elizabeth Harwell's relatives (John's mother) had settled.[6] The Baughs stayed in Giles until approximately 1820 when they moved across the Tennessee border to Lauderdale County, Alabama.

In the mid-1800s, the MacGowan siblings—who by then were living great distances apart—kept in close contact with one another by writing wonderfully detailed letters.[7] Perhaps the MacGowan children took after their parents. If so, we can imagine that in the early years, Frances MacGowan wrote her brother, Richard, many letters about life in Rutherford County. Young John must have listened intently to the glowing reports of the beautiful country, fertile soil and gentle people. Rutherford had all the old world charm, with new unlimited possibilities. Reverend Ebenezer and Aunt Frances, no doubt, sent warm invitations to any family member who wished to visit, and John Baugh—a young man full of restless energy and ambition—was eager to accept. New challenges and adventures would be things he welcomed throughout his life.

In 1828, the journey from the Lauderdale to Murfreesboro by stage-coach took approximately five to six days. The stagecoach, with six to nine passengers, traveled day and night taking only short breaks. On these stops, the passengers could buy poorly made food to fill their empty stomachs. The coach also had a "round boot" behind to carry the mail.[8] The ride was rough, but pleasant for the sites along the way. Going north to Murfreesboro, travelers viewed rolling hills and thick forests edged by rivers and playful streams.

Shortly before arriving in Murfreesboro, the stagecoach stopped in the small village of Millersburg, which lay in an area that had been settled before Tennessee was even a territory. Many of the old homes there have rifle slots in the walls, which attest to the need of the early settlers to defend themselves against Indian attack. By the 1820s though, all was peaceful.

Millersburg was basically a "shop lot"—a U-shaped lot open on one side to the road. Not much different than many small villages of its kind, there were a string of log buildings containing stores. On the east side sat a blacksmith shop and tannery. On the west side, was the stagecoach station run by Miller and White. There was also a small post office, and in the center of the shop lot, an auction block where slaves were sold on weekends.[9] The town made an impression on John; one he would not forget. After a short stop here, the stagecoach left. The next stop was about ten miles away.

Finally, after many days of bouncing up and down on the rough roads, the driver sounded his horn and announced their arrival into Murfreesboro. Up they went over one last hill, and then down again. The clop, clop, clop of the horses' hooves sounded as they crossed the wooden bridge over Lytle's Creek. Entering the town, the passengers became aware of the mingled odors of smoke, livestock and cooked food. Traveling up the slight incline toward the square, the driver pulled back on the horses' reins and brought the coach to a halt.

John Baugh's heart must have quickened, as he looked out the window at all the activity on Murfreesboro's public square. It was much busier than Waterloo, Alabama! The square was lined with one and two-story framed buildings with every kind of shop imaginable. There were merchants, a Masonic lodge, a boarding house, tavern and a house of entertainment. In the middle of the square stood the new brick courthouse, built a few years earlier to replace the old log one. The original courthouse, John would later learn, had been burnt under suspicious conditions.[10]

Men of every type were standing about in the square, talking and conducting business. Some wore fine broadcloth suits with tails, high rolled collars and tall hats. Others were dressed simply in ruffled shirts. John also saw older men wearing blue and brown denim jeans with red and yellow bandana handkerchiefs around their necks.[11] On the far side of the courthouse, a group of about thirty black men, women, and children were milling about in a sort of line, laughing and chattering away. It appeared they were waiting their turn to get water out of the well, for they all had buckets or jugs.[12]

John was fully aware that Murfreesboro was now serving as the state capital. It was no wonder there were such a variety of persons on the street. No sooner had John and the other passengers gotten down from the high step of the stagecoach, than they were surrounded by a variety of citizens eager to know where they had come from, where they were going, and whether they had any news.[13]

After a short rest, the coach was off again. Jefferson would be the next stop; it was the closest stop to Bethel where the MacGowans resided. The picture of sixty-one year old Reverend MacGowan, five foot tall, and thin, with intense blue eyes, standing next to the fresh-faced, curly headed, John, eager and naïve, is a sharp contrast.

Once Rev. MacGowan and John Baugh reached the McGowan house, Aunt Frances ran out to greet them. She was dressed in a high-waisted calico gown with five to seven yards of fabric, and a bonnet-as was the fashion then. Those present were sure to notice the family resemblance. Frances' sparkling blue eyes were very much like John's. The meeting was full of emotion for in this time every family connection was precious.

The MacGowan home was of medium size; a comfortable two-story log house, surrounded by woods and farmland, not far from the winding lane that would one day be known as "Sulphur Springs Road." The home itself had some unusual features. It had been made of the cedar logs which were prevalent in the area, but unlike most homes, these logs were exceptionally large; the longest measuring 28 feet in length. The width of the house was made by logs of 14 feet in length. The joists at the ceiling downstairs were of walnut. Upstairs they were made of cherry. The ceiling joists were decorated with carved grooves, not usual for a home, but sometimes found in old European ships.[14]

Shortly after Reverend Ebenezer arrived in Rutherford County, he had paid $2,500 for a land grant of 1,184 acres.* At the time (about

---

* $2,500 in 1816 would equal approximately $54,051 CPI in 2007.

1816), this part of Rutherford County was still a wilderness of forests, with only tiny lanes, which the Indians had created, to travel on. Bears were seen so often roaming through the area where the MacGowan's built their home that it was known as "Bear Hollow."[15] By 1828, much of the wilderness surrounding the MacGowan log cabin had been cleared for farmland. Not far from their house, were many small log cabins where the MacGowan slaves lived.

Rev. Ebenezer built his home with the help of his slaves, and Frances had decorated it nicely. Originally, it contained two large rooms; one upstairs and one down. Since the only source of heat during this time was the fireplace, most pioneers left their rooms open, rather than dividing them.[16]

During the MacGowan's first years here, Reverend Ebenezer held Sunday services in the main room downstairs. Since he was not very tall, he preached his sermons from the stairs, so that everyone could see and hear him. In later years, the upstairs and downstairs were divided into two rooms each. Outside, there was a porch at either end of the house. The place had a warm and loving atmosphere. Visiting his relatives, John must have felt the charm of Tennessee life.

At suppertime, the family sat at a long table in the main room. There were seven children: Lucy, 10, William, 11, Samuel, 13, Ann, 15, Martha, 18, Harper, 21, (who was soon to be married in November) and Mary, 23. Several of the MacGowan children had died early, and one, Thomas, was married. All in all, it was a full house, with plenty of lively conversation.

Reverend Ebenezer sat at the head of the table, and folded his hands before him. Bowing his head, he prayed fervently. As he wrote his daughter, Martha, three years later in 1831,

> … live for eternity, keep death in view, cultivate a close walk with God, pray frequently and fervently, and all will be well in the end.[17]

After the grace was said, plates of good food including venison, corn, and cornbread (a staple of Tennessee natives) were passed to everyone by the servants. No doubt, there was a lively inquiry of John's parents and siblings in Waterloo, and tales of the long trips both families had taken from Virginia to Tennessee. As John looked around the table, it would

Figure 1. Reverend Ebenezer MacGowan toward the end of his life, some twenty years after John Aldridge Baugh came to Rutherford County.
(Courtesy of Mrs. Frank Stockard)

be obvious to him how much love there was in this home. Even between the white family and the black servants, there was care and concern.

Although Rev. MacGowan kept slaves, he believed in treating them as human beings, and as family. Later in life, after daughter Martha had married Mr. Hutcheson and moved to Texas, she requested one of the slaves as part of her inheritance. Rev. MacGowan wrote her that this servant was married to someone in Rutherford County, and it would be too hard on her to separate her from her husband.[18]

Still, the Tennessee Methodist Conference held that no minister could be a slave owner and be ordained. Like many people in Tennessee, Ebenezer knew that without the help of his slaves, it would be impossible to farm the land and have the money needed to run his church and support his large family. Because he was a slaveholder, like many other ministers, Ebenezer MacGowan would not be ordained an elder or full minister for many years. Most people in the wild and difficult land of Tennessee were keenly aware that their success, even their very survival, depended on the labor of these dark-skinned men, women and children. It became a way of life.

At night, John Aldridge Baugh retired with his male cousins, likely sharing a bed with them. It was not uncommon to pile many bodies into one bed. They slept on rope beds, covered by mattresses stuffed with straw. Few persons had feather beds.

In the daytime, Rev. Ebenezer was busy overseeing the hundreds of acres on which he farmed. Although the slaves did much of the backbreaking work, there was still alot for him to do. It was not an easy life, but certainly adventurous, and one he found greatly fulfilling.

In the following days, Ebenezer showed John the area and how with the help of his servants, he was farming the red earth. John learned a great deal about life in Rutherford County, and the people who

Figure 2. Cotton

lived there. The MacGowans spoke of the advantages of the area; the rich soil, plentiful space, and the devout and cultured people.

On Saturdays, folks rode into town to buy, sell, exchange or barter their farm goods. Although many people had begun planting cotton—a crop that grew well in the hot sun—there were many other kinds of farming, including tobacco and livestock. Murfreesboro was known also for her cedar trees, which were plentiful and grew well on in the shallow soil where the limestone base had come to the surface.

In the evenings after dinner, John Baugh had time to find out more about Rev. MacGowan's history. He had been born in London in 1767. His father, John MacGowan (1726–1780) was a close friend of John Wesley, and had worked with him to establish the Methodist religion in England. John MacGowan died when Ebenezer was only thirteen-years old, but had left him with a passion to bring the light of Christ to people.

Ebenezer was seventeen when he immigrated to America and settled in Virginia. There he began to study for the ministry. It was not until after his marriage to Frances Baugh that Bishop Francis Asbury, the head of the Methodist Church in America, ordained him on March 10, 1798.[19] This rather fierce looking man, John learned, was also very kind. Aunt Frances, too, was a devout Christian woman who loved her husband. Together they made a fine pair.

Sunday was the one day of rest for these hard-working settlers. For many, it was the only time they had to meet and socialize with persons outside their immediate families. However, with few ministers to go around, and a population spread out across many miles, the local residents considered themselves fortunate if they had a minister come to preach once or twice a month. This made Sunday worship even more special.

As one of the first Methodist preachers in the area, Ebenezer Mac-Gowan held services in various small chapels; sometimes at quite a distance from the area where he lived. As the population grew, he wanted a place for the people of his own community. After using his home for several years, the community grew and Rev. MacGowan donated four acres of land, and helped to build the log church he called "Bethel." The church stood in a grove "across the road and a few hundred yards southeast of his home."[20] By the time of John Baugh's visit, this is where Sunday services were held.

A visit in the 1800s was not a short affair. Travel was difficult and lengthy, and it would be uncertain as to when or if one would ever be able to visit again. Life was busy with chores, but still left people time to socialize and enjoy one another's company. John Aldridge Baugh's visit to Rutherford would not have been considered long if it lasted several months, or even a year.

Sometime during his sojourn in Rutherford County, John must have gone to visit his mother's first cousin, Thomas Harwell, who was fairly well-off. The Harwell land—about ten miles west of the MacGowans— lay in District 7 at Stewart's Creek, next to Joseph Morton and George Buchanan. Thomas Harwell lived with his wife, Martha Smith, and their six children, including two sons who were slightly older than John, and three daughters, of which, Nancy, born in 1808, was probably the closes in age to him.[21] Cousin Harwell also had seventeen slaves.

The Harwell home must have seemed fairly sedate compared to the bustle of the MacGowans. Nevertheless, the visit would have been interesting, for Cousin Harwell seems to have been a man of culture. Some years later, Thomas Harwell moved to a farm outside of Memphis, where he purchased an iron casket popular at the time—commonly known as "the Fiske Mummy Case." The casket, manufactured between 1835 and 1860, was made in the form of an Egyptian sarcophagus. In 1978, Harwell's casket was found beneath ground in a brick burial vault on his former farmland. His remains were reburied. His sarcophagus can be seen on display at the Pink Palace Museum in Memphis, Tennessee.[22]

The other relative John Baugh most certainly came to visit in Rutherford County was his great aunt, Mrs. Lucy Marable, the sister of John's maternal grandmother, Rebecca Barner, and wife of Benjamin Marable. Rev. Ebenezer MacGowan must have known the Marables, since Rev. Marable, was one of the earliest Methodist Ministers in the area. Although Rev. Marable lived north of the MacGowans, Benjamin had settled only a few miles west of Bethel Church. It is very possible that Bethel was the church Benjamin Marable's family attended.[23]

Once again, there are no documents stating why John Baugh came to Rutherford County, or where he stayed. Possibly, he taught school, or attended one. Whatever the real reason for his visit, something was about to occur that would change his life forever.

Chapter 9

Mary Ann

In 1828, only the youngest child of Benjamin and Lucy Marable remained at home, sixteen year-old Mary Ann. The two eldest sons, John and Henry Hartwell Marable, Jr. were married. The eldest daughter, Elizabeth or "Betsy" as she was most often called, was twenty-eight and had been married to John B. Hicks for eleven years.[24] The Hicks couple lived on a farm near the Bethel Church with their young children. Twenty year-old Benjamin, Jr., nearest in age to Mary Ann, was busy studying medicine.

Sometime during John Baugh's sojourn in Rutherford County, he visited his Great Aunt Lucy. It is unknown exactly how Mary Ann Marable and John Aldridge Baugh met. John could have had his first glimpse of Mary Ann at the Bethel Church, or even at a country dance. Whatever the case, it was an unforgettable meeting.

As the granddaughter of Reverend Henry Hartwell Marable, and the youngest member of her family, Mary Ann was a very bright, young woman, who in her short life had met persons of all ranks and professions. It seems she had no trouble holding her own in any conversation.[25] As the granddaughter of two devout souls, she also had learned how to be interested and compassionate toward others.

Like the young ladies of her day and location, during the day Mary Ann dressed in a light gingham dress with high waist and full skirt. Like the other Marable family members, it is believed she had dark hair and blue eyes.

Figure 3. Farmland in Blackman today.

At first Mary Ann would have been only a cousin to John. They may have spent time walking or riding on the family land. The Marable property was rich and beautiful. In autumn, the acres of cotton were fields of white that glowed in the moonlight. These lands were tended to and harvested by the Negro slaves, who sang as they went across the fields, keeping rhythm with the work, communicating in the only way they could—through these songs.

There was much for John and Mary (as she was sometimes) to discuss: their early travel from Virginia to Tennessee, religion, and the future as they saw it. The United States was only a little over fifty years-old. For most young men and women at this time, history and poetry were considered the proper subjects for conversation.[26]

The fading green of early autumn in Rutherford County soon turns a brilliant red that seems like a lit fire. In the chill of the changing weather, the leaves turn from red to yellow, and in the late afternoon sun, those yellow leaves become golden. Toward the end of October, the winds begin to blow, ripping the leaves from branches, and whirling them like snow in a blizzard. The nights are chill, and the days remain cool until noontime when the direct sun of Middle Tennessee still can burn.

Perhaps John and Mary Ann took walks across the rich landscape. The wind may have blown her shawl away. She would have laughed to see John running and leaping wildly to catch it.

When winter arrived, there would be little snow, but morning frost and dark, gloomy days are part of the normal Tennessee winter. John and Mary Ann had time to sit before the fire. Mary Ann kept busy with her sewing, while John read to her. It was considered only proper that young ladies keep their hands busy with knitting or embroidery as they visited with guests in the parlor. The evenings included music—playing the pianoforte and guitar.[27]

John Baugh was obviously quite taken with Mary Ann Marable. It is not difficult to imagine all the attributes that must have attracted him to her. Along with the manners and social graces she possessed, her strength, intelligence and compassion caught his heart as much as her lovely blue eyes.

Mary Marable soon felt the same. John, with his great sense of adventure, his ambition, and his deep blue eyes captured her heart as well. When he asked for her hand, although he apparently had little in the way of property or money, she was ready to leave her family for him. Her parents agreed, finding John Baugh a worthy spouse for their treasured daughter. The only stipulation was that she wait for her 17th birthday.

Then, into the midst of John and Mary Ann's growing feelings came some remarkable history that had all of Tennessee abuzz. It was the romance of Sam Houston, the hero and most eligible bachelor, for whom all the ladies had been mad. The fact that Sam Houston was a friend of Mary Ann's Uncle John—possibly even someone she had met—would have made the event all the more intense.

In January of 1829, Sam Houston finally had his heart caught by nineteen year-old Eliza Allen of Sumner County. That same month, the couple was married by candlelight. Then, suddenly after only three months of marriage, word spread that the marriage had been dissolved. Eliza returned to her father's house, and Sam, who had been campaigning for a second term as Governor, resigned and left Tennessee.[28]

A fury rose as many Tennesseans felt betrayed by the man they had almost worshipped. Houston was burned in effigy. People spoke of almost nothing but his betrayal. Those who were not angry at Sam, placed their anger toward Eliza. Mary Ann may have been spared some of this talk, but all of Tennessee was truly puzzled by these events. What had happened to their great hero? It would be a long, long while before their anger toward Sam Houston subsided. It is interesting though to ponder what affect—if any—these events had on the engaged couple. Meanwhile, John Aldridge Baugh may have returned to Alabama to prepare for his marriage. If he did, it was not for long.

On August 13, 1829, one week after Mary Ann Marable's 17th birthday, she and John Aldridge Baugh were married. The original Rutherford County marriage license has been lost, so is unknown who performed the service. It may be that Mary Ann's beloved grandfather, Rev. Marable, now seventy-six, married them, or they may have been married by Rev. MacGowan.

It seems that many persons were married in the evening during this time. We can imagine a beautiful summer evening with friends and relatives gathered, as the handsome young couple stood before the minister, taking their vows by candlelight. Mary Ann would have worn a beautiful hand-stitched gown and wildflowers in her hair. Her blue eyes sparkling, perhaps with a hint of tears, as she gazed at the tall, young man who was now her husband. John would have stood tall with pride, gazing at Mary Ann with a beaming smile on his face, as joyful shouts rang through the air after the final confirmation of their vows.

Food of all kinds would have been spread on outdoor tables. There would be a fiddler, and possibly other instruments, playing lively tunes as the newly married couple and their guests danced the evening away. All of the Marable family, no doubt, was there, as well as many local residents.

It is unknown how long the couple stayed in Murfreesboro following their marriage, but by early 1830, John and Mary Ann had left Rutherford County and settled in Alabama near John's parents and his brother, James.[29]

~

The road south to Alabama was a rough wagon ride for John and Mary Baugh. Riding alone in the back of the wagon was Miranda, the black servant girl, who had grown up with Mary since the time they lived in Virginia. Miranda may have even been one of the wedding gifts Mary received from her father.[30]

The Baughs traveled for days through the farmland of Bedford County. With the help of the Marables, likely John had procured a covered wagon and other furnishings. Also in the wagon was a chest of hand-stitched linens that brides always carried, along with dishes, cookware and some small pieces of furniture for their new home.

Mary, wearing a sunbonnet to protect her face, sat beside her husband, proud to be a new wife. It was difficult to say goodbye to the family she loved so much, not knowing when, or if, she would ever see them again. Yet, now on the road with John at her side, life was an exciting new adventure. John Baugh kept a firm hand on their new pair of horses. He had left home a boy. He was returning to Alabama, a man, with a wife and servant.

Crossing the state border, the dry land of southern Tennessee changed to the lush green of Lauderdale County, Alabama. Before long, the Baughs and the lovely young Mary would meet for the first time. John's mother, Elizabeth inquired after Mary's mother, her aunt.

John's parents, Richard Baugh and Elizabeth Pepper Harwell, had married in 1800. Both were native Virginians, born during the American War for Independence. The Baughs had seven children, five boys and two girls. Three of the boys were born in Virginia, including John who was born on March 12, 1806. John's older brother, James, who was married and had three children, lived near his parents. The rest of John's siblings had been born in Tennessee. Nancy, seventeen, was the same age as Mary. Mary Eveline, was fourteen, Richard Batts, twelve, and Robert, nine. With a house full of children, John's parents kept busy.[31]

It is thought that Richard Baugh may have given John land at this time, in lieu of an inheritance.[32] At the time of his death, Richard Baugh's will stated that John had received his inheritance already. The 1830 census showed John and Mary Ann living on farmland just next to John's parents.

Lauderdale County, although quieter than Rutherford, was a thriving farm community; however, it must have been a large adjustment for Mary Ann. Although it was a lovely area, autumn and spring often bring severe thunderstorms and tornados.

It would be two years before the Baughs had their first child. On December 20th, 1831, Mary Ann Baugh gave birth to a little girl they named Caledonia V. Baugh. The reason for her name and the meaning of the initial is unknown. Caledonia was a lovely little girl. In little more than six months after the birth of her daughter, Mary Ann found that she was with child again. This time, the baby was a boy. Born on March 1, 1833, they named him Joseph Lawrence Baugh.

Mary Ann missed her parents and the sharing with her mother and sister. "Betsey," twelve years older, was well-experienced as a wife and mother, and could have been useful to her. Many letters must have passed between them during these years. Benjamin Marable also wrote to John and Mary Ann about the great improvements in Murfreesboro.[33] The town square was now paved, and cotton crops were fetching good prices. Most merchants made 100% profit on the goods they sold. Granville S. Crockett had been elected sheriff.[34]

In addition to town news, there was the news of family and friends. The news that touched Mary Ann most deeply came in October of 1833 when she learned that her beloved eighty year-old grandfather, Reverend Henry Hartwell Marable had passed on to his reward.

In the time following Reverend Marable's passing, the exact events are unknown, but one day in 1834, John Aldridge Baugh decided to move his family back to Rutherford County, Tennessee.

Chapter 10

Return to Tennessee

Shortly after Mary Ann learned that she was going to have another child, John Aldridge Baugh packed the wagon, said goodbye to his parents, and headed back to Rutherford County. He may have felt some elation returning to Murfreesboro. Waterloo, Alabama was not the booming place Murfreesboro had become, and life in the shadow of his older brother was not the life for someone as ambitious as he.

Looking at the facts, it seems probable that one reason for the Baughs return to Tennessee was that Mary Ann found life away from the parents she loved so much unbearable. It is also possible that she was suffering from some kind of illness or depression. In an 1897 letter written by her son, Joseph L. Baugh to one of his Marable cousins, he says of his maternal grandmother, Lucy Marable, "She took me, it's my understanding, from my mother's breast and raised me…"[35]

The return trip to Tennessee found the wagon much fuller than it had been a few short years earlier. Besides a wife, and servant, John now had the responsibility of two small children and one more on the way. Mary Ann Baugh must have felt great joy as she came over the final hill, and saw the town of Murfreesboro across the distant fields.

"See Callie!" we can imagine her saying to her three year-old daughter as they looked across the fields to the courthouse on the hill beyond. "See Callie! There is Murfreesboro! We are home!"

This was a new beginning for the Baughs. They set up house on Marable land, and waited for the arrival of their third child. This baby, born January 20, 1835, was given three names, John Mason Marable Baugh. The Marable and Mason names honored each of Mary Ann's Marable grandparents—Henry Hartwell and Elizabeth Mason Marable.

The baby was small, with dark hair and long legs. If Mary Ann was not well during this time, at least she was now close to family, and could get plenty of support, whether from her parents and their servants, or her sister, "Betsey." When Mary Ann Baugh's mother, Lucy, took little Joe Baugh home and cared for him, he was not far. Mary Ann and John could see him every day if they wanted.

That summer in 1835, a terrible cholera epidemic swept through many American cities, and it came to the town of Murfreesboro. It did not last long, but many, many of the citizens died, including General William Brady, one of the first lawyers of the town, who was presently campaigning for Congress, and Dr. A. Hartwell, possibly a relation of theirs, who died after fighting to save the lives of many residents.[36]

During the epidemic, all business in the town ceased. In fact, a good percentage of the citizens fled in terror. There was barely a family that was not touched by the plague. Cholera strikes an individual in such a way that it can deplete hydration in a matter of hours, killing the victim with terrible spasms. As the siege passed, business started up slowly, but there was great emptiness in the town. According to John C. Spence's *Annals of Rutherford County*, here and there people would enquire of others they knew, "where is so and so?" only to find that person also had succumbed to the "plague."[37]

John Baugh seems to have made some kind of agreement with his father-in-law about farming the Marable land. Benjamin Marable may have given land to the couple as a gift. Benjamin, now nearing sixty, was still full of health and vigor, as was his wife, Lucy. They liked John and wanted to help their daughter. On the 1840 census, the Baugh family cannot be found in the area. However, by 1850, there is documentation showing that John Aldridge Baugh owned twenty-five acres in the area of the Marable, Bass and Rowlett land.

The property lay in the western part of Rutherford County, near the Batey and Howse families. The soil was good, dark soil, excellent for farming. Living on the Marable land, and learning from his father-in-law gave John the chance to save money and build the wealth he hoped for.

At home, life continued peacefully. In the year following John Mason Marable's birth, a little girl was born on July 23, 1836. They named her Lucy Elizabeth Baugh, for both Mary Ann and John's mothers. In February of 1838, another daughter was born whom they named Martha M.

As happy as they were, there were some sorrows in the Baugh family during these years. It was a terrible shock to everyone when Mary Ann's brother, Dr. Benjamin Marable died on March 20th, 1839, after an illness of fifteen hours.[38] He had been a very, respected doctor—noted for his work with the poor. Still, in their immediate little family, the Baughs had known no great tragedies. This would change in 1840, when their beautiful daughter Caledonia died.

Death among young children during these years was an accepted fact of life. Wealthier families often left the care of small children to the servants, so as not to get attached to them in case they died. But Caledonia was now nine, and this death on October 11th, 1840, was totally unexpected.

We can imagine Mary Ann sobbing over the thin breast that heaved no more beneath the gingham dress. The pale, little face was washed one last time, and the long hair plaited neatly before she was laid to rest in a small, wooden box.

Mary Ann's servant, Miranda, had thirteen children, of which only five survived.[39] Miranda may have lost a child at this time as well, and cried silent tears for the loss she knew so well.

The comfort of the preacher's voice, and the knowledge that Caledonia was now in paradise with her beloved grandfather would not erase the sadness Mary Ann felt as she saw the empty place at the table and knew she would no longer hear the happy singing voice or see the smile of her child.

If they attended the funeral service, the other children, Joseph, 7, John, 5, Lucy, 4 (now called Bettie), and Mattie, 2, would have watched as the plain brown box was lowered into the ground and buried. Fifty years later, Joseph Baugh would recall the sister who had died so young. If the children had fears, perhaps Grandmother Lucy Marable could quiet them with songs and scripture about the end of life—which must one day, come for all—and of the life beyond in heaven.

Then, on December 17th, Mary Ann's grandmother, Elizabeth, wife of Henry H. Marable also breathed her last, going to her reward in heaven. In 1842, John would receive word that his father, Richard Baugh had died on August 24th. Life changed greatly for the couple in their first years of marriage. During the next few years, Mary Ann would give birth to three more children: Benjamin Marable Baugh, (named for her father) in 1843, Fredonia A.V. (we are uncertain what these initials stand for), in 1845, and Mary Ann L., in 1847. If Joseph were still living with his grandparents, this would have meant that John and Mary Ann had six children at home.[40]

One large change in Rutherford County life occurred in 1841 with the completion of the Nashville, Murfreesboro and Shelbyville turnpikes. This meant that travel was much easier, allowing for greater commerce in the area. At the same time, a Mr. Osborn came to town with his carriage manufactory. Rather than riding in the old wagons, buggies were the latest invention. With the great increase of business and success in of the area, many were soon riding around in these "new fangled" things.[41]

With a growing family to support, John Aldridge Baugh was not wasting time in his goal of becoming a successful businessman. He now took part in the business of procuring African-American slaves to advance his cause.

In the 1840s, slavery was accepted by most business men in Tennessee. Many who may have felt the stirring of conscience regarding these practices, soon blunted those tender feelings, and justified their actions in favor of their personal families and wealth.

Saturdays in Murfreesboro, there were slave auctions on the west side of the courthouse steps. Many persons of color were still being brought in from other areas, but instead of going to individual families for a lifetime—as was the predominant case in the past—some were now sold by local slave breeders who saw very little difference in these persons and cattle. If nothing else, money blinded their sight.

Babies and young children were sold for profit, while the more experienced slaves were kept to work the land.[42] The new owners looked on these young, Negro children as easy to train, with no loyalties. They often went to owners in other states like Virginia, North Carolina, and Mississippi, never knowing who their parents were or where they came from.[43]

Grief among the slaves was hardly recognized any more than the moans of cattle in the pens. The farmers had their attention on raising a good crop of cotton, and keeping the land. Land in Rutherford County would be booming through the 1850s, as would the price of slaves.

While this situation was true for some, others cared a great deal about their dark-skinned servants. Finding this way of life, a necessary evil, they did what they could to make life easier for them. While we do not know how the Marables or the Baughs treated their servants, there is a record of one of their neighbors, the Howse family.

In her book, "Falling Leaves," Elizabeth O. Howse describes how her grandmother, Betty Burrus Howse rode her horse down to the slave cabins each morning with medical supplies to see how the people there were faring. They would always show her great love and affection for the kindness she showed them.

In another case, children of the Frizzel family were raised by one of their black servants, their mother having died young. Some years later, when a neighbor came and offered money to buy the woman, the eldest son told him, "I would sell my soul before I sold my Mammy."[44]

Interestingly enough, in later years, a Union soldier, Col. John Beatty, visiting the area at beginning of the war stated that the slaves in Rutherford County were the middle class, adding, "They are not considered so good, of course, as their masters, but a great deal better than the white trash…"[45]

On December 30th, 1841, John Baugh bought a "Negro woman, Mary, aged thirty-five years" from James Marable, Mary Ann's cousin. The price he paid for Mary was $400.00. The Bill of Sale stated Mary "to be in sound body and mind."[46] The bill of sale further states, "I forever warrant and defend the right title of said Negro against all claims to said Baugh, his heirs and assigns forever." This was standard language for the sale of any property, including black men, women and children.

Only three days later, January 3, 1842, John A. Baugh sold the same woman to James M. Haynes for five hundred and two dollars.[47] There may have been other sales such as this, but none were officially recorded. Perhaps this one sale was enough for John Baugh to decide he did not want to make his living selling other human beings. There were others in the Murfreesboro area that did this, although it was frowned upon by local society. A good slave brought into a family was considered part of that family, and not parted with easily.[48] In the coming years, John Baugh would increase his slave holdings to over thirty. The slave's names and the birth of their children were recorded carefully on a page in the Baugh Family Bible.

In the year 1843, there were two unusual events. One was a sizeable earthquake, which shook the furniture and caused many bricks to fall from buildings. The other took place later in the year, when a large comet appeared in the western skies; its tail equaled "one-eighth of a circle."[49] For several days after this appearance, many people spent their summer evenings outdoors watching for it. There was a fear that this comet portended a terrible calamity—such as pestilence, famine or war. That March there was also a very deep snow, falling around the Ides of March. In fact, the banks of snow were so deep; they lasted for nearly two weeks! Happily, to everyone's relief, the snow did not affect the farm crops.[50]

In the fall of 1843, one of Tennessee's own, James K. Polk was elected President. Although not that popular in Tennessee, the fact that President Polk's wife, Sarah Childress had family in Murfreesboro—her brother lived on a street just off the Murfreesboro square—was a matter of great pride to most people. When war with Mexico began, many men of the area joined the army and went off to fight; though none of the immediate Baugh family did.

During the period of 1830 to 1850, there were great improvements in the roads, making it much easier to get around the county. Before this, when the spring and fall rains came, wagons loaded with cotton and food heading to Nashville often got stuck in the mud. The mud was so deep, it could take three days in the rain to travel the ten or more miles to Nashville. Even on an ordinary day, with the roads in their present state, they could not travel further than ten or fifteen miles a day.[51]

To allow for drainage and settling, the new roads were built with a layer of rock below the dirt. In addition, there were now tollbooths (one every five miles or so) which included little houses where a tollgate keeper and his family lived. In this way, the tollgates could be manned 24 hours a day. The funds collected at these gates were used as payment for the upkeep of the new roads.[52]

With the great success cotton planters were having in Rutherford County, and the increase of commerce due to the new roads, it seems that John Baugh was doing quite well. In October 1848, he made his first recorded purchase of land. The 1849 Rutherford County Tax List states that John Baugh owned 370 acres valued at $3,700, 5 slaves valued at $2500, and other property valued at $150.* His wealth had grown considerably since his marriage and would continue to increase.

May of 1849 brought a new addition to the Baugh family of another kind. A little girl, Eliza A. was born. In the following year, John Aldridge Baugh would sell his Marable land, and move the family, now consisting of ten persons, to another location.

John A. Baugh was an ambitious and energetic man, who worked hard to increase his wealth and holdings. Around this time, he found a new area near the future railroad that interested him. It was not far from Millersburg, just off the Shelbyville Highway—before the crest of the hill going down to Bedford County. The place, once known as Jordan's Valley, had just been renamed Christiana.

---

* $3700 in 1849, equals approximately $103,531 CPI in 2007; $2500 = $69,593; $150 = $4,197.

Chapter 11

Catching Up With the Gums

DURING THE YEARS 1810 TO 1820, MANY OF THE ORIGINAL SETTLERS of Rutherford County had passed away or moved on. Now, the pioneers' children were the residents.

While Norton Gum and most of his family had disappeared from life in Jefferson, William Gum, upon his marriage to Malinda Nugent, settled there and started a family. Then suddenly, sometime between 1827 and 1829, William Norto n Gum—like his father before him—was gone from public record. Left behind were twenty-eight year old Malinda Gum and three small children. Viewing the records, some might assume that William had died, but had he?

Down the road, twenty-seven year old William Crosthwait was back on the scene. When the local militia practiced their maneuvers, William could be seen marching with the 22nd Regiment Light Infantry, a commission he received on October 16, 1828.[53]

During the militia's days of training and maneuvers, the local citizens came out with picnic baskets to enjoy the sight.[54] The Light Infantry wore blue hunting shirts, jean pantaloons and round black hats with red plumes. Marching with them were the riflemen in black hunting shirts, black pantaloons and black hats festooned with white plumes. The cavalry joined in wearing uniforms of deep blue, and boots with spurs. It was truly a magnificent sight. All these uniform were the handiwork of the ladies, who took special pride in their contribution.

In general, the people of Rutherford County were full of military spirit. Every able-boded man was required by law to enlist in these self-governing militia companies. Almost every man carried a title and took pride in it. Men like William Crosthwait enjoyed being addressed as "Captain," "Colonel," or "Major."[55]

In his daily life, William Crosthwait held the title of stone mason; "a person who prepares and lays stones for foundations, walls, and chimneys." This was the apprenticeship that had been arranged by his uncle, Shelton Crosthwait, per the request in his father's will. It was four years since Uncle Shelton had passed away. William, now twenty-nine and still single, was ready for a home and family of his own.

Sometime around 1829 or 1830, William formed a bond with Malinda Nugent Gum. One cannot help wonder whether William had been away for a time prior to this, and whether Malinda was a woman he had cared for long before her marriage to William Gum. In any case, at this point in time she was free to marry.

Although a marriage certificate does not exist for the couple, William and Malinda were married sometime prior to the 1830 census, for at that time he is shown to be living with a woman and two small children. Most likely, the preacher marrying them did not return the certificate to the county clerk (which happened now and then). Because of this, their marriage was never recorded. Historically, this fact, among others, has led to some of the confusion about the Gum family.

In 1830, William and Malinda Crosthwait were living in the area south of Wilkinson crossroads, and the land where Benjamin Marable lived. One of the earliest settlers in this area was Alfred Blackman, who settled there with numerous family members in 1808. The land here was said to be unsurpassed in fertility. Although, according to property records, William Crosthwait did not own the land he was farming, he must have felt fortunate to be in such a fine location.

Also living in the Crosthwait home were Malinda's two children, Sarah, age five and John, age three. The question remains—if William Gum was deceased, where was the eldest son, Billy Norton Gum, who at this time would have been only seven or eight years old?

Billy could have lived with a grandparent, aunt, or uncle, yet his biography as published in *Goodspeed's Missouri*, states that he learned the trade of bricklayer from his father.[56] If this is true, and William was still alive after 1830, it might be assumed that he was a restless man who wished to be on the move, and perhaps had gone to work in Nashville or another area, taking Billy with him.

William Gum never appeared in the Rutherford County census again. If he was not deceased prior to Melinda's second marriage, we expect that he did not live a long life. The truth about this will likely never be known. No records of death were kept in Rutherford County during these years, and burials were often on a family farm, or in an unmarked grave. In addition, during this time many men rode off to the newly opened western territory and began new lives. What happened to William Norton Gum remains a mystery.

The marriage of Malinda Nugent Gum and William Crosthwait seems to have been a happy one. William had taken alot upon himself marrying a widow (or divorced woman) with three small children. It would be a few years before William and Malinda started a family of their own. In 1834, the first Crosthwait child of their union was a little girl whom the couple named Emeline. Two years later, their second daughter, Harriet, was born.

By 1840, the U.S. Federal Census shows the Crosthwaits still living in the area of Blackman, two properties from William Beesley and six properties from Lazarus Blackman. The household now consisted of eight persons and no slaves. Although the U.S. Census, prior to 1850, does not give names other than head of household, we may surmise by sex and age that eighteen-year old Billy Norton Gum was now residing with the Crosthwaits, along with his sister Sarah, 12, and brother, John, 11. By now, the Gum children had an assortment of half-siblings. There was Emeline, 6, Harriet, 4, and baby, Anderson. Two members of the household were listed under the profession of "Agriculture." It may be surmised that the two members of the family farming were William Crosthwait and his step-son, Billy Gum.

~

Around this time, a notable and tragic event took place—one no doubt witnessed by many of the Gums, Crosthwaits, and other persons in Rutherford County. For numerous years Native Americans had been living peacefully—for the most part—among the white residents of the south-eastern states. Then in 1830, with the support and encouragement of President Andrew Jackson, Congress passed the Indian Removal Act. This bill was to provide for the removal of all Native Americans to the lands west of the Mississippi River. Various citizens, including Davy Crocket, disagreed with this decision; however some Cherokees had been persuaded to sign a treaty giving up their land. Thus, their fate was sealed.

The agreed upon time for the removal of the Native Americans was May 1838. Fearing that the move (which was supposed to be voluntary, but soon became mandatory) might result in violence, President Martin Van Buren sent in Federal troops to round up the Indians and escort them on their move west. Despite the fact that many had farms and other attachments to local life, they had no choice but to leave. As the soldiers arrived, they were forced to pack what little they could carry and march west.[57]

In 1838, a long line of Native American refugees, escorted by soldiers, could be seen marching down the Old Nashville Highway. They passed Old Jefferson and Murfreesboro, continuing on through Bedford County.[58] Many were old and ill. Some did not even have shoes. In all, 2,000 to 4,000 Native Americans died along the route they traveled, a trail that became known as the "Trail of Tears." No doubt the citizens of Rutherford County watched this long, sad march with mixed emotions. By 1839, except for a very few who hid in the hills, all Native American peoples were gone from the land that had so long been theirs.

～

Sometime between 1840 and 1850, William Crosthwait and his family moved back to Jefferson. By the time the census taker arrived in 1850, Billy Gum was gone, and two more children had arrived. There was Henry D. born in 1841, and little sister, Lucy, born on April 2nd, 1843. The Crosthwaits had a full house with five children and four adults. Sarah Gum was now 24, and John Gum, 22. Then, there was Emeline, 16, Harriet, 14, Anderson, 11, Henry, 9, and Lucy, 6.

During the early years when William Gum and Malinda were married, Williams's young brother, Hinchey Petway Gum, or "Petie," as he liked to be called, also resided in the area of Jefferson, possibly farming the land. Petie enjoyed the company of his young cousins, and in later years, he would remain in touch with them by letter.

By 1830, Petie decided that Rutherford County did not have enough to offer him. His sense of adventure led him to Kentucky where some of the distant Gum cousins had settled. In Allen County, Petie—going by the name Petway Gum—met a young girl named Julia Welch. The couple was married on March 11, 1833.[59] Julia was 20 and Petie, 21.

In the next few years, Petie and Julia Gum

Figure 4. Wilson Alexander Gum, son of Robert E. Gum and Mary Ann Fulks.
(Courtesy of Ralph Puckett)

started their own large family. There was Sarah, born in 1836 (probably named for Petie's mother), Mary in 1837, Sydney in 1840, Payton in 1842, Catherine in 1844, William in 1846, and Elizabeth in 1854. Many people in Tennessee moved just above the state border to Kentucky, an easy distance from Rutherford County. It seems likely that during the years Petie lived in Kentucky, he came to visit his Rutherford County family at least a few times.

South of Murfreesboro, Robert E. had settled down to farm life with his wife, Mary Ann. Through the years, their family continued to grow. In 1832, Mary Ann Gum gave birth to her 4th child, Wilson Alexander Gum. Following his birth, a child arrived every two years: Melinda (possibly named for her aunt) was born in 1836, Mary Ann in 1838 and William T. in 1840.

Although the Gums and Fulks lived in the country, they were not isolated from the important events of middle Tennessee. In 1839, John Fulks served on the county committee, planning a welcome for former President Andrew Jackson. The following year, John Fulks served as a delegate at the Democratic State Convention.

Robert Gum worked hard, and was quite successful. In 1839, he bought fifty acres of land at the head of Cripple Creek from William Lowe. The property purchase included three horses, three colts, saddles, cattle, hogs and furniture.[60]

Then in 1842, a terrible tragedy befell the family when Mary Ann, Robert E.'s beloved wife, died suddenly at the age of thirty-five. During their twenty-one years of marriage, Mary Ann had given birth to seven children.[61] At the time of their mother's death, the Gum children were between twenty, and two years of age. Possibly, another pregnancy was the cause of her death—as it was for many women at that time. Death was no stranger to most families then. Life was not easy, and there were many dangers, and untreatable diseases.

In *The Story of Murfreesboro*, the author, C.C. Henderson speaks of a good-natured, "Bobbie Gum" who loved to play practical jokes. Apparently, Robert Gum also had an extremely loud voice and knew how to project it. When he was drinking, or as the author put it—"imbibing" in a "certain number of drinks of pure liquor," his enthusiasm could get out of control.[62]

The Presidential campaign of 1844 had two candidates: James K. Polk, who favored expansion, and Whig candidate, Henry Clay, who was opposed to it. As previously mentioned, although James Polk was a native of the area, he was not all that popular in Tennessee. Bobbie Gum, like most Tennesseans, supported Henry Clay. According to the story, Judge Anderson was holding court one day when Robert E., standing on the east steps of the Murfreesboro Courthouse, yelled out in his loudest voice, "Hooray, hooray, HOORAY for Harry Clay!"

With his tremendous voice, Robert E. totally disrupted the courtroom. The Judge had him brought before the bench and reprimanded him. Rather than sending him to jail though, he asked him to please go home!

Bobbie's response to the judge was pleasant and polite. (Remember he had already spent time in jail for riding his horse into the courtroom!) Still filled with enthusiasm for his candidate, he asked the Judge if he might be granted the "favor" of giving Henry Clay just three more cheers. Judge Anderson agreed on one condition—he was not to show favoritism to either candidate, but to cheer for each one in turn.

Robert E. considered this stipulation carefully. He was not really fond of James Polk, but he agreed. The Judge suspended court for a few moments, and everyone went out to the courthouse steps where Robert E. gave three resounding cheers for Henry Clay—so loud, it is said he could be heard two miles away—his voice echoing over the farmland. After that, he took a deep breath and began three more big "hoorays." At the conclusion of each one, he lowered his voice to a whisper for, "James K. Polk." Then, he jumped on his horse and rode away. This story gives us a rare glimpse into the long ago character of Robert E. Gum.

Three years later, in 1847 (five years after his wife's passing), Robert E. Gum succumbed—some thought of a broken heart. There were still many small Gum children to be cared for, so Mary Ann's mother, Elizabeth, took the children across the way to the Fulks' home, and raised them herself.[63] The early loss of a Gum parent seems to have been a sad curse that would occur again and again over the years.

Chapter 12

Life Down by Christiana

B Y 1850, THE BAUGH FAMILY WAS LIVING IN BIG SPRINGS, A SMALL town approximately nine miles south of Murfreesboro, and one and one-half miles east of the Murfreesboro-Shelbyville Pike. The town had been founded around a spring of "crystal clear, cool limestone water" that stage-coaches and other early travelers found "impossible to pass up."[64]

The founding of an inn and stores had led to an entire community. John Baugh discovered that Big Springs was an affordable and desirable place to invest in, and raise a family. There was a school and a Methodist church; both important to the Baughs. The town also boasted a post office, just opened in 1848. Lewis Harrell was the first postmaster.[65] The mail's arrival into town was announced by the stagecoach driver blowing a horn.

The 1850 census taker wrote the Baugh name as he heard it spoken: "Bow." Listed as living in household #956 were: John, 43, a farmer; Mary, 35; Joseph, 17, with no profession at the time; John, 15; Elizabeth, 13; Martha, 11; Benjamin, 9; Fredonia, 7; Mary, 5; and Eliza, 1. John Baugh's income (or worth) was listed as $5,000. This amount being approximately $124,000 in the year 2005, John Baugh was not doing badly.

In addition to the immediate family residing in the home, there were two visitors, originally from England: fourteen year-old Anna Butterworth and her brother, twelve year-old John Butterworth. The children's mother, Mrs. Eliza Butterworth, a short, pleasant British lady, was staying at a neighboring farm with the John Woods family. The father, Mr. Ashton

Butterworth, was a British businessman, who worked in manufacturing, and traveled between the United States and England.

Although the family had immigrated to the United States in 1839, and Mr. Butterworth owned property in the area where the Baughs lived, his whereabouts at this time are unknown. It seems the Butterworths had friends, or church associates, to live with in Rutherford County, while Mr. Butterworth established his business.

When the census taker rode up to the "Bow" home on his horse, what did he see? The house, according to the style of the time, was likely a one-story clapboard house with a large sloping roof to keep out the Tennessee summer heat. There was a chimney at each end of the house with a large room for eating and other activities. All of the boys would have all stayed in one room, and the girls in another, with two or three children per bed. While John Baugh was doing well financially, it was still a common custom at the time for the children of each sex to not only share a room, but to share beds.

This home likely had a long porch across the entire front, with posts or columns holding up the roof. This style of porch was known as a "portico." Here the family could sit during the hot summer afternoons, sewing, or shelling peas, and doing other household chores. In the evenings, when a nice breeze might cool them, they would talk, play music, and watch the huge kaleidoscope of stars in the dark night sky.

John Baugh probably planted corn, oats and wheat, as well as, cotton on this farm. There may have been some livestock as well—at least for use by the family. The school nearby was seasonal, and the children of the area walked there, carrying pails with sandwiches, and fruit for their afternoon meal. In the warmer months, they went barefoot to save wear and tear on their shoes.

Now that the Baugh plantation was established, and their wealth had increased, most of the work was done by the slaves. However, with ten children in the house, and more than twenty slaves, there was still plenty to do. The lady of the house was responsible for seeing that clothing was made for the servants, as well as family members. The cotton had to be made into thread, and then woven on a loom into cloth. The wool had to be spun into yarn, and woven. Dyes were made from berries and herbs to give the cloth color. Finally, it was cut to fit, and sewn by hand.

Figure 5. An old Tennessee home in Big Springs. The Baughs may have lived in a similar house, or even this one.

Life was sweet, but there was hard work for the men as well. Unless they had an overseer, John and the boys had the job of "bossing" the servants. They got up early to start the day, and saw that the work was begun at dawn. There was work to be done in the fields, livestock to be fed, cows to be milked, and taken to pasture. The work did not stop until the sun went down.

On cold mornings from late October to early June, Mary Ann rose early, while the servants started fires in the fireplaces to warm the house. During the day, while the men were out, there was cooking, cleaning, and laundry to supervise. To organize this work, a different day would be assigned for each task. For instance, Tuesday might be baking day, while Friday might be laundry day.

Baths were taken once a week. On Saturday night, or Sunday morning before church, a big tub was placed in the kitchen before the fire. The heated water was cool by the time the last member of the family got in. With all the layers of clothing, persons had to run down the path 100 yards or more to get to the privy behind the house. These outhouses had to be moved periodically, and the old ones covered over. At night, chamber pots were used; they must be cleaned as well.

Despite all the hardships, family members depended upon one another, and found reason for joy and laughter. On Saturdays the men loaded up their wagons and went to Murfreesboro to sell some of the goods they had harvested, as well as poultry, meats, and items that had been made. Families often bartered with each other for goods not produced on their own farm; things like seed, fabric, tools or food stuffs. The women stayed home on Saturdays because often enough the men got to drinking at one of the dozen taverns on the Square, and there was sure to be a brawl or a gunfight.

On May 13, 1851, Mary Ann Baugh delivered her tenth child, a son whom they named Charles Richard Baugh. The very day that Charlie was born, John Baugh's mother, seventy-year old Elizabeth Baugh, passed away in Alabama. John did not learn of this fact for at least several days,

Figure 6. Land and an old Barn at Big Springs.

since the only form of communication he had with his relatives in Alabama was by mail.

Between the servants and older daughters, Mary Ann Baugh, who was nearly thirty-nine, had plenty of help with the baby. In fact, the Baugh family, while living in a house that was not exceptionally grand as some plantation homes, was probably living very nicely.

On July 4th, 1851, there was a huge barbeque in Murfreesboro to celebrate the opening of the Nashville and Chattanooga Railroad, which had been under construction for the last twelve months. As the train came through town for the first time, the noise was so loud and frightening—a sound none of them had heard before—some of the ladies fainted. The cattle were frightened as well.[66]

Quite a few of the Murfreesboro citizens boarded the train that day and took a ride south. The idea of traveling so quickly from place to place—without obstruction—was truly amazing to people. Only a generation before, travelers had come over the mountains in wagons that broke as they passed over tree trunks and through rocky streams. The arrival of the railroad would change everything, and John Baugh, for one, was ready for it.

Shortly after the arrival of the railroad, another turnpike was finished; the Murfreesboro to Woodberry Turnpike. The opening of this turnpike meant that many residents would soon move to outlying areas that previously had not been advantageous to those who wanted to farm and sell their crops.

John Baugh began scouting out some of these new locations. His interest in buying land cheaply—in a new and untried area—might explain his willingness to sell the land he had received from Benjamin Marable. His mind was on business, and gaining wealth.

In September of 1850, Mr. Baugh sold his land near the Marable farm to James Bass, one of the longtime residents of the area. For the sale, John Baugh received $200.00.* The record states that the sale included "all appurtenances," which could mean a home, a barn, and/or various farm tools.[67] The sale was finalized at the Rutherford County Courthouse in Murfreesboro by John Woods, the County Clerk, on August 5, 1851.

---

* $200 in 1851 equals approximately $5,078.26 in 2005.

In October of 1852, John Baugh added to his slaves by buying a Negro woman named Ailsey, twenty-five years-old, and her child, Fanny, twenty-two months-old.[68] He made this purchase from Mr. M.R. Rushing, and paid $750.00* cash on the spot.

John Baugh seemed to be involved in many things. Even with the help of his many slaves, one wonders how he kept up. Now, in the mid-1850s, he took on another responsibility. The county had a system which was a kind of welfare. Persons in need of care, and who did not have families to care for them, were appointed a guardian by the court. The "Trustee"— as the caregiver was called—met with the court every few months for review. At that time, he was either replaced, or given authority to continue looking after the person. The caregiver also held money in trust for the person's care.

In January of 1854, John Baugh apparently volunteered, and was appointed to care for Calvin Creasy, "an indigent and affected man."[69] The court gave John A. Baugh, as Trustee, $50.00 to be used for this care.

For the next four years (1854–1858), John Baugh was also appointed to care for John Creasey. It is not known if this is the same man, a relative of Calvin's, or what if any ties there were to the Baugh or Marable families. The record states that John Creasy was "old, affected and indigent." Again, John Baugh was given money for his care. John Creasy must have died some time after the last court order in March of 1858, as there is no further mention of him.

⁓

As previously stated, the first official record of property ownership for John Baugh was in 1848. He procured the land from Burrell Gannaway White in an area known as Millersburg. This was the very town John passed through years earlier on his way to Murfreesboro. On October 20th, 1848, Mr. Baugh paid Mr. White $4,000 for 370 acres of "land lying on the waters of the East fork of the West fork of Stones River in District No. 25."[70] The property lay on a flat plain, nestled between winding hills, and was crossed with creeks and river branches, making it excellent farmland.

---

* $750 in 1852 or approximately $18,838.71 in 2005.

The families who moved to Millersburg between 1810 and 1839 stayed. There were the Millers who had founded Millersburg as well as the Whites, Broyles, Pruitts, Fox family, and Howlands. Just east of Millersburg were the Hoovers. The area they lived in was known as Hoover's Gap. In this area, many people lived in "hollows" (pronounced "hollers"); communities hidden among the hills, where neighbors became family, and lived for generations. Although the Baughs were not living in Millersburg at the time, Big Springs was only a little more than five miles away.

When, in 1848, the Tennessee Legislature granted a charter for the railroad to be built, they planned for it to run from Nashville to Chattanooga, with stops in Murfreesboro and Christiana.[71] John Baugh—with good business sense—bought property in District 25 with an eye toward this future. The proximity of his land to the new railroad meant that he would be able to easily transport his goods by rail. During this time, John bought two properties next to the future train depot in the small town of Christiana.

Jordan's Valley had its name changed about the time the railway came though. The men working on the railway named the rail station "Christiana," and that name soon stuck to the town. Some say it was named for a black railway cook, others for a sweetheart, and still others for a little girl who used to greet the men working on the rails.

Coming off the Shelbyville Turnpike, one rode through flat farmland, until crossing the train tracks. Then, turning left, there was a bank, a post office and Miller's Country store.[72] One home even had a lookout from which you could see the train coming.[73] The road through Christiana, curved around running parallel to the train tracks, until it turned and went to Millersburg, Wayside, Big Springs and Hoover's Gap.

Life was good in this land of beauty, where the skies were blue and peaceful. Now in his 40s, some twenty years after starting married life, John was a hale and hearty suntanned farmer. Like the other men of the area, he may have had a long beard. He rode his horses and conducted his business with great command and energy.

The people of Middle Tennessee worked hard and lived off the land. They were religious people who did not believe in frivolity. Since the outbreak of alcoholism years earlier in Rutherford County, many had joined temperance societies. Most were thin. Mary Ann's Marble history may have meant that she had gained some girth with the birth of so many children. Still, she retained the charm of her upbringing. She was always interested in others; making strangers feel at home; comforted by her kindly questioning and pleasant demeanor.

"Mirandy," Mary Ann Baugh's long-time servant, was a good cook and did most of the cooking for the family. When not cooking, she sat behind the spinning wheel, spinning wool and cotton into long skeins of yarn or thread that could be knitted, or woven into cloth.[74] Between the Baugh family and their servants, there were nearly fifty people to clothe.

Some slaves were taught skills like paving roads, working a mill, or making shoes. The owners could lend these men and women out for a fee. It appears John Baugh sometimes did this. The only problem with lending your servants was—the person you lent them to, might not treat them well, or might even cause them physical or emotional injury.

Willis' father, Clem Marable (who was probably a slave of Benjamin Marable) made shoes. Willis did not see his father often, but he was lucky to know who he was. Many did not.

The Baugh slaves—as Mirandy's son, Willis, would later recount— lived in one-room log cabins behind the main house. Willis was born on November 20, 1842, and was a year older than John and Mary Ann's son, Benjamin. While we do not know how the Baughs treated their slaves, as a general rule, slaves worked all the time—no matter how they felt—unless they were too ill to rise out of their straw pallets. Some slave owners employed doctors to look after their slaves, and prevent serious illness. These slaves considered themselves lucky.

There were many acres to farm. The field slaves spent their days walking behind a horse with a hand plough. Willis Baugh stated that on the Baugh farm, he spent much of his time plowing, hoeing corn, and "chop[ing] cotton."[75] The land was rough, and each year there was clearing to do.

The slaves were expected to begin work as soon as it was light, and work until dark. In the summer, it stayed light later, which meant they worked longer. Then, they retired to their cabins, until the light of day demanded they went back to work. The "house Negroes" had to finish most of their work before sunset because the light of the fire and candles was not enough to see well.

On a big farm, with so many acres and people, there was always work to do. The servants, whatever they felt, knew that life was as it was. White and black alike accepted the fact that this life was not meant to be all happiness and joy. If the slaves had a kind master, and their loved ones around them, they felt truly blest.

On Sunday, the servants went to church with their masters. They either sat outside, or in the basement—where they could hear the sermon. Sunday was the one day they didn't have to work. The sermon and music often brought them to tears—as they learned of another life to come, when Jesus would wash away each tear, and reunite them with their loved ones. The white men and women wore fine clothes. The Negro, for the most part, wore rough, spun cotton both summer and winter.

Seasonally, the white children went to school, often in the same building used for church on Sundays. The children of the slaves did not take any schooling. It was forbidden for any slave to learn to read, though some did. Some owners even taught them secretly.

Work was considered good for the soul, and respected among white and black alike. According to Willis Baugh, the white men watched and bossed, but the black men and women did all the labor. This is how it was for most persons in the entire community. (This situation may have been truer for the Baughs later, when John Baugh owned more land and slaves. There were those who worked side by side with their slaves.)

Men who owned slaves considered themselves of an upper class. The servants kept you where you were, and symbolized your status in society. Slave owners looked down on those who did not have slaves. The slaves themselves noticed this. In public places, those with slaves did not mingle with those who had no slaves.[76] By the same token, a slave owned by a master with many slaves considered themselves superior to a slave owned by a master with few.

Though slaves could not officially marry, they had their own ceremonies of marriage. The Baugh slaves inter-married among each other, and with the neighboring Hoover, Miller, Howland, and White slaves. The farms were close, and it was easy for them to visit. This would usually be done on a Saturday night or Sunday.

No one could do anything without asking their "Massa" for permission. To travel from one farm to another, a written slip of permission was needed. There were patrollers or "pattyrollers" as the slaves called them, who checked to see that the servant had a permission slip, and that no one was going off on his or her own without the knowledge of their owner.

During the 1850s, the Baugh slaves increased with the birth of at least 24 babies. In the Baugh Family Bible, John Baugh, or possibly Mary Ann, kept a record of the births on the Family Record page. Next to "Births" was written "Servants." There were four births in the 1830s, and four in the 1840s, including Mirandy's children, Willis in 1842, Gilbert in 1844, and Larry in 1845. Miranda also had a daughter, Jane, who was born in 1834.

After the first year when John Aldridge Baugh had bought a woman only to sell her days later at a profit, he did not deal in the slave trade, but kept most—if not all—the slaves he had acquired.

Christiana and Millersburg were small communities where everyone knew everyone. The residents knew the other family's history as well. On Sundays, besides worship, folks went to church to socialize. These were the times the children enjoyed the most. The young boys and girls wore their Sunday best, and got to know who was who. Planning for the future began early. You were almost certain to marry someone "a buggy ride away."[77]

On certain occasions there were dances for the young people to meet and court. Fiddlers played country reels, while young men and women jumped, hopped, and skipped; their feet stomping in time to the music. Young girls under the lantern light, with blushing cheeks and sparkling eyes, were courted by young men who not long before had been gawky boys. These couples might soon find themselves planning a wedding.

So it was with young Joseph and Anna Butterworth, three years his junior. It is unknown how long the Butterworth children lived with the Baughs, but it

Figure 7. Anna Butterworth in the late 1860s.

was certainly long enough to form a bond between the pair. By 1854, twenty-one year-old Joseph was engaged to eighteen year-old Anna.

On October 11, 1854, the Baugh and Butterworth families gathered together to celebrate the marriage of Joseph Law-rence Baugh and Anna Butterworth. Joseph seems to have resembled the Marables, with his broad chest. Anna was petite and delicate with her proper English accent. Although the marriage took place in Rutherford County, a very, short time after the wedding, the couple moved to Winchester, where Anna's parents now resided.

Figure 8. Ashton Butterworth, Winchester, TN, circa 1860.

The town of Winchester was founded in 1807, but it was not until the 1830s that the place took form, and the population exceeded one thousand. Built on a bluff over-looking the Elk River, Winchester is a beautiful spot surrounded by water, forests, farms, and mountains. The trip from Murfreesboro was approximately 66 miles along the Manchester Pike. Now, with the train, it was possible for the couple to travel easily between Winchester and Murfreesboro. Times had changed!

By 1860, Ashton Butterworth had founded a newspaper in Winchester, called the *People's Paper*. In addition, he also owned a mill just outside the town.[78] The amount of water in the area made Winchester a prime loca-tion for mills. Mr. Butterworth understood this fact, and had purchased a cotton mill just over the river from Winchester, on the Lynchburg Road in the Harmony area.[79]

Since Joseph Baugh had little interest in becoming a farmer, Mr. But-terworth's offer of a job at the mill was a fine one. So, Joseph went to work for his father-in-law, and the couple set-up house, right there at the mill.

Chapter 13

Jefferson, 1850

IN THE 1840S, JEFFERSON'S APPEARANCE CONTINUED TO CHANGE. IT WAS still the location for food and cotton inspection, but it was not the place its founders, Weakley and Bedford, had envisioned. The square, which Norton Gum had seen rising, was altered so greatly that had he and his peers returned, they might not have recognized it.

The two-story brick courthouse—once the pride of the town—had burnt, and been dismantled brick-by-brick. Also gone were the whipping post (whipping was outlawed in 1829), and stocks. The jail remained nearby, unused. The bustling line of shack shops along the road leading to the Stones River port, were taken down, and carted away.

In 1824, mill owner Constant Hardeman built a steamboat, which traveled between Jefferson and Nashville, but that did not last long. By the 1840s, the rafting of cedar logs—a local export—was the main form of commerce in Jefferson. Boats came through now and then, but the river was found to be not suitable for much traffic. During the low season, a person could easily walk across the river—or even drive a wagon through it— making the route up to Nashville, or down to Murfreesboro a bit shorter.

In spring, when the rains came, the Stones River rose—often turning Jefferson into an island. The lots along the water's edge were found to be uninhabitable. Only those who lived on the crest of the hill, where the old square had been, were relatively safe from flooding. So, bit by bit, these waterfront lots were abandoned, or sold off for a few dollars. Residents who chose to remain often bought several lots. In this way, the town slowly turned into an area of homes with large gardens, or small farms with livestock.

With the passing of time, Jefferson seemed to be left behind. The final blow to the town's position as a center of commerce was the coming of the railroad. Seeing how quickly and easily goods could be transported by rail, much of the river commerce was no longer needed.

For the rest of its existence, the town would be referred to as "Old Jefferson." In fact, the town had really become a sort of village. Yet to those who lived there, it was still a place of activity. The stores and taverns around the square did a good amount of business; often to travelers stopping on their way to-and-from Nashville.

Among those remaining in Jefferson was the Crosthwait family. On a hill above the town, Elizabeth Thompson Crosthwait, widow of Shelton, resided peacefully in her mansion over-looking the Stones River. The Crosthwaits' eldest daughter, Mary had wed a Mr. Richardson. George Crosthwait attended the University of Virginia, followed by Transylvania University in Kentucky where he studied medicine. He graduated in 1832 with honors, and returned to Jefferson, where for a time, he became the town doctor.[80]

Soon after his return, Dr. Crosthwait met the lovely Frances Elizabeth Burton. Eliza, eight years his junior, was the daughter of Colonel Frank Burton and Lavinia Murfree, the daughter of Colonel Hardy Murfree, for whom the town of Murfreesboro was named. Eliza's aunt, Sally Murfree was married to Dr. James Maney. The couple resided at the Oaklands Mansion.

Eliza Burton Crosthwait was well-educated. Public record shows she even held power of attorney—not at all usual for the women of her day. Together, George and Eliza Crosthwait were as about as wealthy as they came. They were also good people, and remained involved in the community.

Following their marriage in 1836, the Crosthwait children came quickly. Little Shelton Crosthwait, named for his grandfather, was born on November 10, 1837. Lavinia followed in 1839, and Frank Burton Crosthwait in 1842.

Figure 9. Shelton Crosthwait (1837–1862).

Figure 10. Frank Crosthwait (1842–1862).

The youngest daughter, Rebecca married the very respectable lawyer, Bromfield Ridley of McMinnville, Tennessee in 1829. The same year George Crosthwait graduated from medical college, Ridley was appointed District Attorney General by Tennessee Governor William Carroll. The district Ridley served included Warren County. For ten years the couple resided in McMinnville, while he attended to his duties. Following his term as District Attorney General, Bromfield Ridley served as Warren County Representative in the Tennessee State Legislature. When Mr. Ridley became Chancellor of the Fourth Chancery District, he decided that the family (which now included

Figure 11. Bromfield Crosthwait (1845–1862).

five children) should move to Old Jefferson—a much closer location to "the center of his duties" in Nashville.[81]

At the time the Ridleys made the decision to move, they already owned land in the area of Jefferson. George Crosthwait had sold them fifty acres of Crosthwait family land several years prior to this. Two years after the Ridley's move, Bromfield Ridley purchased an additional 500 acres. This purchase included the Crosthwait mills, and the ancestral home known as "Fairmont."

Fairmont sat on a natural elevation of about fifty feet above the surrounding land, and over-looked the curving bend of the Stones River. As later described by the Ridley daughter, Bettie Blackmore, the home was built in "cottage style." The house was one and one-half story, with a long portico that was closed off at each end by lattice-works, dripping with honeysuckle, virgin bower, and roses. To reach the house, the visitor came down a long, winding, gravel drive and though a gate. There they would see the home surrounded by eighty acres of blue grass, clover, gardens and old forest. In the 1860s, Bettie Blackmore described the plantation land in this way:

> "…old, majestic, native forest trees, which stand out on the scene with bold, leafy branches and boughs, continually awakening a sensation of power and protection."[82]

As was customary in many early 1800s homes, the inside of the house had a long hall which ran through the length of the building. The hallway was approximately forty-five feet in length, and along its walls were five doors which led to parlors, a dining room and "chamber rooms" (bedrooms). At the end of the hall was a winding staircase, with ornamental railings. This went to the upper hall, and the "attic rooms."

Beyond the immediate house and garden lay fields of cotton and other crops, as well as the log homes of the slaves. Under Bromfield Ridley's ownership, the plantation grew. By 1860, over one hundred slaves lived at Fairmont, farming the land, running the mills, and caring for the mansion house.

About the same time the Ridleys moved to Old Jefferson, Dr. George Crosthwait and Eliza decided to move to Murfreesboro with their children: Shelton, Lavinia and Mary. Following their move, Frank, Bromfield, Eliza, and George were born. Dr. Crosthwait and Eliza loved each other

*Figure 12. An ancient tree on the location of the old Crosth-
wait/Ridley Plantation, not far from where Fairmont once
stood. Note Jefferson historian, Toby Francis stands at the
base of the tree to show its size.*

deeply, and their marriage seems to have been quite happy. Within a few
years, the Crosthwaits left Tennessee and moved to Iowa.

When Rebecca and her husband moved to Fairmont, they brought with
them their four children, Jerome Shelton, 8, Mary Elizabeth, 6, Virginia, 4,
and James, 2. There would be five more children born in the Fairmont
house over the next ten years: George in 1840, Granville in 1842 (he
died in infancy), Charles in 1843, Bromfield in 1845, and Sarah in 1849.

It is not known how close William Crosthwait and his cousins or Aunt
Elizabeth remained, or whether he and his family visited Fairmont. As
listed in the 1850 census, William and Malinda's home was only two

properties away from the Ridleys. Next door to them were the Mere-diths. Mr. Meredith, listed as "overseer," was likely working on the Ridley Estate. Since there are no property records for William Crosthwait, it seems quite possible that he and his family were living in the same home he had shared with his parents as a young boy. Still, the status of the William Crosthwait family and his cousins—the Ridleys and Crosth-waits—were vastly different.

Malinda Nugent Gum Crosthwait and her children had to be very much aware of the grand Fairmont plantation just beyond their doors. The affect of this is something to ponder. Above them was the beautiful home where their cousins lived, and surrounding them were their vast lands and gardens full of flowers.

The Crosthwaits would always have a sense that they were of a higher bloodline. The family greatly valued education as well. How the Gums felt is unknown. Living where they did, they would also have been aware of the activities of the slaves; their work in the fields, and their songs. They also would have seen the comings and goings of fancy carriages and dignitaries.

The children may have attended school together at one time, but how vastly different their homes, dress and manners must have been. In the mid-1800s, a person's manner of dress alone showed their status in society.

Unlike their rich cousins, William Crosthwait and his family had no slaves or servants of their own. They had to sew their own clothes, clean their home, milk their cows, and other things not thought of in our modern age. They had chickens for eggs and meat, a cow for milk and butter, and a small garden in which to grow their vegetables. The locals often kept goats as well as mules, which were very popular in Tennessee.

Sister Sarah helped her mother, Malinda, with the small children and the house. In 1850, besides half-sister Emeline, who was 16, there was Harriet, 14, Anderson, 11, Henry, 9, and Lucy, 6.[83] William, as a stone cutter, made enough money to support his family fairly well, but they were certainly not rich. Jefferson was a comfortable place to live with plentiful merchants and shops, as well as persons holding trades of every variety.

By 1850, John Alexander Gum had taken the profession of plasterer, a job that kept him busy. The definition of a plasterer as listed in *Frow Chips* is:

"A person who uses a mixture of lime, sand, and water, sometimes with hair or other fiber added, that hardens to a smooth solid and is used for coating walls and ceilings."[84]

There was plenty of building going on in the Rutherford County, and Nashville was only 12 miles away. It could have also been a source of employment. Besides being busily employed, John, now twenty-three, was keeping his eyes open for a wife. He didn't have to look long.

~

Alexander's brother, William Norton Gum no longer lived at home, and had been on his own for some time. He may have been away for a while, but on January 3rd, 1847, he was definitely in Rutherford County. On that day, twenty-one year-old Billy Gum married seventeen year-old Margaret Ward. Margaret was the daughter of Benjamin Ward, a native of North Carolina. Ben Ward, born in 1784, had moved to Rutherford County in 1806.[85]

In 1850, Billy and Margaret Gum were living with their baby daughter, Martha, in the Sulphur Springs area—not far from Bethel Church. During this time, Billy bought fifty acres of land from John Ward (possibly a relative of Margaret's).[86] The property lay in District 9, just outside Old Jefferson, and was connected to property Billy already owned. On the other side of this property, lived Best Ward (possibly Margaret's uncle).[87]

In later years, Billy Gum said he learned the profession of bricklayer from his father. Growing up with William Crosthwait, he had also learned the trade of stonemason.[88] After his marriage, Billy found work in Nashville. His most important job there was cutting stone for the new Tennessee State Capitol Building.[89]

Billy Gum seems to have made a fairly good living because he owned quite a bit of land.[90] On November 3, 1850, he sold four lots in Old Jefferson to a widow with six children, by the name of Nancy Wade. The lots—numbers 125, 126, 127 and 128—lay four blocks back from the public square, on the southern edge of the original 1804 town plat. Billy had purchased them from Edmund Lively in 1848 for $350.[91] In 1850, he sold them to Nancy Wade for $200,[92] suggesting that the value of land in Jefferson had decreased greatly during this time.

Figure 13. Tennessee State Capitol, Nashville.

The Wade family was among the few new families who had moved to Old Jefferson over the last decade. Where Nancy Wade came from, who her husband was, and what became of him is unknown.

The Wade family name originated in England. In mid-1800s, a group of thirteen different Wade family members came to Rutherford County from the East.[93] Among them were Levi, who was extremely wealthy, James, Jeremiah and John. Each of these persons had their own family. No connection has been found with Nancy Wade's family. The only clue as to who her husband was comes from the gravestone of the Wades' youngest daughter, Lucy MacLaine. The inscription states that Lucy was the daughter of "J" Wade. Since the youngest Wade child was two years-old when the census was taken in 1850, it is presumed that Mr. Wade died sometime between 1847 and 1850.

By 1850, Nancy Wade's eldest son, Benjamin, age sixteen, had become the "man of the house." On the census, he was listed as a farmer. There were four other children listed as living in the house: fourteen year-old Martha, twelve year-old Elizabeth, nine year-old George, seven year-old

Lucy and two year-old William. Caring for all these children would have been a heavy burden for any woman alone.

During the years 1850–51, John Alexander Gum became acquainted with the charming, young Martha Wade. He could not help noticing her neat little figure, fair skin, and soft, wavy hair. Most of all, there were dimples in her cheeks when she smiled. Although she was only fourteen, she was likely mature in her ways; helping her mother to care for the children and keep house. In the coming months, with Nancy's permission, John came a-courting Martha, and before long the couple's wedding date was set.

At the same time John Alexander was courting Martha, his sister, Sarah, was being courted by Mr. Littleton H. Johnson. Although there were many Johnsons in Rutherford County, we find no mention of a Littleton. Sarah Gum and Littleton Johnson were married in August of 1851.[94] After their marriage, there is no further mention of them. It appears they did not stay long in Rutherford County. No further record of Sarah has been traced. Possibly, she died young.

John and Sarah were not the only ones busy courting in the Crosthwait home at this time. Before twenty-four year-old John Alexander got married, his younger half-sister, Emeline Crosthwait, now seventeen, married John Mullins, a resident of a the neighboring area. It may have taken John A. Gum a bit longer to prepare for marriage—since he had the responsibility of providing a home and supporting a family. It is also true that Martha was quite young, and her mother depended on her.

During this time, John Alexander Gum made a change in the use of his name. From here on, he would go by his middle name only—Alexander Gum. There may be a few reasons for this. For one, at this point in history the first given name of a person was often in honor of a friend or relative. The middle name was used as the personal name.

The second reason for this change was that John Alexander's cousin, the son of Robert E. and Mary Ann Gum, who was five years his senior, was also named John Gum, or John A. Gum. By the 1850s, Cousin John was doing quite well. He had married Caroline McCracken, and they had one child, Mary Isabelle. In 1851, his grandfather, John Fulks gave him land on Lytle's

Creek.[95] John Gum made his living as a farmer, but in the future, he would also be the County Surveyor. Many Rutherford County property records carry his name and drawings of the properties he surveyed.

John Gum also held the title Squire, signifying that he was a principle landowner and Justice of the Peace for his rural district. In later years, his great grand-niece, Mattie Gum Pucket stated that he was County Magistrate—a civil officer empowered to administer law.[96] It is believed that the area known as "Gum" was named in his honor. From this, one can see that John Gum had made a name for himself, and Alexander did not want his business transactions to be confused with those of his cousin.

So it was on November 25, 1851, that Alexander Gum and Martha Wade were wed. Alexander and Martha may have stayed with Nancy Wade for the first years of their marriage, or perhaps rented a small room nearby. Martha was only sixteen, and Alexander twenty-four. The Gums had no children during the first three years of their marriage.

By April 1852, Alexander Gum was doing fairly well. He bought a piece of property from Jennings Rooker for $300. This land of approximately fifty acres was in District 9, just across the river from Old Jefferson, and next to the property of his brother, Billy. The property also bordered on Best Ward's property—as well as one of the MacGowans.[97] In August of the same year, Alexander sold this property to Billy, for the same amount he had paid for it.[98]

Two months later, Billy Gum bought 50 acres of land from John Ward, next to the property he already owned. Other neighbors bordering his land were Thomas Mullins on the North (possibly a relative of Emeline's husband), and brother Alexander on the south. For this purchase, Billy paid $150.00.

By November, Billy Gum was anxious to move on. He sold his 125 acres in District 9 to William P. Miles. It should be noted that this property was next to Mrs. Ward on the south, and bordered by Old Jefferson Road to the southeast. This was possibly one of the roads Billy's grandfather, Norton helped to build. Next to Billy Gum's property on the southwest was the estate of Bromfield Ridley. For this sale, he received $1500.[99]

Billy, like his father and his grandfather before him, had a restless and adventurous spirit. Billy Norton Gum and wife, Margaret, took their four

Figures 14 & 15. Said to be photos of William Norton Gum and his wife, Margaret Ward. Probably taken after they had moved to Missouri.

children: Robert, Martha, Malinda and William, and moved west to Gibson County, Tennessee for a time. By 1860, they had moved to Weakley County.

Meanwhile, in Old Jefferson, Alexander's wife, Martha Wade Gum, found that she with child. The Gum's first baby, a little boy, was born in 1854. (The exact date has yet to be found.) Alexander and Martha named him William, as was customary for the Gums, but gave him the unusual middle name of Tecumseh (Alexander's cousin, Robert E.'s son, born in 1840 also seems to have carried this name.)

Tecumseh, famed chief of the Shawnee tribe, was a fierce warrior who was also famous for his oratory. He called for the Indian nations to rise up and destroy the white man, sending them "back to the water whose accursed waves brought them to our shore."[100] Tecumseh was killed in 1813 during the Battle of the Thames. Many white men held Tecumseh as a symbol of courage, and gave their children his name in the hope that they too would carry such bravery in their lives.*

---

* It is noted that famed Union General, William Tecumseh Sherman also carried this name.

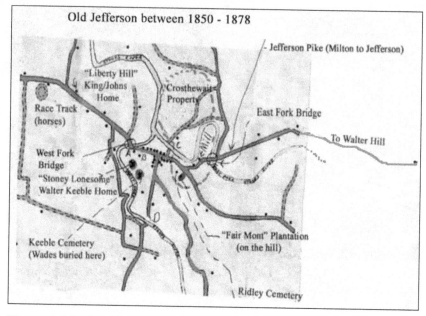

Figure 16. Map by Jefferson Historian Toby Francis. A. Blackmith. B. Ben Wade's Store. C. The East River Fork. D. West River Fork (some called it Creech's Ford).

What particular connection or meaning Tecumseh may have had for the Gums would be interesting to know.

Three years later in 1857, Alexander and Martha Gum celebrated the arrival of their second baby boy, whom they named after his father, John Alexander Gum, Jr. Alexander must have felt quite proud of his growing family.

Not much is known about the childhood of the Gum children. Early in his life, Will T. probably received a great deal of attention, possibly as the eldest son, even preferential treatment. He was, no doubt, a handsome and charming baby.

After Alexander's brother, Billy moved to Gibson County, the Gums spent their time with Martha's mother, Nanny, and the Wades, as well as some of Alexander's half-sibblings, the Crosthwaits.

Late in the 1850s, William and Malinda Crosthwait moved to Nashville, where Alexander's with half-brother, Anderson had settled. It seems Alexander had to sometimes travel a distance to find work. During these times, he might be away several days or even several weeks while he completed a job. He was happy to know that the Wades were close, and Martha and the children were not alone.

On Sept 5, 1854, Martha's sixteen year-old sister, Elizabeth, married William Jones. Mr. Jones was a descendent of one of the earliest families in the area of Jefferson. Only five months later, in February of 1855, Martha's brother, Ben Wade married Susan Robertson.

The Robertson's were an industrious family who lived nearby, possibly in Walter Hill. In time, Ben Wade would give up farming and run a store on the Old Jefferson town square. In 1856, Ben and Susan Wade had their first child, a little girl whom they named Emma. Two years after Emma's birth, their son, Charles, was born.

Little sister Lucy married James McLaine in September 1859. Mr. McLaine's father was a cousin to Ben's wife. As so often happened in the area of Rutherford County, every marriage had a number of inter-relations.

Meanwhile, Alexander Gum continued successfully in his profession. In 1857, Walter Keeble, the owner of a large estate just outside the town of Jefferson, decided to build a larger and more elegant home. The property was just off the Jefferson Turnpike in Walter Hill—a small community across the river from Old Jefferson. The Keeble home, known as "Stoney Lonesome," was built on a hill, surrounded by ancient trees. Alexander was given the job of plastering the mansion's interior. For this, he was paid handsomely. One record of payment still exists. It states that on August 20, 1858, Dr. Keeble signed a note for the final payment to Alexander Gum in the amount of $92.67.[101]

So, life went on in Jefferson, and the Wade, Gum and Crosthwait families lived lives of peace and prosperity.

Chapter 14

Clemmie

MARY ANN BAUGH HAD BEEN GIVING BIRTH TO CHILDREN NOW FOR over twenty-five years. After Charlie's birth, she was fairly certain there would be no more children, and there were none for more than six years. Then, when Charlie was five, Mary Ann Baugh found she was expecting once again.

The little girl was born on April 25, 1857. They named her Clemintine W. Baugh, but the family all called her "Clemmie." (Possibly, she was named after Clemintine White.[102]) Mary Ann Baugh was forty-four years old at the time. She had always been a strong woman, but this time she likely felt a lot more worn and tired. At least, she had the help of the servants and her older girls, Bettie and Mattie.

On the day Clemmie was born, as the doctor, or midwife, lifted her up, Mary Ann learned there was something wrong with her child. It is uncertain as to what the exact problem was, but we do know—as stated by Dr. J.B. Murfree in later years—that she had some sort of birth defect. Mary Ann's good friend, Mrs. A.R. Richardson, said of Clemmie, "She has some spinal disease and has had from childhood."[103]

During her life, Clemmie would be called "lame." How much her condition affected her ability to walk or stand for long periods is unknown. She often spoke of herself as "afflicted."[104] Besides this one defect, Clemmie seemed healthy enough, and the family rallied around to love and protect her, as large families do.

Being the baby and disabled, she no doubt got a lot of attention. Little Clemmie had to struggle to do the things that others took for granted. It was a not easy for her, but she tried to keep up. She was sensitive to any slights she might perceive, and she did not take things lightly. Her spirit was strong however, and she was seldom left behind, even if it meant that her father or older sister Bettie came to her aid. Over time, Clemmie grew accustomed to having her way, and was able to get what she wanted more often than the other children ever had. To survive, she learned to be tough.[105]

Bettie and Mattie mothered little Clemmie, and as older sisters, they always would. However, little sister Eliza, who was only seven years-old at the time of Clemmie's birth, felt a bit displaced. As time went on, Eliza took notice of how easily Clemmie got her way, and she couldn't help feeling a bit jealous.[106]

Only four months after Clemmie's birth, John and Mary Ann Baugh learned they were grandparents for the first time. Joseph's wife, Anna Butterworth had given birth to a baby boy. They named him Ashton Taylor Baugh, after Anna's father. Although Joseph Baugh and family were many miles away, with the railroad, they probably took at least one trip up to Christiana to visit the family.

On November 4th, John Baugh sold one of his properties on the edge of Christiana to P.F. Battin for $50.00.[107] The property was in the process of having a house built on it, but John Baugh had better uses for his time and money. In its place, he bought another property which sat right next to the railroad. This land in District 20 was sold to him by Thomas Atkins for $1200 and contained 43 acres.* Still remaining in the heart of Christiana was a piece of land measuring 50 x 100 feet, and fronting the Grant & Miller Store.

The following year, John Baugh became a stockholder in the Hoover's Gap and Christina Turnpike. This Turnpike was incorporated by the General Assembly March 19, 1858.[108] Along with many of the big landowners in the area, John purchased stock in the turnpike. Other purchasers in the area of Millersburg were Henry Hoover, Burrell G. White,

---

* $1200 in 1857 = approximately $26,697.14 in 2005.

Figure 17. The Railway Station in Christiana about 1903. It had been rebuilt after the war. John Baugh owned property next to it.

Figure 18. The downtown view of Christiana in the early 1900s. It has not changed too much!

Augustus H. White and John Miller. The turnpike was to run from Christiana to Hoover's Gap, going through Millersburg, with only one tollgate allowed.[109] This turnpike was smaller than most; not more than ten miles long, but it was important nonetheless. John Baugh, along with B.G. White, Thomas Jamison, G.W. Bigson, and Lewis Garner were the commissioners.

In early 1859, one of the Baugh girls was being courted. Young Mattie, 19 years old, was very pretty and sweet. She had caught the eye of the tall and dashing Robert L. Howland, son of John Howland and Eleanor Miller. Robert certainly came from one of the well-established families in the Christiana area. Mary Ann was sad to see her go; but she knew this was a fine match. Following their marriage, Father Baugh sent one of the servants over for their use.[110]

In the latter part of the 1850s, everything was changing. Even the town where the Baughs lived changed its name from Big Springs to Carlocksville, after one of the early settlers. (It would not be called Big Springs again until 1904.) Under the control of the Methodist Conference, the Soule Female College in Murfreesboro was established to educate young women. Another institute of learning, Union University, was founded under the Missionary Baptists. In addition to this, two new companies were created: the Cedar Bucket Manufactory, and Rio Mills for milling flour from both wheat and corn. By 1859, the old courthouse in the square was being removed, and a new brick one with ornamental cupola was being erected. Everything in Murfreesboro spoke of advancement and prosperity.

The 1850s were good years for John Baugh as well. His wealth increased significantly during this time, as did the wealth of most people in Rutherford County. With 1860 on the horizon, John and Mary Ann Baugh were well-established. They owned over 400 acres of land, and 32 slaves, who lived in five houses.[111] Two of their ten living children were married. They prayed that the coming decade would be as happy as the previous one, but life was about to change.

The Baugh Family

Richard Baugh (1778–1842) m. Elizabeth Harwell (1780–1851)

James 1801–1835 (Lea)	William (1834–?)	John A. (1806–1870) (Marable)	Nancy (1812–?) (Douglass)	Mary E (1815–1857) (Davis)	Richard (1817–1888) (Leftwich)	Robert (1820–?) (Branch)
Elizabeth (1820s)		Caledonia (1831)	Richard (1845)	Ellis (1845)		
Miss (1820s)		Joseph L. (1833)	George (1848)	Willis (1852)		
William (1827)		John M. (1835)	Rachel (1851)	Richard (1855)		
Benjamin (1830s)		Lucy Elizabeth (1836)	James (1856)	George (1861)		
		Martha (1838)				
		Benjamin M. (1843)				
		Mary (1845)				
		Fredonia Mary (1847)				
		Elizabeth (1849)				
		Charles R. (1851)				
		Clemmie (1857)				

The Crosthwait Family

James William Crosthwait   /   Ann Shelton

Shelton
(1783–1826)
+
Elizabeth Thompson
(1785–1863)

— | Mary   m.   William Richardson
     (1805–?)

— | George Divers.   m.   Eliza Burton
     (1807–1890)   (1816–1860)

— | Rebecca   m.   Bromfield Ridley
     (1810–1869)   (1804–1870)

Thomas
(1785–1816)
+
Elizabeth R.
(?)
| William   +   Melinda Nugent
(1801–1830?)   (1800–1883)

Percy
(1791–?)

Ann Brown
(1793–?)

Endnotes
Book 2—Peace & Prosperity

Note: RCHS = Rutherford County Historical Society

1. We can only approximate the time John Aldridge Baugh went to Rutherford and it is family speculation as to why.

2. *Mecklenburg County, VA Marriage Book* 1765–1810; Killian, Geo W. Descendents of Andreas Killian (1702–1788), *Research of Curry Wolfe.*

3. *Bethel Church History,* Mr. & Mrs. Robert Sanders, May 6, 1962

4. A Collection of Family Bible records in the Linebaugh Library history room.

5. *Curry Wolfe Research.*

6. *Curry Wolfe Research.*

7. MacGowan Family letter (1831–1859). *Courtesy Mrs. Frank Stockard.*

8. *Annals of Rutherford County,* Vol. 1, by John C Spence, RCHS 1991, p. 164

9. Information from John Lee Fults in a letter to me dated Oct. 22, 2007.

10. *Annals of Rutherford County,* Vol. 1, John C. Spence, RCHS 1991, p. 192

11. Ibid, Vol. 1, p. 248

12. Ibid, Vol. 2, p. 1–2

13. Ibid, Vol. 1, p. 172

14. Mr. Martin Rooker—The Ebenezer MacGowan home was moved in 1962. The logs and chimney stones were used to build another home.

15. MacGowan Family from Rutherford County, Deed Book K, p. 537

16. Martin Rooker, Rutherford County, TN

17. Ebenezer MacGowan Letter, May 11,1831 *Courtesy of Mrs. Frank Stockard*

18. Ebenezer MacGowan letter, Ibid.

19. *Bethel Church History*, Mr. & Mrs. Robert M. Sanders, 1962, p.1

20. Ibid, p. 1–2

21. Baugh Family Group Sheet, *Curry Wolfe Research*

22. *The Commercial Appeal*, Memphis, TN, May 4th & 19th, 1970

23. *Notes of Mrs. Frank Stockard*. Not all church records still exist.

24. Family Group Record for Benjamin Marable, *Curry Wolfe Research*

25. This comment is based comments in 1893 RU County court records.

26. *Annals of Rutherford County*, Vol. 1, John C. Spence, RCHS, p. 251

27. Ibid, Vol. 1 p. 251

28. *Tennessee Tales*, by Hugh Walker, Aurora Publishers, 1970

29. U.S, Federal Census 1830, Lauderdale County, AL *Curry Wolfe Research*.

30. This is only a guess—from information collected on Miranda Baugh.

31. Family Group Record on John Aldridge Baugh, *Curry Wolfe Research*.

32. Richard Baugh Last Will & Testament, August 24, 1840, Lauderdale County, AL

33. This is only surmised—no letters of Benjamin Marable are known to exist.

34. *Annals of Rutherford County*, Vol. 2, John C. Spence, RCHS, p. 12–14

35. Letter of Joseph L. Baugh, January 12, 1897, TN State Archives, Nashville

36. *Annals of Rutherford County*, Vol 2, John C. Spence, RCHS, p. 34

37. Ibid, Vol. 2, p. 33–34

38. Letter of Joseph L. Baugh, Courtesy Tennessee State Archives; "15 hr" note from TN State Archives file, notes of Grace Benedict Paine

39. *The Tennessee Civil War Veterans Questionaires*, Vol. 1, The Rev. Salas Emmett Lucas, Jr., p. 294–295.

40. All records above come from the Baugh Family Bible.

41. *Annals of Rutherford County*, Vol 2, Ibid p. 62–63

42. As told me to by Mr. Brandon, age 99, grandson of a man who had been a slave and was sold on the Rutherford County Courthouse steps.

43. Ibid, Mr. Brandon.

44. Frizzel Family story, near Bell Buckle, told to me by Bob Jacobs.

45. *Eyewitnesses at the Battle of Murfreesboro*, David R. Logsdon, Kettle Mills Press, 2002, p. vii, quote by US Col. John Beatty, 3rd Ohio

46. Curry Wolfe, Baugh Family Group Sheet, Rutherford County Deed Book Z, p. 103, #377 & #689

47. Ibid, see Book Z, p. 103, #377, 689.

48. Ernie Johns & Bob Jacobs—local historians

49. *Annals of Rutherford County*, Vol. 2, John C. Spence, RCHS, p. 65-65

50. Ibid, Vol. 2, p. 65

51. RCHS, Pub. No. 20, Winter 1983, p. 44

52. RCHS Pub. No. 20, Winter 1983, Edward C. Annable, Jr., p. 41–44

53. RCHS, Pub. No. 3, Summer 1974, p. 60

54. Ibid p. 34

55. *Annals of Rutherford County*, Vol. 1, John C. Spence, p. 214–217

56. *Goodspeeds Missouri*, Dunklin County

57. http://en.wikipedia.org/wiki/Trail_of_Tears

58. Ernie Johns

59. The Allen County Historical Society, Scottsville, Kentucky

60. Rutherford County Property Records Book X, p. 237, 290, 605

61. Dates here taken from the Gum Family Bible.

62. *The Story of Murfreesboro*, C.C. Henderson, The News-Banner Publishing Co, 1929, p. 66–67

63. Ralph Puckett's passed down family history; also Elizabeth Fulks obituary.

64. RCHS Pub. No. 22, Winter 1984, p. 29

65. Ibid, p. 35

66. *Annals of Rutherford County*, Vol. 2, John C. Spence, p. 99

67. Curry Wolfe, Baugh Family Group Sheet, RU County Books, No. 235

68. Curry Wolfe, Family pages, RU County Record Book No. 1045

69. Curry Wolfe, Baugh notes, January 25, 1854 Court Order

70. RU County Property Record No. 807; *Curry Wolfe Research*

71. *Annals of Rutherford County*, Vol. 2, John C. Spence, p. 81

72. Miller's Store is now a restaurant. The former bank is a gift shop.

73. The lookout was unfortunately removed with renovation in 2006.

74. *The Tennessee Civil War Veterans Questionnaires*, Vol. I, p. 294–5

75. Ibid p. 294

76. Ibid, p. 295

77. Ernie Johns and Glenn Taylor

78. Notes from Winchester, TN Historical Room Card File

79. From the files in the Historical Room, Winchester, TN Library

80. *58th Annual Session of the Medical Society of State of TN*, Nashville, J.B. Murfree, M.D. 1891, p. 249 (TN State Archives)

81. *History of the Ancient Ryedales and Their Descendants*, G.T. Ridon, p. 201; http://members.aol.com/bromnichol/ridley.htm

82. Ridleys of Oxford, North Carolina, p.520

83. U.S. Census of 1850 for Jefferson District, Sept. 25, 1850, p. 10

84. *Frow Chips*, Vol. 26, Issue No. 2, Nov/Dec 2006, RCHS, p. 2

85. *Rutherford County TN Pioneers*, Susan G. Daniel, RCHS 2003, p. 267

86. Rutherford County Property Record Book 5, p. 541

87. *Rutherford County Tennessee Pioneers*, Susan G. Daniel, 2003, p. 267, Best Ward, of NC, bought 7,200 acres on the Stones River in 1804. His deed was witnessed by Ben Ward, possibly his brother.

88. *FROW Chips*, Vol. 36, No. 2, RCHS, November/December 2006

89. *Goodspeeds Missouri*, Dunklin County

90. None of this land has been traced to Norton Gum, but may be yet.

91. Rutherford County Property Record Book 4, p. 589

92. Rutherford County Record Book No. 5, Record No. 1064

93. *Curry Wolfe Research* of Rutherford County records.

94. Rutherford County Marriage Records.

95. Rutherford County Property Record Book 5, p. 639–340

96. www.yourdictionary.com

97. Rutherford County Record Book No. 4, Record No. 500

98. Rutherford County Record Book, No. 5, p. 598

99. Rutherford County Record Book, No. 5, p. 702, 739, record 1013

100. Remini, Indian Wars, 1 Sugden, *Tecumseh, A Life*, p. 237

101. *The Keebles: A Half Century of Southern Family Life*, Thesis by William Foster, Fleming, B.A. Austin, Texas, 1951, p. 55, Dr. Walter Keeble signed a note for payment to John Gum, August 20, 1858.

102. Notes from Curry Wolfe.

103. *J.L & J.M. Baugh v. Rollie Howland & others*, RU Chancery Court, 1893.

104. Clemmie Gum testimony; *J.L & J.M. Baugh vs. R. Howland & I. Jacobs*

105. Surmised from events of Clemmie's life and above mentioned court case.

106. Ibid; Mary Ann Baugh's will, and daughter, Eliza Pruett's comments.

107. RU County Property Record p. 612, July 6, 1858, *Curry Wolfe Research*

108. RCHS Pub. No. 20, Winter 1983, p. 95; Public Acts, p. 388–389

109. Ibid, p. 116; Public Works p. 226–580.

110. *J.L & J.M Baugh v. R. L Howland*, testimony of Robert Howland.

111. Research by Curry Wolfe, taken from the Tax Rolls of 1860; Slave Schedule, 1860, p. 62/63

Civil War

Note: *In writing this portion of the book, it is not the author's intention to take sides, but rather to show the viewpoint and experience of those who lived through the war in middle Tennessee.*

Chapter 15

1860—War Is A-Comin'

THE BEGINNING OF THE NEW DECADE SAW LIFE CHANGING RAPIDLY FOR the Baugh family. On February 10th, John and Mary Ann became grandparents for the 2nd time when Mattie gave birth to her first child, a boy whom they named Rollie Miller Howland.[1] Rollie was a sweet, little boy with blue eyes and blond hair. No doubt, his grandparents were charmed.

Meanwhile, Robert White had come "a-courting" their Bettie. Robert was a solid and responsible fellow; a descendent of two of the earliest families in the area. His mother, Betsey was the daughter of Isaac Miller, the Irish-born citizen who helped found Millersburg in 1796.[2] His father, Burrell Gannaway White was the same man who sold John Baugh his first piece of property in the area. Burrell White, a merchant and plantation owner, had been born in Millersburg in 1810.

Many days in early 1860, the tall, slim figure of Bob White could be seen driving up to Big Springs to visit the Baugh home. Bob was sort of a quiet fellow, but he suited their Bettie just fine.[3] On April 10th, the couple was married. Lucy Elizabeth Baugh was twenty-three, and Robert Miller White, twenty-six. They moved down Christiana Road, and settled in a nice, white frame farmhouse less than a mile from town.

At the same time Bettie was being courted, the Baugh's second son, John Mason Marable Baugh, who was now twenty-seven, had been courting a girl north of them in the Salem area. Maria Murphey was only seventeen and quite beautiful with dark, wavy hair, a slim figure, and a sweet, devout way about her. When John met her, he knew he had found the girl he was looking for.[4]

Maria (pronounced Mah-ri-ah) was the daughter of John Murphey and Louisa Edwards. Mr. Murphey was an Irish immigrant, who practiced law in early Nashville. In 1848, when Maria was six, her father passed away leaving her mother Louisa (Lou-wy-sa) alone with four little girls. Besides Maria, there was Josephine, 11, Sallie, 9, and Mollie, 3.

Two years after Mr. Murphey's death, Mr. Thomas Jarrett, a wealthy farmer, asked for Louisa's hand in marriage. The couple was married in 1850. Mr. Jarrett brought Louisa and her daughters to live in his home, May Place, in the Salem community.[5] While not a fancy plantation house, the May Place (named after its original owner, Thomas May) was a farmhouse of substantial size and comfort. Shortly after their marriage, Mr. Jarrett commissioned an artist to paint portraits of Louisa and him. These hung on the parlor walls for many years.

Mr. Jarrett was a staunch Methodist. The Jarretts and the Smiths were instrumental in founding the Salem Methodist Church in 1812. Because of these two families, and their devotion to the Methodist faith, the Salem Community was created, and grew around the church.

On May 30th, 1860, John Baugh and Maria Murphey were married at May Place before "a large group of persons"[6] which included the Baughs, Jarretts, Murpheys, Whites, and other family and friends. All gathered on this lovely day to celebrate the couple's union. The servants prepared an outdoor picnic, and played music for the guests who danced and laughed late into the night. Little could the wedding party know that this would be one of the last joyous and carefree occasions they would have for a long time. Life, as they had known it, was about to end.

Around this time, the ever-restless John Aldridge Baugh decided the family should move once again. Earlier that February, Mr. Baugh had become a stockholder in the Millersburg Turnpike, a company incorporated by the Tennessee State Legislature. The Millersburg Turnpike was to run from Christiana to Millersburg. John Baugh, along with John Howland, Burrell White, and Henry Prewitt among others, was appointed to raise the capital. Meanwhile, as one looking for greener pastures, John Baugh had occasion to visit the countryside just southeast

Figure 1. *Louisa Edwards Murphey Jarrett.*
(Courtesy of the Holden Family)

of Murfreesboro, around the recently opened Lascassas Turnpike. Construction of the Turnpike in 1858 had opened up hundreds of acres of pristine, fertile land for farming.[7] Here, John Baugh discovered a small community nestled among the hills, called Trimble. It was a place which seemed ideal for his family and monetary ambitions.

Mr. Baugh's decision to move may have been abetted, in part, by the fact that two of his children had recently married and were in need of a place to live while they set up homes of their own. Still, the decision to move his seven children and over thirty slaves ten miles south of their present residence was no small matter in 1860.

The road to Trimble over the Lascassas Pike rises and falls, even as it curves back and forth like a snake. There are times when the road gives the optical illusion of crossing itself. Imagine then, a large caravan of wagons filled with furniture and persons traveling down it; mule-drawn wagons with laughing Baugh children and belongings of all kinds, followed by thirty-five Baugh slaves, mostly on foot. It must have been a sight to behold!

In 1860, the area of Trimble, which lay in the Milton Community, was no more than a post office, and couple of small stores surrounded by hundreds of acres of rolling hills. It is believed that the Baugh Family moved into a big white farmhouse within walking distance of the town. The house may have been larger than the one at Big Spring, enabling the family to spread out and live in greater comfort than they had previously. It was no doubt a new and exciting experience for everyone.

On August 25th, the U.S. Census taker showed up in Trimble. Visiting the Baugh home, he recorded the fact that the family was living by the Milton Post Office. John Baugh was once again listed as a farmer with $16,000 worth of property in land, and $35,000 in personal property. The latter would include silver, gold, and furnishings, etc. This was quite an increase for a man who twenty years earlier had no property. The children listed at home were: Benjamin, 17, Fredonia, 15, Mary, 13, Eliza, 11, Charlie, 9 and Clemmie, 3.[8]

Two weeks prior to the census taker's visit, an unusual site had occurred in the night sky. Anyone sitting on their front porch, resting in the cool air that August evening would have seen it. A meteor about the size of the moon passed across the sky leaving behind it a bright trail of light. This was on August 10th, around 8 o'clock at night. The meteor shower lasted for only fifteen seconds. Then the sky was dark again with only a blanket of twinkling stars. Two days later, the mid-day heat became so intense that all the plants wilted.[9]

On the 14th of September, persons in the area again reported strange things. The sun suddenly appeared at eleven o'clock at night, making it seem halfway between day and night; as if morning was about to occur.

Then, the sun was gone. Was this a message of hope, or a warning of destruction to come? People asked what these signs in the heavens meant. There was a strange feeling in the air.[10]

~

Politics! All anyone talked about in 1860 was politics! There had been soft rumblings for years—disagreements between the Northern and Southern States over slavery—but nothing so near as this, to tearing the country apart. The Federal government wanted the newer states to remain "free"— another words, non-slaves states. The Southern States felt they had a right to make their own laws, without interference by the Federal government.

During that summer, there was a big political rally in Murfreesboro. Supporters of the Whig candidate for president, John Bell of Tennessee, hosted a huge barbeque. People came from all directions and distances to find out what was going on. It is very likely that John Baugh, a Democrat, and John Gum, possibly a Whig, were among those gathered at this grand affair.

Driving their horses, buggies, and wagons along Maney Avenue toward Maney Springs, visitors were surprised by the sight of 300 barbequed beef and hog carcasses. Over "400 yards of tabling" was set up for dinner in the form of a huge **U**.[11] Just outside the Oaklands mansion, the landscape was a beautiful mosaic of men and women strolling along the green in their summer finest. Along the way, children, also dressed in their best, laughed and played.

Lining the street were elevated seats from which viewers could watch the parade. Huge arches of cedar brush had been erected over the streets where the parade was to pass. Flags decorated the route as well. The main arch bore the Whig motto, "The Union, Constitution, and the enforcement of the laws."[12]

The parade was comprised of a long procession of wagons, each pulled by four horses. Many of the wagons carried groups of children waving flags. Along side the wagons, both men and woman rode on horseback.

Near Maney Spring, there were three stands—well-spaced from one another—placed on the lawn under the trees. From these stands, different speakers could expound upon their political beliefs. After escorting the ladies to the tables some distance away, the gentlemen moved from

speaker to speaker, comparing their views. The women would not be voting, and did not need to be troubled by these intense subjects. The men
sat at separate tables from the women, where they could discuss politics
as freely and intensely as they liked, without offending the ladies.

The barbeque gave men like John Baugh and Alexander Gum the
opportunity to exchange news with other men in the area. There were
many conversations that day along the green. Some said,

"If it were not for slavery, we could not have these farms nor supply
the cotton and other produce the north is so eager to buy. They must
understand."

"But you see," a gentleman replied, "Northerners understand nothing
of the kind ... They want nothing more than to control the wealth that
we have created. Their treatment of their factory workers is far worse
than our treatment of the slaves!"[13]

"Do you really think there will be a war?" one brave lady may have
dared ask another that day, but after a moment, the talk returned to
child-rearing, fashions, and recipes.

The race was split between John Bell of the Whig Party, and Stephen
Douglas and John C. Breckenridge of the Democratic Party. Before the
day was out, one speaker would utter prophetic words. After warning
those present of the danger in allowing the Democratic vote to remain
split, thus giving the election to the Abolitionist party, the speaker said,

"The day may come the land on which we now stand, may be drenched
with blood of human beings."

No one could know how true these words would be.[14] Perhaps even
more prophetic were the intense words of a young man, who declared,

"If Lincoln is elected, there will surely be war!"

Not long after this, another barbeque was held for Breckenridge, the
Democratic candidate from Kentucky. "Over two hundred sheep, lambs,
shoats, and beef" were barbequed, but it was not as fancy an event as John
Bell's. Now there was nothing to do but wait for the election.

Meanwhile, summer went along and the crops grew as well as anyone
remembered. The land was beautiful and plentiful, and all seemed good
to those living in Rutherford County—if you ignored the rumblings.

Chapter 16

1861—Off To War

NOVEMBER 1860—THE ELECTION RESULTS CAME IN AND JUST AS JOHN Bell had predicted, the split between the Democrat and Whig candidates had turned the election. The Republican Party won, and Abraham Lincoln, the stanch abolitionist, was elected President.

Shock waves ran through the Southern States. Then, in December,—just as she promised—South Carolina seceded from the Union. By January 1861, Mississippi, Alabama, Florida, Georgia, and Louisiana joined her. In February, Texas joined them. These seven states formed the "Confederate States of America."

By March 4th, when Abraham Lincoln took the Oath of Office, Jefferson Davis had already been President of the Confederate States for nearly a month. Montgomery, Alabama—a city which lay almost 300 miles directly south of Murfreesboro—was chosen as the Capitol of the Confederate States.

On April 12th, the Confederate cannon fired on Federal forces at Fort Sumter, an island off South Carolina. Many thought the Confederacy would go its own way, or perhaps North and South could negotiate a compromise. But after three days of firing on the Fort Sumter, the Northern soldiers there surrendered, and the South took heart.

Three days later, President Lincoln declared the Confederate states in rebellion and asked for 75,000 volunteers to go south, and put it down. Step by step, action-by-action on each side, there was no turning back.

On April 17th, Virginia left the union to join the Confederate States. Any hope for negotiation was now gone.

Many in the South condemned Lincoln for his declaration of war on these fellow Americans. It was an act for which they could never forgive him. It was an act that would cause brother to fight brother; Americans to kill one another.

~

When the news came to Rutherford County that the abolitionist, Abraham Lincoln, had won, people began to discuss what went wrong. Many expressed disbelief at the outcome of the election. There was talk of breaking away from the union; talk of secession.

Riding down to the square in Murfreesboro to do business, John Baugh would have heard this talk. "War is a comin,' that's for sure," said an old man sitting in the tavern. "With that abolitionist Lincoln in the White House, we're goin' to war."[15]

If the Baughs had not left Trimble by now, following the election John Baugh must have made swift plans for their return to the area they thought of as home. There was a sense of impending trouble in the air, and Millersburg was the place where they knew the land, and the people were family. It was the best place to be.

Mary Ann's father, Benjamin Marable had his own sense of the future. He did not trust the banks. According to Baugh son, Joseph, Benjamin gave his money (which must have been in silver and gold) to Mary Ann for her safe-keeping.[16]

With Lincoln's response to the southern states' secession, in Murfreesboro there were intense discussions everywhere, among men and women alike.[17] Which side would they take? When the Confederate states first were formed, Tennessee did not want to leave the Union. But with Lincoln's call for troops, things had changed. Any state that did not take the Union side would be invaded. Those who joined the Union would be required to take up arms against their Confederate brothers. People were horrified. The Southerner's fury against President Lincoln and his measures knew no bounds. A deep rage, which had quietly and slowly been brewing for years, now erupted.[18] Before the vote was called to decide the matter, many Tennesseans, particularly those in Rutherford

County, had already decided they would join their Southern brothers and fight this unjust invasion!

Much of the fight and the anger had to do with measures the Federal government had taken to try to stop slavery from spreading to the new western states. Slaveholders justified their ownership of black men, women and children by citing history, and Biblical quotes. They also justified it by trying to show proof that the black race was inferior.

In the north, writers and abolitionists like Harriet Beecher Stowe were calling the ownership of other human beings, whatever the color of their skin, reprehensible and immoral. They cited the U.S. Constitution with the phrase "all men are created equal"—an idea based on Biblical ideas and the teachings of Christ—and demanded that slavery be ended immediately!

Southerners, in turn, were infuriated by the abolitionists' moral judgment of them. They pointed out that the North was far more immoral than they in its treatment of workers.

John Baugh and the men of Christiana, Millersburg and Hoovers Gap, for the most part, were all slave owners. Residents of Middle Tennessee, with their huge crops of cotton, owned more slaves than either the eastern or western parts of the state. They depended on slavery for their profits, and saw the actions of the Southern States as a simple states' rights matter. They believed they had the right to choose their own laws without Federal government interference.

On April 17th, Tennessee's Governor Isham G. Harris responded to Lincoln's request for troops to invade the Confederate states.

> "Tennessee will not furnish a single man for coercion, but fifty thousand if necessary for the defense of our rights or those of our Southern brothers."[19]

By April 20th, volunteers were gathering in Tennessee. Although a few held out hope that Tennessee would remain part of the Union, many men, felt impelled to rush immediately to the aid of their Southern brothers who were about to be invaded.

~

By 1861, the original Millersburg shop lot, which stood next to the Baugh farm, had become quite run-down. Union soldiers would later describe it as "dilapidated." Because of this, Millersburg residents built a new shop lot for their town, near the church where Hoovers Gap Road meets Millersburg and Wayside. The shop lot was called "New Millersburg," and from here on, the original town lot would be referred to as "Old Millersburg."[20]

On April 25th, fifty-four year-old John A. Baugh climbed on his horse and galloped down the road to New Millersburg. In response to Governor Harris' call for 50,000 volunteers, Thomas White, Bob White's first cousin, was organizing a company. Men were coming in from all directions, and John Baugh intended to be among the first to sign up. Joining him were his eighteen-year old son, Benjamin, and son-in-laws, Robert L. Howland and Robert White. Altogether, one hundred and ten men from Rutherford and Bedford Counties enlisted that day in Old Millersburg.[21]

Thomas White sat on a barrel in front of the general store which his family owned, taking down the names of the men who wanted to sign up. John A. Baugh gave his age as forty-five (or the numbers were reversed.) Bob White's Uncle, Dr. Augustus White, at sixty-five, was the oldest volunteer. Benjamin Baugh, who had just turned eighteen on April 4th, appeared to be the youngest.[22]

If anyone had asked John Baugh about his other sons, he might have told them that Joseph was going to enlist in a local militia down in Winchester, and that Jack Baugh (the name son, John M. went by to differentiate him from his father) would stay behind for a while. Everyone knew that it would not be wise to leave the countryside populated only with white women and slaves. Besides that, Maria was expecting their first child, and Jack did not want to leave her.

As the men gathered outside the store in the New Millersburg town center, feelings of anger, hurt, and betrayal radiated in the air almost as tangibly as the green fields beyond, where soft furred rabbits hopped down the straight furrows. Ordinarily, at this time of year the men would have little more on their minds than planting. Most traveled no more than twenty miles or less from home in a lifetime. All this was about to change.

Each man agreed to enlist in the army for one year, though most expected the war to last only three months or less. After all, couldn't any southern boy "whup" two or three northerners by himself? The men signed up, optimistically sure they would be back home in a short time.[23]

The day after the enlistment in Millersburg, the men met again, saddled their horses, and galloped down the turnpike to Murfreesboro for a big meeting. It must have been quite a sight to see over a hundred men galloping into the town square like a posse on a hunt.

On the square, John Baugh and the others saw a new sign up for T. Robertson and Richard Sanders Gun Store. Stopping to look at the goings on, the men noticed that Robertson and Sanders had hired several new hands to make and sell guns, and the guns were being sold at a remarkable rate.[24] Many of the men from Millersburg hurried to put in orders for the new rifles they would need on their tour of duty.

The men entered Rutherford County's new brick courthouse, where a meeting was being held for volunteers from the area. The first line of business was to vote on the company names. The men in John Baugh's company agreed to call themselves "The Millersburg Riflemen."[25] Following this, in the tradition of the old militias, the men voted for their own officers.

By popular vote, the founder of the company, Thomas D. White, was named Captain; William H. Newman, 1st Lieutenant, Washington D. Ridley, 2nd Lieutenant, and John D. Guest, 2nd Lieutenant. Robert L. Howland was voted, 1st Sergeant; Lewis H. Howland (Robert Howland's uncle), 2nd Sergeant, and John A. Baugh, 3rd Sergeant. Young William D. Robinson was named 4th Corporal. Benjamin Baugh was a private.[26]

While in town, the men listened to the latest news around the square, and learned of other companies being formed. Soon after the meeting broke up, the men mounted their horses, and galloped back down the turnpike to Millersburg and home. There would be much to do in the week before their departure.

～

On April 23rd, the day before Bob White enlisted, Bettie White gave birth to her first child whom she named for her mother, Mary Baugh White. They called the baby, "Mollie." Now she was home in bed, pondering the fact that in a week, her husband would be leaving for war. It must have been difficult to take. They would have to treasure every moment, as God only knew when she might see him again. She would be left at home alone with two servants, but her mother and sisters were not far away.

In preparation for their departure, the Millersburg Riflemen spent most of the next week drilling.[27] Speedy arrangements also had to be made for the care of farms. May 3rd was the date set for departure, and there was little time. They would be leaving from the train depot in Murfreesboro for Nashville, and eventually travel east to Virginia to join forces with the Confederate Army.

On the day of departure, many of the families in the area piled into carriages and wagons, and drove their men down to the train depot in Murfreesboro. It is not known how many of the families from Millersburg and Christiana traveled to Murfreesboro that day, but it seems likely Mary Ann Baugh and the children were among those escorting their men to the train.[28] They wanted to give their local heroes a brave sendoff.

Although Jack Baugh was staying behind, John Baugh handed much of the responsibility over to Mary Ann. After nearly thirty years of marriage, with scarcely a day apart, Mary Ann must have had mixed emotions as she watched her husband and son preparing to go to war. She worried about her husband, but even more, about eighteen year-old Benjamin. At least, John would be there to watch out for him. Despite her motherly worry, Mary Ann felt very proud of these two men.

The servants hitched the horses to the buggy and wagon, and everyone was ready to leave. The personal and passionate goodbyes were done in private. Then—with one last look around—John and Mary Ann walked out the door, and into the early May morning.

Mirandy stood outside saying goodbye to her son, Willis. It had been decided that one of the servants should accompany the men, and Willis had been deemed the best one for this task. Not only had he grown up with young Benjamin, but Willis, now eighteen, was a strong, intelligent, and completely trustworthy young man. In recent years, John Baugh had hired him out to help build the railroad. He also had many other skills, including cooking, sewing, and shoemaking.[29] In his bag, he carried at least one pot, along with other cooking supplies. He was ready to help Massas' John and Ben in any way they might need.

Going to war with "Massa" was an honor. The Feds would never understand how some black men identified with the South, as much as the white men. They also took offense to the Union's invasion. Without

Figure 2. Willis Baugh late in life. Willis was the son of Mirandy Baugh and Clem Marable.
(Courtesy of Mary Elam Fox)

understanding the war's meaning, Willis may have felt as strongly about it as the white men he served.

Mirandy bid her son "goodbye" with pride, while the little black children stood looking at him with big awe-struck eyes. After a quick hug, and whispered prayer, Willis climbed up to the front seat of the wagon, next to the driver. Mirandy would not travel to Murfreesboro. She had work to do.[30]

The Baugh girls, Fredonia, Mary, and Eliza, now in their teens, were dressed in their prettiest clothes. Sitting with them, was ten year-old Charlie, who was excited that his father and brother were going to be soldiers. John Baugh picked up four year-old Clemmie, and climbing into the carriage with Mary Ann, placing the child between them. He would always have a soft spot in his heart for his youngest child.

Standing in the yard were thirty or more Baugh slaves waiting to say goodbye. As the drivers clicked the reigns, setting both carriage and wagon in motion, the servants called out blessings and good wishes to "Mistah Bo" and "Mistah Ben." John Baugh had given instruction to the men and women whom he felt he could trust, to take good care things while he was gone. Now, he would focus on what lay ahead.

As the wagons bounced down the road, the family members could not help noticing what a beautiful day it was. The fields were green with corn, oats, and cotton.

Here and there, along the fence posts, carpets of wild violets, buttercups, and daisies bloomed. In the pastures, the birds sang, and the cattle mooed lazily as they grazed on clover. The tall trees showed their hazy, green branches against the blue, blue sky. Could there be a more beautiful place on earth than Tennessee?

Back down the road, Robert Howland was bidding his wife, Mattie, and one year-old son, Rollie, "goodbye." Mattie would stay at home with their son, while Robert was gone. There was also the servant her father had lent them to help around the house, so she would not be alone.[31]

Along the way, were other wagons with families heading toward Murfreesboro; preparing to say their goodbyes. For those who did not ride to town, there were women waving the men off with white handkerchiefs, while the children hooted and hollered. One hundred and ten men left

Figure 3. Old Millersburg land once owned by John A. Baugh. Beyond these hills is Liberty Gap.

the area on this day. There were the sounds of horses' hooves, creaking wheels, and calls of "God speed." Then, all was silent.

Down at the Murfreesboro train depot, a large crowd had gathered to send the men and boys off with great patriotic spirit. Hundreds were present. Families, all dressed in their best, were piled into wagons. There were fine ladies in buggies, and groups of just regular citizens standing about not far from the great, iron train. The scheduled time of departure was ten o'clock, so at nine the ceremony began.

Beautiful, young girls in fancy hooped-skirts came up to a podium erected for the purpose and gave passionate speeches. They presented the "brave young men" with patriotic banners they had hand-stitched.

> "Receive then from your mothers and sisters, from those whose affections greet you, these colors woven by our feeble but reliant hands ... May it be a sign that cherished ones appeal to you to save them from a fanatical and heartless foe."[32]

In the preceding weeks, the talk of "Yankees" had grown in fancy, and intensity until young girls felt they should be fearful for their safety in the presence of these monsters. Only the protection of their honorable, young men could save them. Following the speeches of the young ladies, a local minister preached a sermon and prayers were said for the success of the soldiers.

Now, it was nearly ten, and the time had come for the men to board the train. These were the last moments to say goodbye. The usual rules of propriety were likely thrown aside. Perhaps, Mary Ann smoothed her husband's coat one last time, and noted the bit of gray in his beard. She may have been afraid to look into his eyes, for fear tears might come. John Baugh had the utmost confidence in her abilities, and in the fact that he would return. In one swift moment, he may have put his arms around her, as she whispered into his chest, "Be safe, Mr. Baugh."

During this time, a man and woman would never dare to use the other's first name—at least in public. Doubtless, the confidence of the South was John Baugh's that day. "God will be with us, Mrs. Baugh," he may have told her. And then, in a whispered message of his confidence in her, "I know you will be fine, Mrs. Baugh,"[33]

After Mary Ann's quick hug and kiss to Benjamin, husband and son turned and walked down that long line of well-wishers toward the train. Perhaps, more difficult than saying goodbye to her husband were the goodbyes to her son. Benjamin Marable Baugh, named after her father, seems to have been a child Mary Ann treasured. On this day, he was close enough to childhood, with barely a wisp of beard on his face. His eyes still held that shining light of idealism. She would not see him this way again.

In a final move of bravado so representative of the Confederate spirit of 1861, we can picture John Baugh turning back to his wife and family, and saying with confidence, "Don't worry, Mrs. Baugh. This war will be over before you know it. We'll show those Feds, they can't push us around!"

As the men walked down the long path, surrounded by cheering well-wishers, a shower of blossoms was thrown over them. Some were offered money, and many a young man like Ben Baugh, found himself red-cheeked as a pretty girl with tears in her eyes kissed him. Then, in the midst of swirling emotions, the bell rang, the steam whistle blew, and the giant iron machine rolled slowly at first, and then with ever-increasing speed, out of Murfreesboro. Left behind were the cheering crowds, the dear familiar faces, and the words, "Hurrah for our brave and daring men who will soon return in victory!"

Within an hour, the steam-engine train arrived in Nashville. Here, another passionate, cheering crowd awaited them. How exciting! For young Benjamin Baugh, this was probably first time he had been to a big city. The great welcome only added to the excitement.

In 1862, Nashville was a bustling city, with buildings as tall as five stories. With a population of approximately 17,000 people,[34] Nashville was far more sophisticated than Murfreesboro ever dreamed of being.

The one hundred and ten Millersburg Riflemen marched through Nashville's streets to the Square, drawing much attention, and many cheers from the crowds along the way. Arriving on the square, the companies were dismissed and went off to the Maxwell House Hotel on 4th Avenue for dinner.

The Maxwell House Hotel, (later the creation site for Maxwell House Coffee), was a five-story building, which covered an entire city corner. The hotel was only half-finished in May of 1861, but it was completed enough to provide shelter for the men. Even half-finished, the hotel was likely the largest and grandest building any of them had ever seen.

Following their meal, the men spent the balance of the day marching in formations, and organizing with others to form the 2nd Regiment of Tennessee Volunteers of the Confederacy. When evening came, the company marched back to the square where they were dismissed.

That night, the Millersburg Riflemen returned to Maxwell House Hotel, and were joined by other companies converging on Nashville. There were volunteers from as far as Memphis, and as near as Bell Buckle. After such a busy day, men like John Baugh were ready to retire. Young men, like Benjamin, stayed up late into the night, talking about their visions of chivalry, and hopes for a speedy victory. Finally, exhausted and spent, the young men retired as well.

On Sunday, May 5th, the Millersburg 110, now Company F, officially began their life in the army as they marched to the old Nashville Fairgrounds, pitched their tents, and built their first campfires.[35] The next day, John, Benjamin, and the rest of the company boarded a train, and traveled to Camp Trousdale for more training.

Camp Trousdale, just north of Nashville, lay on the Tennessee/Kentucky border. The Louisville and Nashville Railroad had just been completed, ending on the Union side. Kentucky wished to remain neutral in the conflict, which made this an extremely strategic spot. But for now, all was peaceful. The men remained here three days, after which, they boarded the train again, and traveled east.

—

They were gone. The men were truly gone far away, and they wouldn't be back tomorrow, or next week, or even next month. Mary Ann Baugh was now in charge of a household with five children, and a farm with over thirty slaves. Although her son, Jack, was not far away, this sudden change of position, even for a very smart woman, must have been daunting.

In 1861, Mary Ann was forty-eight. Some women her age were old, but she was still quite strong and full of energy. Like hundreds of women all over the South, Mary Ann would soon discover she had far greater strength than she had known. Over time, she would find satisfaction and pride in how well she managed, while the men were away. Crops were grown, harvested, and sold. Some were sent to the railroad in Christiana. It was Mrs. Baugh's duty as a Southern woman to take care of these matters for "the cause." There was no other thought about stepping into her new role.[36]

The "servants" went on with their work. The children knew that they must put their hands together and help as well. Neighbors like the Whites, Pruitts, and Hoovers checked in on one another. Many women in the area were in exactly the same position as Mary Ann. Living in a small community like Old Millersburg made things much easier.

Mary Ann wrote her husband and son as often as she could, and they wrote her. From their letters, she learned that the Millersburg Riflemen had traveled by rail to Lynchburg, Virginia on May 12th. On their arrival, they were officially mustered into the Confederate Army, and became part of the 2nd Tennessee Confederate Infantry Regiment. The other company from Rutherford County—formed under Maney—was now part of the 1st Tennessee Regiment Infantry.

In Virginia, the men received their uniforms. There were pale gray suits made of a mixed cotton and wool for the privates. The officers, like John Baugh, wore butternut or navy pants of jean, with light blue long coats. Most of the soldiers also carried a cotton bag, called a haversack, which was slung across their shoulders. In this bag they were able to keep special items like a Bible, letters, or photos of loved ones. In the future, these bags would also be used to store extra food. As the war went on, meals would be few and far apart.

Additional items carried by the soldiers included canvas bag canteens for water, and a musket 5 feet long, weighing approximately 15 pounds. Each soldier was also given a rough gray wool blanket for sleeping at night. Although it was difficult for a man of John's years to sleep on the ground, there were no complaints.

Returning to Virginia, some forty years after he had left must have stirred many feelings in John Baugh. He had been born here, as had his father before him. Now he was returning to fight a war for Virginia, and the entire South. There were stories he could share with Benjamin; stories of the past which may have come flooding back to him.

As the days in Lynchburg passed, there was no noteworthy news to send back home. Besides maneuvers—which were done several times a day—there was little to do. To escape boredom and pass the time, many men took up gambling, which was considered a great vice. Throughout the war, it would be difficult for the army to rid itself of this practice. Some boredom was relieved by the visits of friends from Murfreesboro, who brought food, clothing, and news from home.[37] These visits did much to raise the spirits of the men.

Meanwhile, Willis was kept busy preparing meals, washing clothes, and keeping their tents clean.[38] In addition, he repaired any clothing or other item that needed it. Still, even he had free time, which he spent among the other servants traveling with the army.

Although rumors of skirmishes persisted, until June 1st, no real battles were fought. Toward the end of May, the 2nd Tennessee traveled by rail toward the sea. At Aquina Creek, they came under the fire by three U.S. gunboats. When John wrote Mary Ann again, there was sad news to report. One member of their company, Private William Lynch, had been mortally wounded, and died a few days later at Fredericksburg. Following the battle, the only excitement was the capture of a large amount of coffee on some Federal mail ships![39]

It was during this time, that the men learned Tennessee had seceded the Union. It was said that only six men in all of Rutherford had voted against separating from the Union.[40] After this, all their actions took on an official air. Although the war was not moving as quickly as they had hoped, it was clear that other Tennesseans would soon be joining them, and things would be heating up.

By July, the volunteers started to feel the difficulties of soldiering life. The heat and humidity of Virginia made travel during the day extremely difficult. Trying to march under a burning sun, through air as thick as a stew pot, weakened them greatly. In addition, they found that their uniforms, which consisted of a cotton and wool mix, were unbearably hot. Many soldiers who were carrying overcoats threw them away, thinking the war would be over before winter.

Frustration grew as the men waited for a battle that even remotely resembled the visions of glory they had when enlisting. Their idea of battle changed soon enough as their brigade joined Beauregard's forces at Manassas. Although the Millersburg Company did not actively engage in fighting, on July 21st during the Battle of Bull Run, they were placed in support of Brigadier General Richard S. Ewell's Brigade, and came under heavy fire. The Battle of Bull Run resulted in five deaths for the 2nd Tennessee.[41] Robert Howland's cousin, 2nd Sergeant Lewis H. Howland, was wounded and later discharged. 2nd Lieutenant John D. Guest was wounded. When Guest resigned at Fredericksburg, Corporal William D. Robinson took his place.

Meanwhile, the men continued to drill two or three times a day in preparation for the battles to come. The news of casualties and wounds, sad as they were, were part and parcel of war. The men believed that honor was a far higher goal than life.

Sometimes in the evenings, someone would pull out a musical instrument—a violin, banjo or harmonica—and start playing a song they all knew. The song might be "The Girl I Left Behind Me," "Oh Susannah," or "Home, Sweet, Home." All the men would join in singing; their spirits lifted by these rousing and familiar airs. These musical moments were often followed by sudden quiet, as thoughts of home and loved ones overwhelmed them.

During the quiet times, the soldiers took out the letters from home; letters that were often carried close to their hearts. If they were lucky, they might also have a photo. Gazing into the eyes of a wife, mother, sweetheart or child, they imagined themselves at home. In these moments, a feeling of homesickness sometimes came over the men with an intensity they could never have imagined. They had to believe home was everything they were fighting for.

To bolster themselves, the soldiers sometimes spoke with hate of the "Yankee" and of what they would do when they finally met. This was done more and more often, to keep the men riled up in preparation for the battle that was sure to come.

After the long, hot summer, September finally arrived. On the thirteenth of the month, the Millersburg Company learned that their regiment was being transferred to Colonel J.G. Walker's Brigade, now stationed at Fredericksburg, Virginia. Joining them were the 1st Arkansas and the 12th North Carolina Volunteer Infantry Regiments. The soldiers remained in Fredericksburg until the end of the year.

After nearly eight months in the army, the men realized that the three-month war they boasted about had not materialized. The new reality was they had no idea when this war would end, for it had not even begun.

~

As head of the family, Mary Ann not only looked out for the children at home, but for her married daughters as well. There was Bettie White, Mattie Howland, and daughter-in-law, Maria. On October 29th, when Maria gave birth to her first child, Thomas Saunders Baugh, Mary Ann was likely there to welcome him into the world, and help Maria along. This would be wonderful news to pass on to Mr. Baugh, but before Mary Ann could send the letter, another event occurred.

Shortly after Thomas' birth, Bettie and Robert's baby daughter, six and one-half month-old Mollie became ill. Perhaps she had always been delicate, but the fact that Dr. Augustus Miller, the local physician was away in the war effort, did not help matters. Mollie died on November 2nd, and Bettie was left alone in her grief. This was news, Mary Ann also had to write the men.

The saddest event of the year, however, was yet to come for Mary Ann Baugh. On December 12th, Mary Ann's eighty-three year old mother, Lucy Barner Marable passed on. Her passing was a great loss to the family. In his 1897 letter to a Marable cousin, Joseph Baugh described Lucy Marable as "noble," saying, "I have not language to express or to do anything like justice to her."[42]

Mary Ann was the last of the living Marable children. Her sister, Betsey, had passed away the previous year at the age of sixty, and her brothers were all gone. Mary Ann's father, eighty-four year-old Benjamin Marable was living in his home, somewhere between Blackman Road and the Nashville Turnpike, almost in Smyrna. He had two house servants, a couple who had been with him many years. Now, after over sixty-two years of marriage to his beautiful wife, Lucy, Benjamin had no desire to be anywhere but in the home they had shared, and near her grave, which he likely visited every day.

Although Mary Ann Baugh must have been concerned about her father, he was where he wanted to be. She visited him when she could, though it was a buggy ride of about twenty miles—a day's trip at that time.

So, the year 1861 drew to a close. It had been a difficult year, but hopes were high that 1862 would bring the men home to happier times.

Chapter 17

The War Comes Home

B Y THE SUMMER OF 1861, THE RESIDENTS OF RUTHERFORD COUNTY knew that war was coming to Tennessee. For a time after Tennessee seceded the Union, the citizens lived peacefully enough. In Old Jefferson, life went on as it had pretty much for the last fifty years. Except for those who had married and moved to other locations, three generations of Gums, Wades, and Crosthwaits still lived close to one another. On the neighboring Keeble plantation, Stoney Lonesome, Fanny Keeble, the wife of Walter Keeble, fished in the Stones River, took carriage rides, and drew pictures for her children to color.[43] It was unimaginable that life could change.

In the autumn of 1861, John and Martha Gum were living just off the Old Jefferson Square with their three children: Will, 7, Johnny, 4, and Baby Laura, who was about a year old. Not far from the Gums, lived Martha's brother, Ben Wade, his wife, Susan Robertson, and their three children: Emma, 5, Charlie, 2, and Baby Sallie. Since the Wade children and their Gum cousins were so close in age, it is easy to imagine they spent many happy days playing together. Then, in the autumn of 1861, tragedy struck.

It began with a sudden illness in little Charlie Wade, who by now was nearly three. Ben and Susan soon learned that the fever, with chills and diarrhea, was typhoid fever, an illness sweeping through Jefferson.[44]

Ben and Susan may have called in local physician, Dr. Thompson. The treatment at that time was bathing in warm salt baths, cupping, mustard plasters, and chamomile for calming.[45] In the case of typhoid fever, there

Figure 4. The Wade Home in Old Jefferson, late 1800s. Susan Robertson Wade stands center.
(Courtesy of Lucy Mae Lenoir)

was little more the doctor could do to help.[46] The Wades watched their beloved son fade to a pale creature of skin and bone. On September 16th, little Charlie died.

The sorrowful parents had barely laid Charlie to rest when seven month-old Sallie became ill. One week after Charlie's passing, Baby Sallie was gone too. Then, in one more terrible blow, one week after Sallie's passing; sweet, five-year old Emma, the Wades' oldest child, came down with typhoid fever, and closed her eyes for the last time.

In the Keeble cemetery, three little graves with headstones lay side by side.[47] From a household of happy, laughing children, all were gone. There were no little voices calling "Mama," no sounds of running feet, or babies to dress and feed. There was only silence and emptiness. One can only imagine the agony of the parents, who were too stunned even to weep.

John and Martha Gum must have felt the deep sorrow of Brother Ben and Susan. In their home, there were three little children; all alive and well (though possibly one or more had been ill and survived.) They could only trust in God's will, and try to comfort the Wades.

"The Lord gives and the Lord takes," they prayed in church. Susan believed in the goodness of the Lord, but she must have felt like Job— bereft of her beautiful children. Through all this, Susan had been six months pregnant. When the Wades' baby, James, was born on December 29, 1861, it was a blessing they feared to rejoice over too much, in case he too might be taken.

A few months later, early in 1862, Martha Gum found she was expecting her fourth child. With three small children and another on the way, Martha must have worried about the conditions her baby would be born in. It appears that John Alexander Gum was still at home with little inclination to enlist in the army. Circumstances, however, were about to change.

～

The beginning of 1862, Old Millersburg seemed peaceful and safe, far from the ravages of war. In Murfreesboro, the citizens turned Union University into a hospital for the soldiers. The ladies formed the Soldiers Relief Society, and spent every spare moment making clothes, and bedding for their men.[48] Mary Ann and the women of Old Millersburg and Christiana likely added their handiwork to this organization, or created a similar one.

After several large victories by the Confederate Army, including Bull Run, the residents of Rutherford County were hopeful that the war would not last much longer. Meanwhile, unbeknownst to the citizens of Murfreesboro, the Federal Army was moving closer and closer to the town. They had come down through Ohio, and along the Mississippi River. By the beginning of February, news reached Murfreesboro that the unthinkable had occurred; Fort Donaldson near Nashville had fallen! Four days later, Nashville was invaded by the Federals.

Stories filtered down to Murfreesboro, of how the Nashville citizens had been thrown into a panic, trying to escape before the Union soldiers arrived. Many of these people came to Murfreesboro, giving first-hand accounts to the citizens of the chaos that ensued. Stores in Nashville had been thrown open and looted so that the Feds would not get anything.[49]

Soon, General Albert Sydney Johnston entered Murfreesboro with his bedraggled Confederate troops. They were exhausted from the battle, which had been fought through the rain and sleet over many days. Entering the town, they looked broken, wet, and hungry. It was February 15th, and the weather was growing even colder. Snow began to fall.

When the Confederate boys pitched their tents in town, the citizens were sure that they would stay; Murfreesboro would be well protected with their own soldiers in town. But a few days later, the people of Murfreesboro woke up to the noise of galloping cavalry, clanking wagons, and marching feet. Their army was leaving them![50]

The smell of smoke began to fill the air. Across the landscape, high shooting flames could be seen as the fires burned intensely. The residents learned that Captain J.H. Morgan—a man the Yankees hated for the trouble he gave them—had ridden in with a cavalry group of about fifty men. It was they who were setting fire to the bridges, and destroying the railroad.[51] When Captain Morgan galloped out of Rutherford County, he rode out with a much greater group of men than he had ridden in with. Many men, attracted by his passion and energy, were eager to join him in the Cause.[52]

~

One day in mid-February of 1862, the women of Old Millersburg had a great surprise. The sound of galloping horses' hooves, met by the yells of slaves and any other resident who happened to be out, brought women like Mary Ann Baugh and her daughters rushing to see what was going on. Their men were back!

On February 1st, the 2nd Tennessee Infantry (Bates), which now included the Millersburg 110, the 1st Tennessee (Maney's), and the 3rd Tennessee (Vaughn's) had been sent to Knoxville where they were given a sixty-day furlough. At the time, they were to report back to Nashville, but the news of Nashville's fall to the Union changed everything. The men were now told to meet before the end of March in Huntsville, Alabama, a small town about seventy-five miles south of Old Millersburg.[53]

The time at home passed quickly. What joy there was on both sides! For the men, it was a welcome respite from nine lonely months of camp life. For the women, there was rejoicing in the fact that their men had returned alive and well. It was but a little while that the Baughs, Howlands, and Whites could laugh and talk about good times, and "when the war is over."

The men also had not so welcome news. They had to tell their families that having completed their original enlistment, they had all signed on for three more years. "Of course," they told their wives, "the war will be over long before that." Together, the families prayed that this indeed would be the case, and that everyone would return safe and unharmed.

By mid-March, the time was nearing for the husbands, sons, and brothers to return to duty. The news that Union troops were filtering down towards Murfreesboro may have sent John Baugh and the others packing sooner. Now, on a cold spring morning, the men kissed their wives and children goodbye, and headed south to Huntsville.

~

On March 10ᵗʰ, a huge group of Federal Cavalry headed by General Mitchell galloped into the Murfreesboro town square. A crowd of citizens, who were out shopping and going about their business, gathered to see what was going on. The Commander of the group asked, "Have the citizens here been in favor of the burning done by Captain Morgan?" Some of the men standing in the square yelled out boldly, "Yes!" From the back of the crowd came a voice saying, "Maybe yes and maybe no." Oddly enough, no one seemed afraid. Neither did the Union soldiers feel any threat from the citizens.[54] Then, to everyone's shock, the Union Commander rose in his stirrups and declared, "I am the master of this place, and I intend to set this town in order."[55]

The audacity of the commander deeply offended the local citizens. John Spence recorded the commander's words in his *Diary of the Civil War*, and no doubt, these words were repeated as far as Jefferson and Millersburg.

During the Federal occupation, the citizens of Murfreesboro had nothing but distain for the "Feds" or "Yankees"—as they called them. Soon,

Figure 5. The Murfreesboro Courthouse under Federal Occupation.
(Courtesy of the Albert Gore Research Center, Middle Tennessee State University)

even women and children began to speak contemptuously of them in a manner that was quite open. They felt the Feds were invaders who had no place being there. Even the sight of the U.S. flag, which the Yankees had hoisted on the courthouse, offended them. In later days, when one poor man who owned no slaves was asked, "Why are you fighting?" he replied, "Because you're here."[56] To many, the answer was just that.

In early 1862, the Union Army was still hopeful of bringing the renegade Southerners back into the Union. They believed that secession was only a matter of misunderstanding, and that with guidance the South might return. This belief led the Union general to be surprised and insulted when he was not invited to any of the dinner parties in Murfreesboro.[57]

Generally, there was still some sense of friendly disagreement between the two sides. Each side believed the conflict would not last long. When the area was put under martial law, this situation, and the lives of citizens in and around Murfreesboro changed.

During the day, the Union soldiers began riding out into the surrounding countryside. As their explorations continued, they became bolder, and began to take anything they wanted from the local residents. First, it was the cotton, the most valuable item to the people of the Middle Tennessee. Then, they began to invade homes.

Federal soldiers, in the name of security, began to search through personal items such as bureau drawers, trunks, boxes, pantries, smoke houses, and cellars. Local citizens could do little but stand by as the Feds took their family heirlooms, wedding rings, and even the provisions they had for meals.

The soldiers taunted the locals with contempt, calling them "sesesh" (secessionists). The ultimate goal was to make life as difficult as possible for the "Rebs," in the hope that they would return to the Union.[58]

In time, many of the citizens, now fully aware of the dangers of war, and the madness that can overtake men when they become soldiers, began to hide their valuables, and their food. They hid them in wells and caves, buried them, and placed them behind secret walls, and under floorboards. Others, aware that the Northerners likely did not know about springs, and cold places built under houses on swampy land (where the food was put to keep cool), placed much of their food there. Mary Ann probably was one of those citizens working to hide her food, and the family's few precious items.

Of course, some of the larger items, like horses, cows, and pigs were more difficult to hide. These were among the most valued items to the army. One local farmer in the area of Old Millersburg was able to save his horse from being drafted into the army by driving nails incorrectly through its horseshoes. Because of this, the horse appeared lame, and was rejected by the military. By the end of the war, this horse was one of the very few left in the area.[59]

In May, a group of citizens asked for a meeting with Federal officials, requesting that for this purpose, "all peaceable citizens will be permitted to visit Murfreesboro and return without military passes." Included on the list were persons from Jefferson, Old Millersburg, and the Blackman area. A large group of people showed up.[60]

Following the meeting, the Governor issued an order that all persons in town who engaged in business would be required to take "An Oath of Allegiance" to the United States. If they did not, their businesses would be closed. John C. Spence, in *A Diary of the Civil War*, states that few people were doing business at this time anyway, so few took the Oath. Local citizens soon learned that if they chose not to take the Oath of Allegiance, their ability to travel anywhere, or transact of any kind business would be vastly limited.

One little girl in the town of Murfreesboro, Mollie Nelson, was accidentally shot through the neck by a Union soldier while playing on East Main Street. The girl's father ran to get a doctor—to save her life—but was stopped by the Union soldiers who told him he would not be able to procure the doctor's services without taking the Oath.[61]

Although the Baugh and Gum families were not living in the town of Murfreesboro, news of the various events taking place there must certainly have reached them. In the long run, these new regulations would affect them as well. Most citizens felt so passionately about the Southern Cause, that no matter what, they would not take the Oath. The Union was working hard to wear them down. It would certainly have been easier to concede, but to the Southerner it was a matter of honor not to.

A few citizens in Rutherford County sided with the Union. Some, who were interested in making money from the Yankees, took the Oath for reasons of their own.[62] It is doubtful that Mary Ann Baugh or any of the Gums took the Oath in the beginning, but over time, many found it necessary in order to survive.

In the name of order, the Federals began setting up files on the men of the town. Using these names, soldiers were ordered to go to their homes and search "for guns and ammunition, and anything else that had the appearance of danger in the way of shooting."[63] While the searches were being conducted, often many personal, sentimental, and other items of value would disappear. Nothing dared be said about it. Unless a citizen showed themselves to be a local "Fed," or was willing to give some information on another citizen, complaining was dangerous and might only open the complainer to more trouble.[64]

During this time, many persons were arrested for little or no cause. The majority were held in the courthouse jail. Others were sent to the Nashville penitentiary.[65] A young man found walking along the road without a pass was in danger of being picked up, accused of treason, and thrown into prison. Sometimes these accusations ended in hanging, with little or no evidence. The women in town often went to the jail with food and bedding, offering to write a young man's parents or loved ones. While in many ways life seemed to go on as before, it also had its dark side.

~

Over the next months, with the crops ripening in the heat of the Tennessee summer, the Yankees visited nearby farms, and piled their foraging wagons high with corn and other crops.[66] If a cow, hog, or chicken disappeared, "well," the Feds would say, "it's the fault of the owner who did not keep his animals secure enough."[67] Meanwhile, the Feds were removing fence rails and using them for firewood, or any other need.

The locals began to rise up in retaliation for the Union Army's seizure of their goods and land. These new, homegrown soldiers were known as "Bushwhackers." The groups took part in a kind of guerilla warfare against the Federal soldiers and pickets from under cover. Their hidden, plain-clothes attacks both infuriated and endangered the Union Army's stance in Tennessee.

In turn, the Union Army took retaliation for these attacks. When they did not have a culprit to blame, they made the locals pay. God help you if a Bushwhacker occurrence took place near your property, or where you happened to be at the time. The Yankees burned houses, and took anyone in sight to jail. It should be noted that the Bushwhackers could also be brutal toward citizens they suspected of being Union sympathizers. Many feared them.

Between May and July of 1862, the force of martial law began to be felt intensely in Middle Tennessee. Now, ordinary citizens on the street had to fear for their safety. Should any citizen, by chance, happen to be in an area where a gun was fired, or a skirmish took place, that person, or persons, would be in danger of being placed in prison, and tried for treason. Innocent citizens often were sent to the penitentiary in Nashville, or even hung, as a lesson to those who dared to fight them.[68] For the residents of Middle Tennessee, this was an increasingly fearful time.

Down in the Millersburg/Christiana area, citizens became more guarded. The Federals had certainly been through the area. In fact, skirmishes took place not far from the Baugh home. Because of this, most residents chose to remain at home. Children no longer attended school, nor did the families attend church. It was dangerous for citizens to congregate; they might easily be accused of treason. That was not the only reason for staying home.

A family away from home could find themselves caught in a skirmish, or return to find that Federal soldiers had come and stripped their home bare. Even worse, they might return to find their home burnt to the ground. So, school lessons were taught at home. And each day, both morning and night, families gathered for "devotions," just as they always had; reading the Bible, and praying for loved ones both near and far.

Then, a new and unexpected issue began to occur; it was perhaps the most worrisome of all to the locals. The Union soldiers had begun telling their black servants to leave them. The Feds knew that without the help of their slaves, the South would be crippled. This would be one of the most important strategies for winning the war—to get the slaves away from their owners. Union soldiers began inviting black men and women to come to the Army camps where, they said, they would be paid for their work. Many slaves accepted these offers.

In some cases, the African-American slaves had a deep bond with the families they had served for one or more generation. Women like "Mirandy" and her family had little desire to leave the place they considered home. This surprised the Federals. Other persons of color, mistreated and deeply unhappy with their lives, were eager for freedom and opportunity. Some would even find the Union camps as bad, or worse, than life on "Massa's" land.

In the ensuing months, many slave owners found their former position of power reversed. The Yankees took the word of former slaves over that of the white Southern Rebel. Now, they had a power previously not imagined. One word from them, and a white man could go to jail. He could even be hung!

Slowly, the war situation had come upon the citizens of middle Tennessee. Daily, the citizen's predicament became more frightening. Despite all these things, with the men at war, the women carried on. They had to for the sake of their families and the honor of the South.

Chapter 18

The Boys at War—1862

IN LATE MARCH, JOHN AND BENJAMIN BAUGH, ROBERT HOWLAND, BOB White, and servant, Willis, met the others of Company F at the appointed place in Huntsville, Alabama. On April 1st, the troops reorganized, and the Millersburg Riflemen became part of the Army of Tennessee. Of the original 110, one hundred remained. Leroy B. Howland, 4th Sergeant was demoted to Private, while nineteen year-old Benjamin Baugh, deemed an able and heroic soldier, was promoted to 4th Sergeant in his place.[69]

Meanwhile, Alexander Gum's cousin, forty year-old John Gum, had joined the 23rd Tennessee, on the contingency that he be allowed to go home seasonally to plant his crops.[70] At same time the men of the Millersburg 110 were reorganizing in Huntsville, John Gum, as part of the 23rd Tennessee, was also there, and wrote to his wife, Caroline, and daughter, Mary Isabel, about his recent experiences.

Mr. Gum's letters to his wife were written on torn scraps of paper—anything he could find. Paper was scarce during this time, but John Gum made do. In his "History of Murfreesboro," C.C. Henderson describes John Gum as a large man who was gifted in mathematics, but "careless as to his grammar."[71] The following letter has had some punctuation added to make it readable, as well as a few repetitive words taken out. The spelling has been left as it was.

At Huntsville, Alabama

March 1862

Dear and Affectionate Wife and Daughter:

I this night take the opportunity of riting you a fiew lines to let you no that I am well . . . Hoping that these lines will find you and Mary well.

Well, Dear Caroline, I have nothing to rite you that would interest you at this time . . . I got to Shelbyville the next Day after I left home. my health improved tolerabl fast. On Sunday aftr I got ther it being the 9th of March about 12 o'clock we tuck up the line of march but I did not no where. we marched 7 miles and camped for the night.

It rained all night so we did not start early but we waded the mud that day. I give out before we got to our Camp . . . me and Solomon stopped on the road and rested and then we went on to the camp. So the next day we passed Fayett-ville, crossed Elk River which is about one mile from town and there camped.

I did not give out that day. Bill Brown's wife was put out of the wagon Satur-day by orders of Col. Neal.[72] So Wensday there being a detail for 6 privates and one non Com officer to go with the wagons so I made the detail for the privets and went myself[.] . . . we had a hard time of it but we reached Flint River and camped on its bank and it commenced raining about night and rained all night and nearly all next day.

We did not move . . . that day. We could not cross the river, so Friday we tuck the line of march. Our Boys waded Flint River and then they tuck the mud wich was from Sohoe [shoe] mout to nee deap. When we reached Fishing Creek, which was waist deap the Boys gu[n]s plunged in. It is about one hundred yards wide. Then we reached Beaver Dam Creek. It had to be waded too but it was not quite as deap.

We reached our camp too(2) miles this side of Huntsville about tree o clock and it commenced raining at nite and rained all night so we stayed hear all Day to Day.

I Recon that we will leave hear tomorrow. I under stand that we will take Cars[the train] but I don't know where we will go to.

Caroline, my shoes is nearly wore out. My feet is wet every day, but it don't hurt me. Caroline, I hope we will get back before long. Caroline, the Boys cant rite at this time. You mus send them folks word how they ar. Soll is well, so is David. Jim Benson and Jim Collmon. They are all well. You must go or send

Figure 6. John Gum and his wife, Caroline, 30 or more years after the war. It is said the Community of Gum was named in honor of him.
(Courtesy Ralph Puckett)

their folks word that they ar well fir they have no c[h]ance to rite.... Send
Aregile Benson wife word that he is well, so is all of the Benson Boys.

Well, Caroline, I have not time to rite much at this time. I send these lines
by Tom Lee. I will rite to you every chance. I am tolerabl well, stouter than I
could expected. I think I can stand it. We have a good fier to night so we can
dry our feet

So ever more, Dear wife, but remains your Husband [til] death

John Gum[73]

There was word the Union was on the march, and the Confederacy needed to protect its rivers and railroads. The men marched to Corinth, Mississippi, and then toward a place named Shiloh, meaning "peace." The name was taken from an old log church, which stood on the hill overlooking the green pastures that descended to the Tennessee River. The journey to Shiloh had been down a series of meandering cow-paths leading to the pasture.[74] The Union Army was camped at the bottom of the pasture hill, on the banks of the Tennessee River. The plan was to surprise them, and drive them into the river.

It had been stormy for the several days of travel; a miserable journey. The winds were blowing, and the rain was coming down. Still, they marched forward. Sergeant Robert L. Howland, 23, Captain John Pruitt, 22, and 19 year-old Sgt. Benjamin Baugh all knew that this time they were preparing for a serious engagement with the Federals. A large battalion of soldiers was expected.

The Confederate Army was under the "direction" of General Albert Sidney Johnston, 59 years old; an imposing man with longish hair and a thick mustache. General Johnston was a West Point graduate, who had fought in the Mexican War. Now he was accompanied by the large and powerful Army of Mississippi, approximately 44,699 men strong.

It was a beautiful Sunday morning, when the battle began. April 6th at 5:30 AM, the Confederates began their march down the hill. The lines of soldiers descending toward the river frightened a mass of wild birds and animals. Terrified, they fled into the Union camps, awakening the men. The Union was so completely unprepared for battle that many were captured in their tents, wearing only underwear. Some ran to hide in the bluffs along the Tennessee River, but thousands stayed to fight.

This was the largest group of soldiers any of the men had encountered. The Union Army, under
General Ulysses S. Grant, was a
force of approximately 48,894 men.
There was chaos as some of the Confederates ran to loot the abandoned
Union camps. The other men went
on blindly; through the continual
boom of the canons, the sound and
smell of gunshot, and the cries of the
soldiers who fell, some screaming in
pain, while others were ripped apart
by bullets too quickly to know what
had happened.

No matter the age, this battlefield was a horrifying sight. It was
one thing to talk with hate of the

Figure 7. General Albert Sidney Johnston.

Yankees, but another to see the faces of their countrymen as the enemy
they had to kill. This encounter, a first of its kind, was shocking. It was
kill or be killed. The men had to go ahead.

The Confederate Army rolled in, going over the Union positions, one
after another. General Grant's orders had been to "hold the sunken road
at all costs." The Feds established a line that stopped the advance. Bullets whizzing through sapling trees sounded like nests of hornets, buzzing
around. Later this spot would be known as the "Hornets Nest."

The Confederate Infantry launched eleven attacks, but the Union line
in the sunken road did not break. Then, the Confederates lined up their
sixty-two cannons at point blank range, and fired at the Illinois and Iowa
farm boys in the sunken road. They fell, and the Confederates moved
in, taking over the road. The Feds, who had held the road for six hours
against the Rebs, were forced to surrender.

Nearby there was a peach orchard in full-bloom. The battle was rag-
ing here, too. Soon, the bodies of countless soldiers lay dead beneath the
trees; the blossoms falling like snow upon them. General Johnston came

out of the peach tree orchard riding his horse; his clothes in tatters from the bullets that had grazed by. A soldier, seeing him a bit wobbly in his saddle, asked him if he had been hurt. He said, "Yes," but refused any help. He sent his surgeon to care for some of the soldiers—both Union and Confederate—who lay moaning in agony out on the field.

General Johnston's aid helped him off his horse, and sat him down near a tree. He had been shot through the back of the leg. It would have been easy for the surgeon to stop the bleeding. Even a tourniquet placed around the leg would have stopped the flow. General Johnston bled to death under the blossoms of the peach trees. His death would be a great physical and moral loss to the men he cared for.

Willis and the other black servants, who had stayed out of the fighting, stood on the hill above in terror. They wondered if they would ever see their white masters alive again. One servant found that both his masters had been killed. Soon, some of the black men joined in the fight.[75]

As evening approached, dead men lay everywhere. The orchard was covered with blood, and the nearby pond ran red as men tried to bathe their wounds, and get a drink of water. As night descended, the screams of men in pain rang out across the land. The most terrible calls were the voices crying for water. As the cry went on, it seemed God had heard them, for the skies opened up, and the rain poured down. Flashes of lightening revealed a horrific sight. There were vultures and pigs feeding upon the dead. This battle was a turning point. Both sides would be scarred and toughened by what they witnessed this day.[76]

By nightfall, the men had been in battle nearly eleven hours. There was a small lull. Then, coming up the Tennessee River, the Union reinforcements began to arrive. They had come on steamboats, with gunboats traveling alongside them. To protect the soldiers disembarking from the ships, the gunboats fired eight-inch shells onto the shore for fifteen-minute intervals. A torrential rain fell, drenching the troops, but the gunboats did not stop their barrage.

For the exhausted Confederate Army, there were no reinforcements. Their commander ordered them to withdraw. As dawn shown on the distant horizon, the men, including John and Benjamin Baugh, Robert White, Robert Howland, and John Gum marched wearily, broken, and shell-shocked up the hill and back to Corinth. Behind them, they left a field of nearly twenty-four thousand dead men—13,047 Federals and 10,694 Confederates.

Arriving at Corinth, the soldiers viewed the body of General Albert Sydney Johnston. He had been carried there to lie in state. Later that day, his body would be shipped to New Orleans for burial. Following this, the Millersburg Riflemen had the sad duty of burying their own fallen comrades: Lt. Ridley and Private Samuel Daughtery.[77]

John Baugh's regiment lost 235 men in the Battle of Shiloh; approximately two-thirds of the regiment. Some were killed, others wounded. In Company F, Captain Thomas White, who had survived the initial battle, was wounded in the fight with the replacement troops. By June, he would resign, and William D. Robison would take his place. Robert L. Howland took the place of 2nd Lt. Washington D. Ridley. The men took over their duties proudly, knowing that they might be gone as soon as the men whose places they were now filling.

Coupled with the tragic loss of their general and so many soldiers, was the knowledge that they had failed. The Confederates had needed to win this battle in order to save the Mississippi Valley. Now, Memphis and Vicksburg were vulnerable to Union attack.

From here on, there would be no rest for the men of the 2nd Tennessee. They went from one battle to the next with little stopping. Retreating to Corinth, they traveled to Tupeo, Mississippi. Reorganizing at Verona, they moved north to Kentucky.

In the rare moments away from battle, the men often sat and stared into the distance. Sometimes they were nearly deaf from the cannon and rifle shot. For many, flashbacks of horrors taunted them.

In an effort to lift the soldier's spirits, their black servants made music. These men knew how to provide a ready smile or laugh to cheer their white masters. The sound of old familiar songs, and the treasured letters from home could bring back the feelings of goodness and beauty, if only for a moment. Home was a place the men dreamed of.

The Battle of Richmond, Kentucky resulted in victory for the Confederates, but the Battle of Perryville was a huge loss. Two of Millersburg 110 were killed in this battle. One wounded man was taken prisoner by the enemy.

In October, the men marched to Knoxville, where they received the news that they would be going to Shelbyville to camp for the winter. This was welcome news since Shelbyville was just over the hill from home. Once the company arrived, they were given a brief furlough.[78]

Seven months had passed since The Millersburg 110 had been home, and those seven months had exposed them to nightmare battles that would forever change them. Nevertheless, the soldiers looked forward to the peace and comfort of familiar surroundings. They assured themselves that this situation must surely be settled by spring.

~

In July of 1862, a group of Yankee soldiers were riding through an area just outside of Murfreesboro when they were fired on. In revenge, a Federal scouting party was sent out to arrest as many as a hundred men and boys. Stragglers along the road, and anyone a neighbor might have named (some did so just to be in good with the Feds) were picked up and taken to the Rutherford County Courthouse jail. Still angry, and looking to make a big impression on the local citizens, the Union soldiers rode out to Woodbury, and arrested "most of the men and boys of the community."[79]

Figure 8. General N.B. Forest.

By the 12th of July, six of the men arrested had been condemned by die by hanging. Many of the men's wives and mothers came to Murfreesboro to beg for the release of their loved ones. Around midnight, some of the local citizens came to the jail, and offered shelter to the grieving women. At this point, the women resigned themselves to the fact that their loved ones would die at dawn.

Somewhere out in the dark night, General Nathan Bedford Forest was riding. Although he was suffering from a wound he had received at Shiloh, he was on a mission to fulfill an order—

to disrupt Federal communications along the Nashville-Chattanooga Railroad.

Close to midnight, General Forest entered Woodbury, and found himself surrounded by the women of the town, who with tears in their eyes, told him of the unjust imprisonment of their men. Forest quickly declared that their husbands and sons would be returned to them before sunset the following day. At this news, the women hurried home to bring food for the hungry soldiers and their horses. Within two hours, Forest and his men were headed for Murfreesboro, about eighteen miles away.

Sending his scouts ahead, Forest learned the positions of the Federals, and divided his troops, arranging a plan that would have each group engaging a portion of the Union troops, so that "none could go to the aid of another."[80]

Usually a Federal Guard, or "Picket," was being posted in the road about a quarter of a mile from town. When Forest sent his advance guard on a road such as this, he had them turn off the road and run through a field shortly before reaching the picket. Then, the advance guard would return to the road ahead of the picket, thus advancing toward their goal. The advance guard apparently found the next pickets sound asleep, and captured them. Word was then sent to General Forest that the way was clear.

Early that morning, the town of Murfreesboro was sleeping peacefully, as were some of the Federal pickets. Suddenly, the sound of thundering hooves was heard. General Forest had given the order to advance, and the men were going at a gallop, yelling like a bunch of Indians, as they entered the camps by Maney Spring.[81] It seemed to the Union soldiers that the Confederates had come out of no where. The Yankees jumped out of bed still in long-johns, and scampered for their rifles.

Following the attack on the camp at Maney Spring—which did not last more than three-quarters of an hour—General Forest headed for the Courthouse in Murfreesboro's town square. The soldiers let out Rebel yells, and fired shots into the air, letting the Yankees know the Courthouse was under attack. In response, the Union soldiers locked the Courthouse doors, and set the place on fire.

Time was of the essence now, because the men behind bars were in danger of burning to death. Finding the walls too thick to damage, Forest ordered his men to secure battering rams and knock the doors down.

Then in a fury, Nathan Bedford Forest rode his horse into the Courthouse entrance. Bullets were flying in all directions. Some bounced off the walls, and some were embedded there.* Once the prisoners were set free, Forest set off to complete his plan of action.[82]

Having achieved his purpose in releasing the imprisoned men, General Forest rode back to the Oaklands Mansion, and declared victory. Even though he had not gained full control of Murfreesboro, he told Union General Crittenden, who was resting with a broken leg as a guest of Dr. Maney, that he had no choice but to concede, which he did.

Following Forest's victory, there was great celebration in Murfreesboro. General Forest was their savior. Not only had he saved the innocent men in the Courthouse, who had been waiting to be hung. He had relieved the citizens of their sense of hopelessness under Federal occupation, and the rough treatment it imposed on them. Because of this one day in July, Nathan Bedford Forest would forever remain a hero to the residents of Murfreesboro.

After the Union's concession to Forest, the Confederates did not remain long in Murfreesboro. By October 1862, the Federals were back again. This time, they took over the town and roamed the county, doing pretty much as they pleased. Murfreesboro was a strategic location, and it was clear the Union intended to stay.

By the time the Federals returned to Rutherford County in the Fall of 1862, Jack Baugh had had enough. He made the decision to enlist in the Confederate Army. Besides, his original reason for remaining at home no longer existed.

In September of 1862, President Abraham Lincoln issued the first of two Executive Orders toward freeing all slaves. The first order stated that all slaves were free in any Confederate state which did not return to the Union by January 1863. Although Tennessee was exempted, because it was already mainly under Union control, Lincoln's executive order opened the door to freedom for thousands of African-American slaves. In the next months, many would leave their masters to go work in Union camps.

---

* When the Rutherford County Courthouse was renovated around 2005, bullets from Forest's attack were found embedded in the walls.

The farms and plantations were not only suffering from lack of hands to work them. Local farmers soon found that whatever was grown, would likely be foraged by either the Federal or Confederate Army. Further, the "Oath of Allegiance" had made it nearly impossible for anyone not taking it to do business. With his wife and child safely situated at the Jarrett home in Salem, Jack Baugh had nothing to hold him back from joining the army.[83]

Down in Winchester, Joseph Baugh had enlisted with the local Militia as soon as the War Between the States began. In the tradition of all Tennessee militias, the company voted for its own officers. Joseph had been voted Major, but when it came time for the men to leave for war, twenty-eight year-old Joseph, who was the youngest member of the company, felt he did not deserve to be "Major" and refused the appointment.[84]

As the months passed, the two oldest Baugh brothers kept in contact about the progression of the war. Then, in the autumn of 1862, Joseph Baugh decided to come up to Rutherford County, and enlist with his brother. He left his wife, Anna, and their two sons, four year-old, Ashton Taylor Baugh, and one year-old Henry with Anna's parents, Ashton and Eliza Butterworth. Mr. Butterworth was still running his cotton mill in Owl Hollow, however within a few months it would be burnt to the ground.[85]

Once in Rutherford, Joseph went to stay with Jack. On October 4th, the two brothers rode their horses over to a place in Salem where a new Confederate company was being formed under the name, Douglass' Tennessee Partisan Ranger Battalion. October 4th was the final day General Joseph Wheeler had given Major Douglass to complete enrollment. Each man enlisted for a three-year period. John Lytle was their captain.[86]

Joseph and John M. (Jack) Baugh were each paid $24.40 for the use of their horses.[87] Jack would ride with the battalion. Joseph was put in charge of the Commissary Department, a position in which he would remain until the end of the war.[88]

In his official records for the war, Joseph was described as 5 feet tall with gray eyes, fair complexion and dark hair. Men and women were shorter then, but either this was a mistake, or Joseph was less than average height. From an early photo taken after the war, Joseph Baugh had a broad frame, like those in the Marable family, and a neatly trimmed beard.

Jack, not described in his war papers, was much thinner than his brother, with dark hair, a beard, and the dark, deep-set eyes of the Baughs. From photographs taken after the war, Jack Baugh's beard was similar to many of the farmers in the area.

At the same time Jack and Joe Baugh were signing up for Douglass' Partisan Rangers, Anderson Crosthwait came down from Nashville and signed up as well.[89] As a member of the Crosthwait family, he was a passionate Southerner.

At the time the men enlisted, the company reported to General Nathan Bedford Forest. Then, in December, Forest left for a raid in west Tennessee, and turned the company over to General Joseph Wheeler. Wheeler remained in charge until February 1863 when the company was reorganized. Anderson Crosthwait would forever be proud that he had served under Wheeler.[90]

For the next two months, Douglass' Partisan Rangers spent most of their time traveling between Murfreesboro, Smyrna, and Franklin. The Company took part in several skirmishes in the area between La Vergne and Nashville. Although they kept quite busy, Jack Baugh—when it was safe—was able to visit his wife and son. No large battles occurred during this time, but the men made enough trouble for the Feds to feel they doing their part to win the war, and protect their land. While other soldiers were fighting battles far from home, these men had the advantage of fighting on their own turf.[91]

With the Feds in Tennessee, there were daily attempts to destroy bridges and cut railroad supplies. By now, both sides were aware that Tennessee was perhaps the most important state in the war. Strategically placed close to the center of the present United States, Rutherford County contained the railroad, which ran east to west, and north to south. Tennessee was basically supporting the Confederacy.

~

When the war began, John Alexander Gum, a non–slave-holding citizen, seemed to have little interest in joining the Confederate Army. His cousin, John Gum, and brothers-in-law, Ben and George Wade had all enlisted in the Confederacy, but Alexander stayed home with his family. Then, with the Federal occupation of Murfreesboro, things changed.

By 1862, the Union occupation of Middle Tennessee left Confederate hands tied. There was a great need for information on the comings and goings of Union troops. General Benjamin F. Cheatham, a Tennessean, was assigned the job of setting up an intelligence system of trustworthy men and women to act as scouts who could supply the Confederacy with this information. Cheatham was very familiar with the area around Nashville, and turned to local people he knew he could trust. In many cases, the servers and carriers of important missives were women and children. When this intelligence was passed on to Confederate Generals (sometimes containing no more than troop whereabouts and numbers), it could made the difference between a battle's victory or defeat.

There were at least two groups of scouts in the area during this time: the Coleman Scouts, and the Carter Scouts. General Cheatham had chosen forty-year-old Captain Henry B. Shaw to command the Coleman Scouts. Shaw was a former steamboat owner who lived in Nashville. His company consisted of approximately one hundred men. The identity of the scout members was kept secret for obvious reasons. Even after the war, many lived in fear of retribution. Some names would never be revealed. Shaw, who was killed in a boat explosion after the war, was possibly the only person to ever know the identity of every member.

Although the "Coleman Scouts" were the most famous in the area, the Carter Scouts from the area of Smyrna, also did important work. Some of these members were enlisted Confederate soldiers who periodically took leave of their companies to pick up or deliver key information.

Alexander's half-brother, Anderson Crosthwait, while serving in Douglas' Battalion, joined the Carter Scouts. Around the same time, Anderson joined the scouts; Alexander Gum also joined a group of scouts. Although it is unknown which group he joined, it seems very possible that because of Anderson's membership, he may have joined the Carter Scouts. The only knowledge of Alexander's scout membership comes to us from his granddaughter, Martha Fox Todd, who recorded this information in her membership application for the Daughters of the Confederacy.[92]

Scout members were considered by the army to be "men of marked ability and daring."[93] Knowledge of the back roads was a key matter, as well as the ability to appear innocent, or even stupid. The men often

disguised themselves as farmers or peddlers. Confederate soldiers in official uniform, if captured, were protected, but they could hardly hope to
obtain information about the Union that a man in plain clothes might.
However, if a scout was caught, they would likely pay with their lives.

One member of the "Coleman Scouts" said he would rather fight
ten battles than go on even one intelligence mission.[94] A number of
scouts said they never went out on a mission without expecting to die.
Except for a few instances, little is known about scout missions during
the Civil War.

Frequently, scouts memorized information so they would not carry
anything incriminating on their person. When transportation of papers
was necessary, they cleverly sewed the papers into the lining of their
hats, jackets, and even boot soles. Most information was sent in code, so
the scout did not know what information they carried. Frequently, the
documents were left in the hollow of a tree, or a similar spot for pick-up
by another.

A Confederate Scout never dared to stay very long in one place. It was
urgent they not be seen going home. On rare occasions, they might hide
their horse in the woods, and sneak into the house for a few moments
with their family. Neighbors were not to be trusted. This was particularly
true in Jefferson. There were those who were secretly Union sympathizers, or eager to gain favor with Federal occupation by betraying someone.
The scouts slept in the woods, and sometimes went without food for days
rather than risk discovery. Most of all, they did not want to cause trouble
to anyone by association.[95]

We can only guess where Alexander Gum went, and what he did
during this time. The fact that between the years 1862 and 1865 there
were no new Gum arrivals, suggests that Alexander was not around. He
may have checked in with his family from time to time, but as the war
progressed, women were considered safer alone than with men.

Two "Coleman Scouts" are famous for their heroic lives and deaths.
Sam Davis was born in the log house that Reverend Henry Hartwell
Marable built. The Davis family lived on the property a few years after
Reverend Marable's death. When Sam was about five, the family moved
to a larger plantation in Smyrna. Shortly before Tennessee seceded the

Union, Sam enlisted in the 1st Tennessee Infantry, and like the Baughs, took part in the terrible battle at Shiloh.

In 1863, Sam Davis became a member of the "Coleman Scouts." He was captured in November of that year while traveling toward Chattanooga. Along with soap, toothbrushes, blank books, slippers, gloves and socks for Colonel A. McKinstry, Sam was found to be carrying 11 newspapers, and other detailed writings on Union troop movement. The papers hidden on Sam's person were something that could only have come from Union General Grenville Dodge's desk. General Dodge's soldiers were the ones who captured him.[96]

Although Sam Davis' Confederate uniform should have protected him, discovery of the papers he was carrying meant he had received information from a spy. The Federal soldiers in Pulaski, Tennessee threw him into jail. General Dodge offered him his life and freedom in exchange for the name of the person who had given him the information, but Sam refused to betray his source.

Sam Davis was tried and convicted of being a courier and a spy. The punishment was death by hanging. On the gallows, twenty-one year-old Sam Davis, given one last chance to reveal his source declared, "I would die a thousand deaths before I would betray a friend."[97] His behavior toward his captors, and bravery in facing death impressed even the Federal soldiers, who felt sorry to execute this fine, young man.

Much later, it was revealed that unbeknownst to the Federals, Henry Shaw, the leader of the "Coleman Scouts" had been in jail with Sam the entire time—disguised as a doctor.* During their time together, Sam never gave any indication that he knew Shaw. A few days after Sam's death, Shaw was sent to prison. Over time, the story of Sam Davis inspired countless persons. He became known as a "Boy Hero of the South"; a symbol of what true honor means.[98] His statue stands on the Capitol grounds in Nashville, Tennessee.

Dee Jobe was also a member of the "Coleman Scouts." He was a young man of twenty-four when the Yankees caught him hiding in a bush as

---

* Shaw was not charged as no papers were found on him, but he was sent to Johnson's Island, a prison in Ohio. Interestingly, the Union relay prison at the time was Maxwell House where the Millersburg Riflemen began their service.

he attempted to chew and swallow a document he was to deliver. The fifteen Yankee soldiers tried to make him tell what information had been on the paper, and who he was working with. When he refused, they cut out his tongue.[99] After committing this atrocity, they gave him another chance to reveal the information, and save his life. When he refused, they took his horse's bridle rein and strangled him to death. Later, some of the soldiers apologized to his family, saying he was the bravest man they had ever seen.[100]

We can only imagine the fear Martha Gum felt as a woman alone with three children. She had no way of knowing whether she would ever see her husband again. Alexander Gum and Anderson Crosthwait, having grown up in Blackman and Old Jefferson, knew every back road, and as some said, every "pig path" of the area. Whether by cleverness, God's blessing, or fate—they survived the war, but the dangers were real.

Chapter 19

The End of 1862

BY LATE AUTUMN 1862, TWENTY-FOUR YEAR-OLD MATTIE BAUGH HOWland was big with child. She had not seen her husband Robert for seven months, and was impatient for news of him. The Union troops had pulled out of the area some time ago, but life was still difficult. Mattie's one comfort was little Rollie, who at two and a half looked like a miniature of his father.

On November 16th, Mattie gave birth to a baby girl, whom she named Mary Baugh Howland. Not long after the baby's birth, Mattie became ill. Because of the war, there was likely no doctor available and no means to fetch one. Conditions were poor, but the women did the best they could to care for Mattie.

Around November 24th, the men of the Millersburg 110 reached Shelbyville by train, and were released for a one-week furlough. By the time Robert Howland reached home, he found a new baby, and his wife, Mattie, seriously ill. There was little anyone could do to help her, and on December 6th, Mattie died.[101]

Mary Ann Baugh took over the care of her two grandchildren, nearly three year-old Rollie and baby Mary, but without her mother, or possibly even a cow to give milk, baby Mary did not survive. Death among women and children was common, but that did not make it any easier. The only solace for Mary Ann was knowing that Mattie and her baby were now together in heaven. One day they would all meet again.

Rollie Howland stayed with Mary Ann. He was a good boy; quiet and thoughtful. His pale little face with the big blue eyes and wispy, gold-blond hair contrasted sharply to Clemmie, who was now five.[102]

Mary Ann's heart broke as she looked at Mattie's small son asking for his "Mama," but she found Rollie was no trouble at all to care for. More than no trouble, he was a comfort. "Why he's the best boy I ever saw," she would say in later years to friends and relatives when speaking about Rollie.[103]

The servants hung black crepe over the front entrance to the house and windows—a message to all who passed that those inside were griev-ing. Not yet out of mourning from her mother's death, Mary Ann would probably remain in mourning for the rest of her life.

At the homeplace, most of the Baugh slaves had fled by now. Some like Mammy Ran (as Mirandy was now called) remained faithful to the family, but the shift of power had definitely changed. The slaves who stayed on with their former masters knew they could leave anytime, and no one could make them do anything they didn't want to do. Looking at marriages among the black Baughs in the area of Christiana after the war, we can guess that at least eight to ten of the former slaves remained with the Baughs throughout the war. With few servants, and eleven year-old Charlie the only white male at home, the Baugh women did the best they could to survive.

In the weeks preceding Christmas, all of Murfreesboro was in a festive mood. There were plenty of parties, and enough to eat. Now that the Confederate troops were once again in control, the dark, tense atmo-sphere that Federal occupation had held over them was lifted. People walked about the town with a sense of freedom and hope.

The Confederate troops arrived in large groups, with plans to winter in town. With their arrival, people began to feel, the coming New Year just had to be the year the war would end!

There was quite a stir when the citizens of Murfreesboro learned that President Jefferson Davis was coming to town. A large battalion of Con-federate soldiers pitched their tents around the grounds of the Maney fam-ily's Oaklands Mansion where President Davis was to stay. That evening, residents who had homes along the road to Oaklands lit candles, and put them in the windows as a greeting for Jeff Davis. There was a parade attended by black and white, young and old alike. Cheering and celebration were everywhere.

Jefferson Davis had come to Murfreesboro to discuss strategies for the war with General Braxton Bragg. While there, he was apprised of the fact that Union troops were coming down from Nashville in massive numbers. It seemed the Confederate troops were not going to have a winter rest. There was going to be a battle, and soon!

Later that evening, the celebration continued as people from the town came to serenade President Davis, who decided to extend his visit so he could attend the wedding of General John Hunt Morgan to Mattie Ready. The marriage took place in a home just off the Murfreesboro Square.[104] Early the next morning, Jeff Davis left town, returning to Montgomery, Alabama.

Skies were cloudy on Christmas Eve, though the weather was warmer than usual. That night, there was a ball on the corner of East Main Street and Courthouse Square. The house was brightly lit, and four large "Bs" of cedar and evergreen—signifying Bragg, Beauregard, Buckner and Breck-inridge—adorned the walls. A ball was being held inside. Elegant ladies in gowns and men in uniform laughed and danced. The sounds of music, the clinking of glasses, and laughter wafted through the open windows. "It was a magnificent affair," a member of Bragg's escort remembered.[105] Outside in the camps, men drank, had fights, and rolled their dice.

In the days following Christmas, something in the air changed. A cold wind was blowing, and the rumors of Federal troops coming down from Nashville spread. Something was about to happen.

Up on Wilkerson Pike where Benjamin Marable lived, the local families noticed a long line of Federals coming down the Pike. The Batey, Bass, House, and Beasley families had large farms, but the majority were related and kept in contact with one another.

General Braxton Bragg, in town, and the officials and troops out on the highways passed messages back and forth frantically. At first, they thought only one group of troops was coming down from Nashville. Then, they realized the Feds were coming toward Murfreesboro from three directions! They would just have to dig in and wait.

~

North of Murfreesboro, Douglass' Partisan Rangers, under General Joseph Wheeler, had seen Union soldiers coming down along the Nashville Pike, a fact that Anderson Crosthwait—as a scout—would have reported to his superiors.[106] Jack Baugh, a patroller, was also keenly aware of what was going on. The cavalry were ordered to slow the Union soldiers down, weakening them before they got to Murfreesboro. The Partisan Rangers did just that, but they had some help.

The rain had been coming down, and while the Nashville Pike was paved with ground rock and a mixture which held the earth together, the Union soldiers felt it would be wiser to take a side road. These roads contained the red-brown earth of Tennessee, a kind of clay affair. Anyone from Middle Tennessee would know that these roads, once wet, would be impossible to pass on—especially with heavy wagons and cannons—but, of course, the Union Army didn't know. It didn't take long for their cannons and heavily loaded wagons to sink deep in the mire.

Wheeler's men showed up and decided to have some fun catching those Union boys trying to get their wagons out of the mud. When the Yankees saw the Rebs coming, they were in such a hurry to get away, some of the men left their boots behind! In this manner, General Rosecrans lost half the troops he planned to have in Murfreesboro by December 30th. Men like Jack Baugh and Anderson Crosthwait were excited to turn the tide in their own way.

During this time, Wheeler's cavalry as a whole destroyed twenty wagons in one Union division, and an entire wagon train in another. Nearly a million dollars in damage was done. One witness described the destruction near La Vergne in this way:

> "... the turnpike, as far as the eye could reach, was filled with burning wagons. The country was overspread with disarmed men ... The streets were covered with empty valises, trunks, knapsacks, and broken guns ..."[107]

Sleep deprived for three days, the men were given a few hours of rest beyond Nolensville. Then, returning south they stopped in Jefferson, just behind the Yankee camps, to feed and water their horses. From here, they returned to La Vergne, and continued their raids, taking possession of 300 heavily-laden wagons, and 300 prisoners as well. Of their escapades, Captain George K. Miller said, "We also had an immense deal of fun."[108]

By December 29th, John Baugh and the men of the 2nd Tennessee Infantry had left Shelbyville, and were positioned north of Murfreesboro along the Lebanon Pike. William H. Newman was the new captain for the Millersburg Riflemen; and twenty-one year-old W.D. Robinson was now in direct command of the 2nd Tennessee. From here on, this division would be named for him (Robison's). Directly above "Robison" was General Lucius E. Polk, who was in charge of eight regiments. The

Figure 9. *Major General Patrick Cleburne.*

2nd Tennessee was now a part of Polk's Brigade, under Cleburne's Division, in Hardees Corp of Bragg's Army of Tennessee.

Because of his outstanding leadership in the battles of Shiloh, Richmond, and Perryville, Patrick Cleburne, an Irish born citizen who had served in the British Army, had just been promoted to the position of Major General. The men of the Millersburg 110 had fought all these battles, and were well aware of who he was.[109]

John Gum, who had fought in many of the same battles as the Millersburg 110, was now stationed in Murfreesboro with the 23rd Tennessee Infantry. The 23rd was also a part of the Cleburne Division. John Gum, like the others, waited out the cold night to see what would happen.

The night of December 30th, General Bragg ordered Hardee's Corp to move to the west bank of the Stones River.[110] Bragg expected a long battle because he ordered his troops to prepare three days of rations.

~

Down in Old Millersburg, Mary Ann Baugh had no idea anything had changed. Looking out the window, she noticed the sky. It looked like a winter storm was brewing. The children would definitely stay in tomorrow.

Christmas was quiet and sad with Mattie's passing and the men gone. They would look to the New Year; an end to the war, and the return of loved ones. This was the prayer each night in hundreds of homes. Mary Ann thought of her grandfather Reverend Marable, of how powerfully he had prayed, and she worried about her father all alone up in the Blackman Community.

~

Up in Old Jefferson, Martha Gum tucked her children safely in their beds. On September 12th, she had given birth to her fourth child, a beautiful baby girl with dark hair and blue eyes, whom she had named Lucy.

There had been a skirmish, just across the river from Old Jefferson that day. Many from Walter Hill ran to Jefferson for safety. On this night, December 30th, all was peaceful as Martha prayed with the children, and then rocked baby Lucy to sleep.

Not far away, on the hill over-looking Jefferson and the Stones River sat the beautiful Fairmont Plantation. Rebecca Crosthwait Ridley and her family were having a small gathering to celebrate the coming year. Seventeen year-old Bromfield Ridley, Jr. was entertaining a group of young people, including his cousin, Frank Crosthwait.

George and Eliza Crosthwait had moved the family to Iowa some years earlier (1852). Two years prior to this, on December 22nd, 1860, Eliza Burton Crosthwait had passed away. At the start of the war, all the eligible Crosthwait sons rushed to join the Confederate Army. Frank Crosthwait's youngest brother, seventeen year-old Bromfield Ridley Crosthwait had been killed two months earlier in the Battle of Corinth. His eldest brother, Shelton had been killed in the Battle of Fishing Creek the previous January. But tonight, Frank was in good spirits.

Around midnight, someone rode up to the plantation, which looked eerily enchanted in the misty light of the moon. The visitor had news for the men: "Union soldiers are coming down the pikes, and positioning themselves for battle," they were told. The party broke up quickly as Frank Crosthwait rushed out to join the 20th Tennessee Infantry, Company E.[111]

The same thing was happening all over Murfreesboro. At the ball on the square, soldiers hastily ran out, leaving behind startled ladies in ball gowns. This was not what they had planned, but they had to get ready.

The Confederates were suffering in the freezing cold. John Baugh, Benjamin and the others had no tents and little with which to keep them warm.[112] As part of the Cleburne Division, the Millersburg 110 was stationed (according to various war maps and diagrams) within two miles of Benjamin Marable's home.

As the men of the Confederacy lay down to rest before the battle that would take place in a few hours; there was a stirring in the air. Music was being played in some distant place, and echoing across the land. Then the Confederate boys heard the voices of the Union men singing:

Mid pleasures and palaces though we may roam,
Be it ever so humble there's no place like home!

Now the bands began to play—a band here, and a band there, until the night was full of heartfelt music.

I gaze on the moon as I tread the drear wild,
And feel that my mother now thinks of her child;
As she looks on that moon from our own cottage door,
Thro' the woodbine whose fragrance
Shall cheer me no more."

The men and boys of the South, feeling the yearning of the song, began to join in:

Home, home, sweet home, there's no place like home,
*Home, home, sweet home, there's not place like home.**

The song ended, and for a long while after there seemed to be a lingering vibration of music in the air.[113]

---

* "Home Sweet Home," music by Henry Rowley Bishop, 1821, lyrics by John Howard Payne, 1823. The song was very popular in the mid-1800s.

Chapter 20

The Battle of Stones River

A S THE LAST GRAY DAY OF 1862 DAWNED, THERE WAS TERRIBLE CAN-nonading in the distance. BOOM! BOOM! The sound echoed across the land and shook the plates in the cupboards down in Old Mill-ersburg. Distant though it might be, the battle noise was powerful. It was heard as far as one hundred miles away, and it went on all day and into the night, echoing across the land until the girls held their heads and cried to Mammie (as they called their mother) to make it stop.

Mary Ann's thoughts were distracted. Where were Mr. Baugh and Benjamin? And where was her father? The sounds of battle seemed to be coming from up near Blackman, but it was impossible to know. Was it Murfreesboro? Oh, dear God, where were all the people? What if it was Blackman? Certainly her father would know what to do, or someone there would look after him.

They had talked of war, of confronting the Yankees, but now the war had come to them. It was right here, on their own land. Many had lost sons and husbands. Was it her turn now? She could not know, and the anxiety was too painful to bear. Have faith, pray to God; *He* will protect us. That was what she told the children.

It was cold and dark outside, and soon the smell of smoke drifted down to them. The little children, Rollie and Clemmie, huddled together with the older girls, who tried to amuse them. The remaining servants were ter-rified out of their minds. Some came crying at the door, while others ran and hid in the woods behind the house. Mammy Ran stayed in the house, along with two of her children, Jane and Gilbert. Eventually, seven-year old Clemmie and three-year old Rollie seemed to adjust to the noise. How amazing children were. The girls, Fredonia, 17, Mary, 15, Eliza, 13, and Charlie, 11 sat quietly by, keeping their minds and hands busy. It would be days before the family had any idea what truly had occurred.

~

At 6 AM, the morning of December 31st, General Hardee ordered the men forward. When the first wave of Rebels came through the woods, they found the Union soldiers sleepily rubbing their eyes as they rose from their camp beds. It was a gray, bone-chilling morning, and believing the battle would start later in another location, the Union men camping along the Stones River were just about to prepare breakfast and coffee. When the Confederates came running out of the woods, it was a slaughter. The Union men who survived ran for their lives.

The Millersburg Riflemen, as part of the Cleburne Division, followed up the initial attack. They were hungry for victory this time, and determined to have it on their own land. By the end of morning, the right wing of the Union Army had been knocked out.[114]

Some Federal soldiers were backed up against farm fences that they could not get through. The volleys of the iron rifle ball with metal spikes were brutal. They could rip a man apart. In terror, the men who could escape ran across the farmland, and into the cornfields. They ran south of Wilkerson Pike and west. The Rebels left their formations to chase them into the cedar brush, where the cannons could not go.

The Yankees lodged themselves in an area that would come to be known as "the round forest." Here, they fought back. By the afternoon, the tide had begun to turn, and soon the ground was covered with the bodies of Confederate soldiers. By night, it was clear the Confederates had not won this battle. Along with this depressing reality was the bleak, biting cold of winter.

John Baugh, and the others of the Millersburg Riflemen, spent the night along the Stones River. Some men were given whiskey by their commanding officers. The fumes alone were strong enough to make a man drunk, but helped them get through the night.[115]

Figure 10. A local farm where some of the battle took place.

Up on Lebanon Pike, the men of Wheeler's Division could hear the battle some thirty or more miles away. Jack Baugh, and the others in his company, continued the work of slowing the Union troop movement. On this day, Wheeler's Cavalry captured 1,100 men, and destroyed 320 wagons by setting fire to them.[116] At the end of the day, Wheeler's men rejoiced, feeling that they had had a great victory.

Down on Blackman Road, the ground shook with every volley of the cannon. It seemed the dishes in the china closets would shatter at any moment. It felt as if the world was coming to an end.

The Howse, Batey, Bass, and Marable slaves gathered chickens, pigs, cows, and sheep, and ran up into the cedar lands where they knew the trails. "The Yankees is comin' ... The Yankees is comin,'" they cried, and ran for their lives. They stayed up there for weeks after the battle, hiding under trees, and in caves. It was not a place the Yankees should come. For those who did not know their way, there were sinkholes and bottomless pits. Bushwhackers also stayed up in those hills, and Yankees following them might never be seen again.[117]

During the battle, the white folks in Blackman stayed in their homes for the most part, waiting with apprehension. As long as the fighting did not move west, they were fine, but the sound was fearful; ear shattering, and the air was black with horrible smoke that burned the throat and singed the eyes. You could taste it.

It seemed the battle would never end, but on Thursday, New Years Day, everything stopped. The men went out on the battlefield to collect the dead and wounded. Overnight, a frost had formed across the farms, turning the ground white. The dead men were completely white. The wounded, but living, had a small outline of earth around them where the frost had not formed. In this way, the soldiers gathering bodies could tell quickly who was alive, and who was dead. The cold was also a blessing in that it slowed the bleeding, and prevented many wounds from becoming infected.

The number of men who had fallen on one day during the Battle of Murfreesboro was so vast; there were not resources to handle them. Men were transported to farmhouses, and to Murfreesboro, but still there was not enough room. They lay everywhere—in the streets, the square, and the railway station.

Doctors, and others in the freezing cold, would reach a home to discover it had been abandoned by terrified residents, who had run for their lives. The men entered to find tables neatly set for dinner, and fires burning in fireplaces. These homes were soon filled with wounded men, who were placed on beds, tables, and floors.[118]

One room in the home was set aside for surgery. There were few cases where wounded men needed simple treatment to save their lives. In most cases, bones were fractured, and flesh torn. The solution of the 1860s was simply to remove the wounded limb before infection set in. A swig of whiskey or a sniff of chloroform might be all a man got to ease his pain. Then, saws were taken out and a hand, foot, arm or leg was sawed off, and thrown into a pile. To this day, there are many homes in Murfreesboro, and the surrounding area, which contain the bloodstains of men wounded in this battle. In some cases, the foot imprints of a surgeon, who stood for hours amputating limbs, are outlined on the floor in blood.[119]

~

When the battle stopped, ambulances with the wounded began to descend on Murfreesboro. The doors of homes along East Main Street were opened, and hospitals set up in every place imaginable. The Union Seminary could not hold them; neither could the churches or houses. The wounded lay in the square along side those who were dead. With the cessation of the cannon and gunfire, many from the surrounding areas came into Murfreesboro to search for loved ones.

Rebecca Crosthwait Ridley was one of those who came, desperate to find her husband and her son. Later, she would write of what she saw that day:

> "On entering ... what a sight met my eyes! Prisoners entering every street, ambulances bringing in the wounded, every place crowded with the dying. The Federal General, Sill, lying dead in the courthouse—killed Wednesday."[120]

On the courthouse counter, Mrs. Ridley found the dead body of her nephew, Frank Crosthwait.[121] Only a few days earlier, he had been at her home, laughing with her sons. Now, he had been lying dead for three days. Numb with the horror of it all, Mrs. Ridley ran out into the street, desperate to find her family. On Vine Street, where the large of Methodist Church stood, she witnessed worse sights:

> "The churches were full of wounded, where the doctors were amputating legs, arms. I found my (husband and son) ... safe, and being informed that another battle was expected to begin, I set off on my way home, and passed through our cavalry all drawn up in line. I had only gone a mile when the first cannon boomed, but I was safe."[122]

Now the battle began again. The Confederates pursued the Union troops east, where they descended down a slight incline of trees and rock to the Stones River. They were so intent on their pursuit of the Yankees, and their attempt to catch them up against the river, that they failed to see the line of fifty-eight cannons on a hill above them. The cannons were fired, and hundreds of men were mowed down. In a little over an hour, 1,800 Confederate men lay dead, their blood flowing into the waters of the Stones River. It was here the Battle of Stones River would conclude.

Figure 11. Land along the Stones River, where the terrible final battle took place. This land is now part of the Stones River National Battlefield.

Jack Baugh's company took part in this terrible final battle. Then, they heard the order to retreat. From this devastating place by the Stones River, Wheeler's Cavalry galloped down the road to McMinnville. The men were shaken and shattered by what they had witnessed. They would never forget this day.

~

On Saturday, January 3rd, General Bragg initiated a withdrawal of the Confederate troops as a whole. Moving his headquarters south to Winchester, Hardee's Corps went to Tullahoma, and Polk's to Shelbyville.

John Baugh and Benjamin, following the command, began to move en masse with their companies down the Manchester Highway to Tullahoma. Along the way, a woman ran out in the road and screamed at them for giving up, and leaving Murfreesboro in the hands of the Federals. Another woman, watching the retreat wrote in her diary,

"It was the grandest saddest sight we ever saw ... No other sound broke the stillness ... only the ceaseless footsteps of the retreating heroes that followed each other in rapid secession ... "[123]

Then, too, was the moment they passed the road going to Old Millersburg. How tempting to go home, but there was not time for that now. The defeat and the devastation were heart sickening, but the Army was not ready to concede. It had been a victory for the Union soldiers; a victory that never hurt so much because they were leaving their wives, mothers, sweethearts, and children in the hands of the Yankees.

Of the Millersburg 110, four had been killed, and fifty-nine wounded. Some wounded, like Private Nathan Hatchet, were able to be taken home for care. Others lay in the snow, waiting for treatment, or waiting to die. In the retreat, several young men, believing the company to be Georgia-bound, decided to desert. Home was only three miles away, and they ran for it while they could.[124] John and Benjamin Baugh continued on with the rest.

On Blackman Road, where the lane curved, Benjamin Marable's home sat vacant. His servants had run to hills, but where was he?[125]

Down the road, closer to the Wilkerson Pike, Dr. Manson opened his doors to the wounded soldiers straggling in. Some would make it, but many would not. Dr. Manson set a table in front of the parlor window, not far from the fireplace. In this spot, where he had light to see, and could keep the patients warm, he set to work; operating to save men's lives.

As the day went on, more and more homes were turned into hospitals. There was the Horde home, the Gresham home—which sat right in the middle of battle—and on a hill over-looking the embattled farmland sat the white Jenkins mansion, an elegant and roomy oasis. The battle had gone all the way around this hill, and the cannons thundered—scaring the family half to death—but the Gresham land itself seemed to be declared a free zone.[126] Here lay hundreds of wounded and dying men.

Two days after the Battle of Stones River began (also called the Battle of Murfreesboro), suddenly all was quiet. The reports were that

Figure 12. Dr. Manson's home on Wilkerson Pike. The home began with a log cabin and, like mainly other homes in the area, was covered by boards and built on to. (Courtesy of Charles Batey)

thousands—*thousands*, not hundreds, had been killed! It was unthinkable that such horror had taken place on their own land; the land where the Gums, Marables, Baughs and others had lived for two and three generations. The land they had helped create out of a wilderness was now covered with the bodies of their own countryman.

In Murfreesboro, the smell of death, and the cries of the dying filled the air. Every home that had room had been turned into a hospital, and was housing those wounded in battle. Surgeons worked day and night, operating on the hundreds of men waiting with bullet holes, and mangled arms and legs. The winter cold, which kept the germs down, also made the men vulnerable to illness. These poor soldiers waited for days to be taken care of, moaning in pain, as the stench of their bloody wounds filling the air.

The courthouse, schools, and churches had also been turned into hospitals. From the Nashville Pike to the Wilkinson Pike, the wounded lay on parlor floors, and in the yards surrounding homes. The homes people

Figure 13–15. The Gresham Home sat on a hill, just southwest of the area where most of the battle was fought. It was not far from Blackman. In 2007, the mansion was razed by its owner, against great protest.

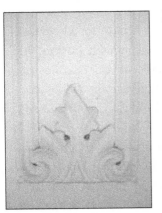

Detail on front entrance double doors and entrance hall staircase.

had vacated in terror had had furniture moved, and bleeding men carried in. Outside the homes, the bodies, and body parts were piled high for burial. Eventually, many of the wounded soldiers were transported by train down to Tullahoma. There was simply not enough room, or enough doctors in Murfreesboro to care for all these men.

As a result of the battle, the Union troops, under General Rosecrans, lost 12,800 soldiers—dead, wounded or missing. The Confederates, under General Bragg, lost approximately 10,306. Cleburne's Division lost 2,066, with 229 dead, 1630 wounded, and 19 missing.

~

Mary Ann Baugh knew she had to get to her father. Had she learned that the fighting was taking place near his home; or had someone slipped a message through the lines to her? Only a few days after the battle ended, the Yankees were swarming over the landscape like flies. There was not a road or a pike that did not have a Federal guard.

When the battle ceased, Mary Ann Baugh ordered one of the servants to hitch a horse to the buggy, and set off toward Blackman to find her father. At the Shelbyville Pike, she could see the shapes of the blue uniformed pickets. "Halt!" they cried.

She explained that she was going north to the Blackman area to try to find her father, but no matter how she begged, the soldiers refused to let her pass.[127] They had orders that "no one" was to pass "for any reason." They had just survived a three-day battle of unimaginable horrors, and they would go by their orders. The Union soldiers could not be concerned with the problems of a "sessah" woman, who for all they knew was spy.

It was no use. Mary Ann had to turn around and go home. She would never see never see her father alive again.

Some time during or after the Battle of Murfreesboro, eighty-three year-old Benjamin Marable left his home in the freezing January cold. He was taken in by a Mr. Hunt—possibly a relative through marriage of Rev. Ebenezer McGowan. Here, he died. Where he is buried, is unknown.

Chapter 21

War Comes to Old Jefferson

URING THE PREVIOUS MONTHS, OLD JEFFERSON HAD REMAINED A fairly quiet, out of the way place. Then, beginning in December, the town's location (lying halfway between Murfreesboro and Nashville) made it the inevitable target for Union raids. In addition, the fact that there were a few large plantations in the area—most particularly "Fairmont" and "Stony Lonesome"—made it of special interest.

Martha Gum, as the wife of a Rebel Scout, and a woman alone with four children, must have been fearful for her family's safety. Willie was eight years-old now, John Jr., five, Laura, two, and Baby Lucy almost four months. Nearby, sister-in-law, Susan Wade was living with Baby James, and Martha's elderly mother, Nancy Wade. Sometime during the war years, it appears that William and Malinda Crosthwait also may have returned to the area. Life was not easy for these families in Old Jefferson. The Confederates, and then the Union soldiers pretty well cleaned out most of the livestock, and other means of food supply in the area.

Beginning in December 1862, the residents heard skirmishes in the vicinity. At one time, shots were fired directly across the river from them. The sound of galloping horses, and gunfire often kept the families of Old Jefferson indoors.

Then on December 30th, a large skirmish began at Walter Hill near the Espey's Chapel. The skirmish sent local residents running across the river to the town of Jefferson for safety. Throughout that day and the next, the families heard the constant boom of cannons, and the shots of riflemen.

Figure 16.

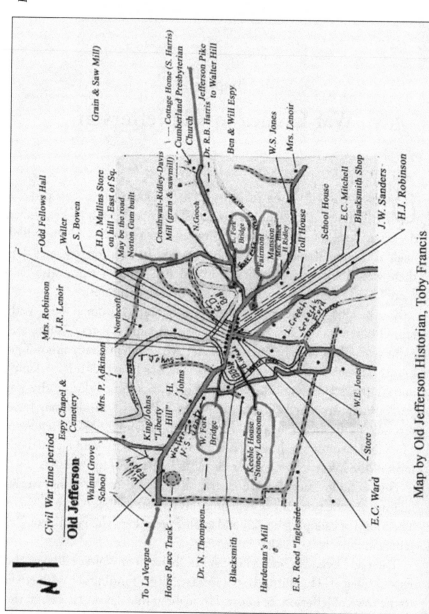

Map by Old Jefferson Historian, Toby Francis

Between the battlefield south of them, and the actions of Wheeler's Cavalry, who were burning wagons of supplies just north of them, the families must have been exhausted from the stress and fear that they soon might be in the midst of the battle. They had nowhere to run; they could only sit in their homes, and wait, and pray.

During the Battle of Murfreesboro, the deafening noise continued for three days. The cannons, shots, and yells of the soldiers exposed them to horrors no mother would want her children exposed to. What might be visible outside the doors of their home was even worse.

On the hill above Old Jefferson, Fairmont Mansion remained solid, and peaceful. Yet from their elevated position, the Ridley family was able to witness even more of the "atrocities" taking place in the fields beyond.

Bettie Ridley Blackmore, the daughter of Rebecca Crosthwait Ridley, kept a diary about this time. To our knowledge, it is the only known account of what took place in the area of Jefferson during the war, and the closest we may come to knowing what the Gum family experienced. Mrs. Blackmore wrote:

> "During that time, we witnessed from our gallery a severe skirmish between the contending parties. The flash, smoke and deafening noise of the artillery, the clicking of small arms, deploying troops in an open field, the shouts and curses of the infuriated soldiers, was a scene we will not soon forget."[128]

With the Confederate Army in retreat after the battle, the Union soldiers secured the area. Judge Bromfield Ridley returned home after the Battle of Stones River, but soon realized for his own safety, he had to leave Fairmont. It seems that local Union officials had confused him with another Ridley who caused great trouble for them. This confusion would cause

Figure 17. Judge Bromfield L. Ridley.

the Union soldiers to harass the Ridleys, and treat them with even greater harshness than they would have otherwise.

Mr. Ridley decided to take the couples' thirteen-year-old daughter, Sarah, out of the area with him. The dangers of war for a young girl in occupied territory, and the horrors she might witness or experience if she stayed were not something he wanted to risk for her.

In other circumstances, Mr. Ridley would have taken his wife, but now he was forced to leave her, and their eldest daughter, Bettie, behind. Rebecca Ridley refused to leave Fairmont because her mother, seventy-eight year-old Mrs. Shelton Crosthwait, lay dying in the back bedroom. At the same time, daughter Bettie Blackmore had been seriously ill for weeks, and was also thought to be dying. Mrs. Ridley, left alone in a house now in the midst of enemy territory, said, "I have no help but God."[129]

On January 14th, just two weeks after the Battle of Murfreesboro, Elizabeth Thompson Crosthwait's suffering ended. The family placed her in a coffin made from a neighbor's cherry wardrobe. Despite their sorrow, there was great relief that their mother and grandmother would suffer no more in this terrible time. Bettie wrote,

> "... she rests calmly and sweetly now on the bosom of that saviour she delighted to glorify while on earth."[130]

Whether William and Malinda Crosthwait or any of the Gums were present at her burial is unknown.

During this time, the Union soldiers came foraging every day. They were rough, and rude. The survivors of this last battle—on both sides—became hardened by the events of those few, brutal days. From now on, it would be survival of the fittest, and no one would be trusted.

The residents of Rutherford County had not lost their sense of dignity or entitlement. The sweet southern ladies of the past were now women of steel. They were not afraid to fight or tell the "enemy" exactly what they thought.

Bettie says the soldiers were "insolent" and "taunted" her "ma" with the fact that her sons were in the "Rebel Army." The soldiers also tried to get the former slaves—who were still living with them—to tell them where valuables like the family silver were hidden.

In order to avoid any disturbance that might further harm Bettie's health, Rebecca allowed the soldiers to take anything they asked for: chickens, meat, horses, and other goods.[131] Meanwhile, Rebecca—with a view toward survival—had hidden a quantity of food up in the rafters of their home: corn, wool, dried fruit, wheat, and fifty bacon hams! But with each succeeding visit by the Federals, the tension heightened, and things got worse.

From the windows of their home, the Ridleys had seen other homes being burnt. The soldiers made constant threats, saying that they would do the same to Fairmont.

In the following weeks, Rebecca wanted to take at least a few of their precious belongings to some of the neighbors' homes, in case such a calamity should take place, but she was unable to find anyone who would take them. Bettie writes:

> "… our neighbors were fearing the same calamity, and we knew of no place of safety. An additional source of alarm was almost every night being aroused to witness some conflagration in the neighborhood—either a dwelling house, gin or stable. In four weeks, seventeen cotton gins had been destroyed by fire and several dwelling houses. Our nights, you may imagine were full of terror, but no serious cause for alarm occurred until the 1st of February."[132]

On February 1st, one of their neighbor's former slaves came to Fairmont with a group of armed Federal soldiers. He demanded that his wife and his child—two slaves owned by the Ridleys—be released to him. The former slave, feeling the full flavor of freedom, had two pistols, and walked confidently into the Ridley mansion, expressing his pent-up rage loudly, much to the alarm of the women.

Mrs. Ridley, feeling entitled because of the beliefs she had grown up with since childhood, refused to release the man's wife or child, and told him that his demands were "outrageous." She said she would shoot him if he came through the door. In response, the man told her he would return in two weeks.

Ten days later, on a cloudy, moonless night, the family "assembled on the gallery to witness a burning house two miles distant." That night they went to bed with feelings of "impending evil."

Some hours later, their dog, Carlos, who was outside, ran barking from door to door, insistently banging on the glass, and growling in order to wake them. Rebecca finally rose to see what the matter was, and discovered that the house was on fire. She called for the servants, Susan and Leila, to ring a bell, sounding an alarm.

Bettie, who was unable to walk on her own, had to be carried from the home, by "faithful Hardin," one of their servants. No sooner had Bettie been carried out, than the roof of one part of the home caved in. Hardin took Bettie to a slave cabin, and laid her there to rest.

The fire spread quickly through the old, wooden mansion—from the office, up along the roof and across the mansion. As the roof came crashing in, the burning Fairmont lit up the night sky. Among the many family treasures lost that night were the Ridley baby cradle, the family Bible, and a portrait of Elizabeth Thompson Crosthwait.

As Bettie Ridley Blackmore lay on the ground, watching the home she loved burn, she saw the gravestones of her family lit like day by the fire. She thanked God that her grandmother, and sister were not alive to experience the pain of seeing their home destroyed. She writes:

> "Only four neighbors dared to come to our relief. The soldiers watched from the ice house, madly exulting in their midnight work, and all were afraid to come to our relief or go anywhere in the yard."[133]

The light of fire on the hill above the river, and the sounds of the mansion crashing in would have woken residents in Old Jefferson. How many persons had lost their homes, or been vandalized by the Yankees there? Who were the four neighbors who came, unafraid to help and comfort them?

The burning of Fairmont—which graced the area of Jefferson, and had long represented wealth, beauty, and culture—symbolized the end of an era for those living in Old Jefferson. Life would truly never be the same again.

In the early morning hours, the Yankee soldiers came to the family who had lost their home, and demanded breakfast, while laughing over their midnight work. Rebecca Ridley, in a fury, hurled insults at the men who had burnt her home; a place sheltering four "defenseless women." (The other two women were the servants who had remained with them.) Many of the neighbors came to offer the women shelter in their homes.

Mrs. Walter Keeble sent a carriage so that Bettie Ridley Blackmore—still too frail to move or stand—could be brought to her home. The servants carefully placed Bettie in the carriage on a bed, but before they could drive away, the Federal soldiers surrounded the carriage threatening to cut loose the mules that were pulling it. Friends of Bettie's begged the soldiers to at least allow the mules to pull Bettie and Rebecca to Mrs. Keeble's—about a mile away. The Yankees agreed to this, but upon their arrival at the Keebles, took out their knives, cut the harness off the mules, and took them away.[134]

In the days and weeks following this event, the Ridleys went to live in a small cabin, belonging to someone in Jefferson. While there, Bettie noted in her writing, that some persons, including "Mrs. Crosthwait," came to ask if they could take the wood remaining from Fairmont, for their own use.

Bettie Ridley opened a small school for the children of the area. Her school grew from a few children to about twenty-five. It's very possible that the Gum and Wade children attended this school. Bettie wrote of teaching in her diary:

> My school occupies me entirely ... I give music lessons every night ... I love the care of children. The association seems purer than any other now. Their young hearts have not yet learned the duplicity & wickedness of the world & are only full of pure thoughts.

Sadly, Bettie's health was not good. Some of the older boys in the area were rowdy, and she had difficulty handling them. It was not easy to keep a school going under Union occupation.

Finally in July of 1864, the Yankees came, and said they would burn the house that Rebecca, Bettie, and four lodgers were renting—accusing them of harboring guerrillas. Then, in anger, they said they would burn the entire town of Jefferson, but finally, were satisfied with burning the one block on which the house they were renting stood.

After this, Bettie was never the same, but sank until four months later, she died. Rebecca remained alone until the end of the war.

The war took its toll on many. Rebecca Crosthwait Ridley passed away four years after the end of the war in 1869. Bromfield Ridley was financially destroyed, and although he had always been a strong man, passed away one year after Rebecca in 1870.

Chapter 22

The War Goes On—1863

IN JUNE OF 1863, THE WAR CAME CLOSER TO MARY ANN BAUGH AND
family than they could have ever imagined. After the Battle of Stones
River, most of the Confederate Army of Tennessee had moved to points
south. When General Rosecrans did not pursue them, Hardee moved his
troops back up to Wartrace, an area along the railroad, about six miles
south of Old Millersburg.

The area between Old Millersburg and Wartrace consists of a hilly landscape with winding roads, ravines, and hollows. Amidst these hills lie the
towns and communities of Bell Buckle, Fosterville, Fairfield, Liberty Gap,
and Hoover's Gap. The area also has many hills and "knobs," with fine
lookouts. During the war, local citizens kept a good watch on these hills,
where they could see as far as Murfreesboro. Then, in June of 1863, citizens
observed Union troops coming down from Murfreesboro to Hoovers Gap.

As a result of this siting, the Confederates placed two regiments, and
artillery at Liberty Gap; a town about two miles directly south of the
Baugh home. Liberty Gap was one of the few places between Old Millersburg and Wartrace that had enough open space to hold a regiment.

Around June 24th, the "Bluecoats" (as the locals sometimes called
them) came through Hoover's Gap. Here they met Confederate troops,
and a battle began that raged on for two days. At the battle's conclusion,
the Union soldiers continued south on Hoover's Gap Road. Reaching
New Millersburg the Federal troops surprised a group of Confederates by
crossroads, and a large skirmish began.

In time, the Federals continued on, marching past the Baugh home, where they turned, and headed south on the pike toward Liberty Gap. Passing through an area of tall hills on either side of the road, the "Bluecoats" surprised the Confederate pickets, and another skirmish followed. The Confederates fought to keep control of their lookout, Knob Hill.

On this day, the weather was not good, but despite a huge downpour, the battle continued.[135] At New Fosterville, about 4 miles southeast of Old Millersburg, the Confederate band played "Dixie,"—a sign that yet another battle had begun. The heavy rain continued throughout the day, until the streams were near to overflowing, and the roads turned to mud.

What the Baugh family experienced during this battle is unknown, but rifle and cannon fire was coming from all directions around them. They would have seen the line of "Bluecoats" swarming across their land, a frightening sight—especially for children.

Later that day, the Confederates moved south about a mile and half. By dusk, it was raining even harder, but the Union soldiers persisted, with even more men coming down Liberty Pike. The battle continued the next day, but only in the form of skirmishes. By evening, the Yankees were seen moving back through the Gap toward Old Millersburg with a large number of wagons and ambulances. When the Confederates followed—attempting to engage the "Bluecoats"—they returned, and another battle began.[136]

That night and the next day, the fighting did not let up. Confederate Captain Swett had pulled out the twelve-pound Napoleon Guns, which made a big racket.[137] There was such terrible noise from the big guns on the hills, no one in the area could sleep.

Down by Liberty Gap, a widow with three young children and their servant girl climbed the hill to see what was going on. The widow, "Ma Emily," later reported that she was able to see battles at Liberty Gap, Millersburg, and Fosterville.[138]

On June 26th, when the Confederates found they were low on ammunition, their superiors ordered them to withdraw.[139] Until now, despite being outnumbered by the Yankees three to one, the Confederates had held their position. Their superiors, however, decided that they needed to concentrate their energies on larger and more important battles. Old Millersburg and the neighboring areas were now clearly in Union hands.

During the battle, the Feds needed to eat, and some of the local plantations were raided. Although what occurred at the Baugh home (if anything) is unknown, John Lee Fults states that his ancestors, Henry Pruitt, and daughter, Elizabeth Pruitt Fox, had their homes raided by Union soldiers. Elizabeth Fox had three small children at the time. When one of the raiding Yankees—who was loading up every bit of food he could find—saw the youngest, a three year-old boy named Henry, following the soldiers around, he remarked, "That sure is a fat little fellow you have there." Eliza Fox, without missing a beat, responded, "Well, he ain't going to be fat long after you get through taking all he has left to eat." Shame-faced, the Yankee soldier left behind a few chickens, and some sides of ham.[140]

~

In the months following the Battle of Murfreesboro, John Baugh and the men of Company F, 2nd Tennessee Infantry had not traveled far. They were stationed in Allisonia Springs near Tullahoma, Tennessee, approximately 40 miles from Old Millersburg. They remained in the area until late spring 1863, acting as Provost Marshals, and guarding the Confederate army stores.[141] It was not difficult work.

Following this assignment, the Millersburg Company was given the job of guarding the railroad. News came shortly after, that they were going to be transferred to Alabama. During this time, more members of the original Millersburg 110 were lost. Some were wounded, some died, and quite a few deserted. Faith in the war had begun to dwindle, and living conditions were getting worse.

By the autumn of 1863, less than half of the original Millersburg 110 remained. Those who stayed included: John and Benjamin Baugh, Bob White, and Robert Howland. These men experienced fierce battles including the battles at Chickamauga, Lookout Mountain, and Missionary Ridge.

On September 19th, the Confederates had a significant victory in The Battle of Chickamauga. Immediately following, General Bragg ordered the men to retreat. At the same time, Forest and Polk felt they should continue to pursue the enemy. Over Major General Bragg's orders, four generals ordered the men to go ahead.

General Bragg later reported to President Jefferson Davis that "a vigorous pursuit followed." In the following days, those officers who had gone against his orders—namely Forest, Hill, Hindman, and Polk—were relieved of their commands.[142] As John Lee Fults writes in his book, *The Millersburg 110*, "Such a ruckus followed that President Davis had to come to town to try to restore order."

Forest and Polk were not only furious with General Bragg for recent events; they felt he had caused unnecessary deaths in the Battle of Murfreesboro, as well as the loss of key battles where the Confederacy needed victory in order to win the war. Word spread among the soldiers that Forest and Polk refused to serve any longer under Bragg. When relieved of their duties, these two men were given independent companies in Mississippi. Before leaving, Forest was heard to say, "If Bragg comes to Mississippi, I will shoot that son-of-a-bitch on the spot!"[143]

Meanwhile, the 2nd Tennessee traveled south into Georgia. In late November, Union and Confederate soldiers in the area met, and called a short truce. During this time, they visited each other's camps, sampled each other's cooking, and swapped newspapers and tobacco. Once Sherman took command of the Army of the Cumberland and started his march in their direction, it was back to war.[144]

As part of Cleburne's Division, the men were camped on Lookout Mountain. It was here, at Tunnel Hill, that they faced Sherman's Army. On November 24, 1863, when the battle—which is sometimes called "The Battle Above the Clouds"—began, the Yankees stormed the mountain, and Cheatham's Confederate Division ran for their lives down the other side. Brigadier General Patrick Cleburne kept Sherman's men back, though they outnumber his division three to one. Then, they formed a position, blocking Ringgold Gap where the Western Atlantic Railway passed through, thus stopping General Grant from pursuing them.[145] Following this battle, the Confederates retreated to Dalton, Georgia.

Arriving in Dalton on November 28th, General Bragg turned in his resignation. Three days later, he left. Now, winter was at hand, and the men were suffering. There was not enough food for either the soldiers or their horses. In fact, the animals of the 2nd Tennessee were so weak, they were unable to pull the cannons, or even be ridden.

During this time, Willis Baugh was cooking for the men. He fixed anything he could find to feed them. Sometimes, it was "pickled meat," and sometimes "stock." According to Willis, they were "hungry often."[146]

There was also not enough clothing for the soldiers. Many had no shoes, and were walking around barefoot. It would be twenty-six days before General Joe Johnson of Mississippi arrived to take command. Once he arrived, he saw that the men got the supplies they needed. Meanwhile, things did not look good.

Early in December, John A. Baugh, now 57 years old, made the decision to leave the army. He asked for an honorable discharge—which was granted. He had seen enough—maybe even lost his faith in the war, and he was tired. It is also possible Mary Ann asked him to come home. Some women of the South, after struggling alone to survive for two years, did just that.[147] In any case, John Baugh now left the war to younger men.

Nothing could have meant more to Mary Ann in the winter of 1863 than to see her husband walk through the door of their home. Since the war began, she had bore the death of a daughter, two grandchildren, and both of her parents. An entire way of life had disappeared, and for nearly three years, everything had rested on her shoulders. Now, there would be two of them. At least 1864 would begin with her husband by her side.

Chapter 23

1863–1864—On the Front

WHEN JOE AND JACK BAUGH JOINED THE CONFEDERATE ARMY, AS members of Douglass' Partisan Rangers Battalion they had the enviable job of being allowed to keep much of the booty they captured from the Union. Now in 1863, General Robert E. Lee received reports that men were leaving the army for the battalions so they might have this same benefit. When Lee recommended changes that would put an end to this practice, there was not a man in the Rangers who did not protest this decision, but to no avail. In February of 1863,—at the command of General Wheeler—Douglass' Partisan Rangers were organized as a regiment, and became part of the 11th (Holman's) Tennessee Cavalry. John M. and Joseph L. Baugh both became members of Company D under Captain John Lytle.[148]

On March 5th, 1863, the 11th Tennessee Cavalry, under General Nathan Bedford Forest, captured Thompson's Station, and took 1,200 Yankee prisoners. From there, the men were ordered to Florence, Alabama, where again under General Forest's leadership, they captured 1700 prisoners, approximately three times the troops General Forest had at hand![149] This was an exciting time for the soldiers, and a great boost to morale.

Both Jack and Joe Baugh would be forever proud that they had served under the brilliant leadership of General Forest. Even those who did not like him had to admit that he was one of the most brilliant military men ever.

Then, while they were in Cleveland, Tennessee, on October 1st, the troops were taken from General Forest, and put under General Joseph

Wheeler. Most of the men were not happy with this change. The soldiers were truly fond of General Forest. Beside his brilliant leadership, they felt he truly cared about them, and their well-being.

General Wheeler, although small in stature, was an intense man, who drove his troops relentlessly and recklessly toward victory. Many complained that Wheeler would lead them to slaughter if he thought he could do damage to the Union, and help win the war. Since the companies had had such great success under Forest, many wondered why General Bragg made the decision to bring Wheeler in.

Figure 18. General Joe Wheeler.

When Wheeler took over, Forrest protested that his soldiers and their horses were in no condition to take on a new campaign. He even rode to Bragg's headquarters to speak to him—a meeting that resulted in Forrest "cussing" out the General, and telling him, "… if you ever again try to interfere with me or cross my path, it will be at the peril of your life." As stated previously, General Forest did not care for Bragg, and made no effort to hide it.

In the midst of the arguing, General Wheeler decided to meet with Forrest's men near Cottonport. On arrival, he found Forest had not been exaggerating. Some of his troops were "mere skeletons," without enough food to survive. Joseph Baugh, as part of the commissary, must have suffered knowing he did not have enough food to feed his fellow soldiers.

In addition to the lack of food, the 11th Tennessee Cavalry barely had any ammunition, and their horses were not well. The groups joining Wheeler's men numbered about 4,000. Between them, they only had about six pieces of artillery, obviously not nearly enough for such a large number of men.[150] By some accounts, the present state of the entire Confederate Army was "pitiable."

After taking care of his troops, Wheeler accomplished much for the Confederate cause. Under his leadership, the troops cut the line of Union communications from Sequatchie Valley near Chattanooga, to the north, and west toward Nashville. They tore up the railroad, and destroyed supply depots. When Wheeler led the men on raids of the Union supply line, he ordered destruction. There was no time for spoils now.

During this time, Joseph Baugh continued to accrue money every three months for the use of his horse. By July 1, 1863, he was owed $146.40. The Confederate Army, now cash poor, was possibly too poor to pay him.

By late 1863, the South had little ability to grow cotton or any other crop. The war had lasted far longer than anyone expected. The railroad was broken, and they had no ability to sell the goods they had. There were even blockages to prevent goods from reaching foreign countries. No crops and no sales meant that no money was coming into the Confederate coffers. The average citizen was also suffering from a lack of basic foods, and goods. Although Joseph and Jack were not doing too badly, they witnessed much suffering. Still, neither of them was ready to give up the fight.

In March of 1864, President Lincoln called General Ulysses S. Grant to the White House for a conference, and made him Lt. General of all the Federal Armies.[151] After this meeting, Grant divided the South into three territories, putting William Tecumseh Sherman in command of Georgia, Alabama, Tennessee and Mississippi. Sherman established his headquarters in Chattanooga, and by May 5th, 1864, he had begun his campaign to conquer the South.

The men of Joe Wheeler's Cavalry were now under General Joe Johnston's Army of Tennessee, a force of approximately 62,408 men.[152] In May, as part of Company D of the 11th Tennessee Cavalry, Jack Baugh was in Georgia, heading toward Resaca. The fighting had been vigorous. All of Wheeler's men, who were not on picket duty, were ordered

Figure 19. General Joe E. Johnston.

to "guard the Confederate fortifications until the last wagon was on its way."[153] Under General Joe Johnston's orders, the Confederate Army was retreating southward toward Atlanta.

Halfway between Calhoun and Atlanta, just north of Rome, the soldiers had entered a level valley between the Etowah and Ostenaula Rivers. Suddenly, Sherman caught up with them. Shots were fired, and out of no where they were in a battle.

Jack Baugh spurred his horse forward in the midst of whizzing mini-balls. Then, suddenly there was a piercing blow so hard he was thrown from his horse.[154] In the two years he had been in the Army, he had never been hurt. Now, he lay on the earth, with blood flowing from his shoulder, and a pain so intense he could not move.

Maria Baugh waited for news of her husband, Jack. It was likely a long wait, but finally that news came. He had been wounded, badly. She could not go to him, and the daily wait with no news must have been almost unbearable. Maria was staying with her mother in Salem, a place overrun with Yankees. Frequent skirmishes took place as the Rebels attempted to take the area back.

Jack Baugh was in a Georgia hospital for some time. The surgeon there cut out the bullet, which was lodged between the joints of his shoulder. Jack Baugh lost the use of his arm, but he did not return home. Following the example of his superiors—Forest, who rode with numerous bullet wounds, and Wheeler, who was back in the saddle shortly after loosing his leg—John Mason Marable Baugh returned to the 11th Tennessee Cavalry (Holman's), where he remained until the end of the war.

Chapter 24

Atlanta

Atlanta was a large manufacturing city, and an important railroad junction. It was the heart of the South's most prosperous stage for cotton, as well as its principal arsenal and supply depot. Because of that, General Grant aimed for battle here. To capture Atlanta, would be the downfall of the Confederacy.

For General Joseph E. Johnston of the Confederate Army, the single railroad track to Atlanta—120 miles away—was also the Federals' lifeline. Along this track passed the supplies for 100,000 men, and 23,000 animals. The Confederate raiding parties aimed for this line.[155]

The skirmishing began May 7th, and by May 8th of 1864, a battle had grown in size around Dalton. The railroad passed through this 1500 foot high Rocky Face Ridge at Buzzard Roost Gap. Sherman found the narrow gorge too strongly held by the Confederates to be carried by frontal assault. Instead, he sent McPherson's Army of Tennessee on a right-flanking march to threaten the Rebel rail supply line at Resaca, 18 miles further south." The Union Army marched along Snake Creek Gap—an undefended pass—and encountered a body of 4,000 Rebel troops blocking the path into town. The Feds retreated.

In June, Episcopal Bishop turned General, Leonidas Polk, sat on his horse, looking through his glass at the scene below him, when a Union soldier took aim, and shot him squarely in the chest, tearing out his lungs. At first he remained erect, then he slipped to the ground. General Joe Johnston ran to his side, and raising the general's head cried without restraint, "I would rather anything than this."[156]

Seeing that General Sherman was heading toward Atlanta, General Johnston had to cross bridges quickly in order to place his army between the Federals, and the outer defenses of the city. Johnston rode bareheaded beside the body of his general. Then, he returned to the front, and broke the news to his assembled army:

> "In this distinguished leader, we have lost the most courteous of gentlemen, the most gallant of soldiers. The Christian patriot has neither lived nor died in vain. His example is before you. His mantle rests with you…"

Figure 20. General Leonidas Polk.

The funeral for Leonidas Polk, officiated by Dr. Charles Quintard, took place the following day in Atlanta at St. Luke's Episcopal Church. There lay Polk in his worn and greasy uniform, his sword by his side. Across his breast, white roses were laid. The Confederate flag was draped across the casket, and overhead was a bower with hundreds of magnolia blossoms. A huge crowd of mourners stood on line to pay their respects, and many took a leaf, flower or twig from the General's bower in memory of him.

Fully aware that Sherman and the Union Army was on its way, Atlanta had hoped to hear of General Sherman's capture, but no news like this came to be. When the citizens learned that the Union had torn up the railroad tracks between Atlanta and Decatur, panic set in. Many citizens had planned to leave by rail. Now, there was no escape.

The Confederate soldiers prepared earthen areas called "Bob proofs" or "Gopher holes." These were excavations of six to eight feet, with eight to twelve squares for a family to hide in. Planks were laid over the holes, and covered with 304 feet of earth.

Now, soldiers moved through the woods in silence, like ghosts. They slept from exhaustion, lying on the ground with their horses lying beside them.[157]

For a while, soldiers from both sides bathed in the Chattahoochee River, and lay sunning themselves on its banks. Not a single shot was fired at those on the other side. When General Sherman learned of this, he ordered that each man be given 100 rounds, declaring that if the rounds were not used up, each man would be given extra duty. Some threw theirs away.[158]

By mid-July, the Union Army had crossed the river, changing Sherman's preplanned strategy. Wheeler's cavalry kept an eye on the Decatur and Georgia Railroad.

The hot, heavy air of summer had descended upon the region. It was hardly cooler in the night than it had been in the day. Robert Howland, now 1st Lieutenant in the 2nd Tennessee, was ready to defend Atlanta. The fighting went on for days as the Union Army pushed forward. Atlanta's citizens deserted the city in terror, taking all they could, and running for their lives.

The Army of Tennessee was occupying the earthworks they had created on the north bank of the Chattahoochee River, just ten miles from the city. To enter Atlanta, Sherman created a diversion downstream, and while the Tennessee Army followed that, 15 miles upstream he pushed his main force across the river.[159]

On July 17th, while General Joe Johnston sat discussing the matter of extending the breastworks, he received a telegram notifying him that he was to turn over his command immediately to Lt. General John Bell Hood.

The soldiers from the Army of Tennessee had utter confidence in Johnston. For four months they had complained about him, but even though they had been heavily outnumbered, no lives had been lost wastefully. They were a tougher army now, inspired by his leadership.

When the Confederate outpost on Peachtree Creek heard General Johnston was leaving the Army of Tennessee, they told the others, "Boys, we've fought all the war for nothing." Then, all five pickets at the outpost threw down their guns, haversacks, and cartridge boxes remarking that they would not have further use of them, and crossed the creek—presumably casting their lot with Sherman's Federals."[160] It is said that men cried over his loss.

Now John Bell Hood, a thirty-three year-old who had lost his right leg, and the use of his left arm in previous battles, took over. General Hood's approach was—"see the enemy and charge."[161]

General Hood planned to smash the Army of the Cumberland at Peach Tree Creek, before it could join the Armies of Ohio, and Tennessee. The latter two armies were trying to cut Atlanta's rail links to the east. Some of the local citizens were so sure of a Confederate victory; they got dressed up, and drove out for their last chance to see the Yankees in Georgia. The planned assault was for July 20th.

When Lt. Robert Howland was sent out to check on the position of the troops, he was captured by a group of Union soldiers. As it turned out, they were part of General W.T. Sherman's army. Lt. Howland and his fellow soldiers had no choice. They were tied together, and had to wait out the battle. Robert Howland waited in hope that the battle would turn, and they would be rescued. The fight was "savage," and rescue was not to be.

That summer, only thirty-six of the original Millersburg 110 remained in service. During the Battle of Atlanta on July 19th, Robert L. Howland and twenty-seven other men were captured at Peachtree Creek. When asked to take the Oath of Allegiance, Robert Howland refused. Within days, he was transported to Louisville, Kentucky, where he arrived on July 27, 1864. Here, he awaited sentencing. On the 28th, twenty-nine year-old Robert Howland was sentenced to a military prison. The dream of the Confederate States was now nearing its end.

Had it been earlier in the war, the Union likely would have let Lt. Howland go after a few days with a simple promise not to bear arms or appear in the same area again. But after a certain point in 1863, both sides began to hold thousands of men, who had little hope of being released until the end of the war.

Chapter 25

1864—On the Home Front

THERE HAD BEEN EXCITING DAYS DURING THE WAR, AND THERE HAD been hopeful days like the time General Forest came storming into Murfreesboro. Yet, as 1864 progressed, the Southern war effort looked more and more hopeless.

People elsewhere could not know the deprivations Southern citizens were suffering. After three years of war, the land was stripped bare of trees, brush, and fences. When wood was needed for fire, or building a fort, the Yankees simply took whatever they could find. Many times a family stood grieving and helpless as they watched their beloved home torn apart, and carted away. Then they would seek shelter with a kind neighbor, not knowing if tomorrow the soldiers might return for the neighbor's home.

The Union soldiers continued to forage, taking food, blankets, heirloom pictures, wedding rings, and even pets. Families had to beg for needed and treasured items, particularly items needed by small children. With little food, clothing, or blankets, many grew sick and died. The elderly and the young were most vulnerable. In addition, many a family portrait was slashed by a Union saber, and other items destroyed. To the people of the South, it seemed strange to be considered enemies in their own land.

Stories handed down through the years recall hardship and courage among the common citizens. In one story, a little boy had only his pa's shirt and under-drawers to wear. After a soldier came by, he was left with only the drawers. Another story told of an old man down in Hoover's Gap, sitting by the kitchen fire, watching as the Yankees rifled through his daughter's home, taking whatever they pleased. There was a chicken cooking in a pot over the fire, and as one soldier approached it, the old man said, "Take anything you want, but if you touch that chicken, I'll shoot you." The Union soldiers left without a word.

It is said that sweet potatoes were the saving grace in Millersburg, and perhaps in a good portion of the South. The Yankees didn't know what these odd looking roots were, and wouldn't touch them. As a result, sweet potatoes were a major food source during the war.

The former slaves who stayed on did not do much work, but whatever they did was a mercy. Mary Ann's lifelong companion, Miranda, was there, living in her little log house just as she always had. She was family, and would not leave. Each day, "Mirandy" cooked the meals. In her spare time, she helped with the sewing and spinning. Perhaps during these moments, she and Mary Ann shared memories of the old days when Mary Ann's parents were alive. When they spoke of the boys still away at war, in silence they must have wondered if they would ever see their sons again.

As the war progressed, it is doubtful that John and Mary Ann Baugh heard much—if anything—from their sons, or sons-in-law. There were only rumors of tremendous battles, and of terrible losses.

~

The summer of 1864, Bettie's husband, Robert White, came home unexpectedly. Bob had deserted the 2nd Tennessee, and signed the Oath of Allegiance.

During the Battle of Stones River, Robert M. White, a Sergeant Major, had received a slight hip wound.[162] In March and April of 1863, he was detached as a conscript officer, and received a bounty of $50 for bringing soldiers into the army. They were young men, some of whom were dead now, or irreparably wounded.

One day Bob White just couldn't take it anymore. By leaving the army, he had little to be ashamed of. He was only one of many who had given up hope about the outcome of the war. "It's just a matter of time before the Confederacy falls," they said.

The Whites settled down in their little house. They had only been married about a year before Robert went away. Now, they would begin

Figure 21. Bettie Baugh White in a photo taken shortly after the war.
(Courtesy of the White Family)

anew. Poor Robert was so thin, he looked like a skeleton. Bettie worked at nursing him back to health. In the past three years, her pretty, young face had grown thin. Her eyes contained a sad, haunted look that had not been there before. Looking into Bettie's eyes, you could see the horror of the war.

Bob and Bettie were aware that the greatest blessings were the simplest things: sitting at table together and praying over their food, watching the sun rise, the sound of the other's footsteps on the floor. They had to be keenly aware that all these moments were gifts from God, which many others would never have.

Appropriately, on July 4, 1865—one year after Bob's return—Bettie gave birth to a baby boy whom the couple named William White. For a while, the couple rejoiced, but sadly, seven months later William died.

During her fifty years of life, Mary Ann Baugh had survived the childbirth of eleven children, and remained a strong woman. But nearly four long years of war had changed everyone irreparably. While John may have been thin, and suffered from his years with the 2nd Tennessee, Mary Ann and the children had suffered as well. If Clemmie, now seven, and Rollie, now four, cried from hunger, what could she do?

The children would probably remain small for life, due to their lack of nutrition during the war years. Charlie and the girls had suffered as well, but they were older and stronger. As Mary Ann watched Clemmie and Rollie play together, dreaming of what they wanted when the war was over, she must have worried about them; especially poor little Clemmie with her twisted spine.

The servants may have known better than their white masters how to make do. In the evenings, they took out their instruments, and made music. Hearing the old songs brought smiles and comfort to everyone, as they recalled happier days. Home—this was home.

And as always, the family prayed for those lost, and for those still fighting. Most of all, they prayed for an end to sorrow in this land that had once been so beautiful, and for them, free.

⁓

Following the Battle of Stones River, the Union soldiers had been ordered to build a supply depot just outside of Murfreesboro, next to the

Nashville and Chattanooga Railroad. To protect the depot, a huge fort covering approximately three and one-half miles, was built. On January 23rd, the fort was officially named Fortress Rosecrans in honor of the Union General.

The outer walls of the Fortress were earthen. To complete the interior buildings, which included blockhouses, sawmills, warehouses, and commissaries, the Union soldiers tore down houses for lumber, and carted away bricks from the remainder of the First Presbyterian Church.[163] With the building of Fortress Rosecrans, it was clear the Union intended to stay.

Among the soldiers stationed at Fortress Rosecrans for guard duty was Corporal Daniel C. Miller, a German immigrant. While stationed in Murfreesboro, Corporal Miller wrote a series of letters to his family back in Ohio describing his stay in Rutherford County during the war.

In the summer of 1864, Corporal Miller was sent to a blockhouse, "Stockade #6", at Stewart's Creek, just north of Murfreesboro, near Smyrna. Miller wrote home that he was so well-fed, he was getting fat. His letter to his parents adds, he was eating strawberries, blackberries, applesauce, pie, biscuits, and in season, even peaches, and watermelon. For additional nutrition, he and his fellow soldiers went fishing in the Stones River, catching "... enough fish for all 30 men almost every day."[164]

Then, in September of 1864, Corporal Miller experienced the most dramatic event of his entire stay in Murfreesboro. General Joseph Wheeler and his troops, a group of 6,000 to 8,000 men—including Jack Baugh and Anderson Crosthwait—burnt 30 miles of railroad. In the process, Wheeler attacked the blockhouse Miller had been guarding, burning it to the ground. The captured Yankees, including Miller, were taken to Nashville, where they were kept in a house. Eventually, Wheeler's men let them go, and Miller and the others walked 30 miles back to Murfreesboro.

Although Forest and Wheeler continued to be active in the area, it was becoming clearer by the day that the Confederacy could not last much longer. On January 3rd, 1865, Miller wrote,

> "The Rebels desert by the hundreds every day and they say that the South would be better off to give up because they do not have a chance."

At the start of 1865, Corporal Miller had been sent to guard a block-house by the railroad in Christiana. As opposed to life at the Stewart's Creek blockhouse, people in the area of Christiana were suffering severely from the effects of war. Miller told his family that conditions were poor, adding, "... Yarn is short here. Sometimes you have to walk ten or twenty miles before you see a sheep ..." Eggs were also scarce. Nevertheless, the soldiers were able to procure some food, including "four sacks of corn from a good rebel lady," and an ox who had strayed from the herd.[165]

On March 24th, Corporal Daniel Miller wrote:

> "... A lot of soldiers pass by here every day. The South has just about had it. And instead of staying in the Army, they desert ..."

Now, the Union men were just waiting for the end, so that they too could go home.

Chapter 26

Prison

ACROSS THE COLD, DARK WATERS OF LAKE ERIE, THE PRISONERS WERE taken to a place about a mile off-shore called Johnson's Island. It had been named for the farmer who owned it. Asking where they were, Lt. Howland learned that they were in Ohio. The Union had reserved this prison for Confederate officers. In the dusty light, all was unclear except one thing—there would be no escaping this place. Arriving on the rocky shore, Bob Howland with another officer from his company, and a score of others were flanked by bands of solders with rifles, who marched them inside the gates.

Prison in 1864 was a dangerous proposition on either side. Expecting the war to end soon, provisions were not made for prisons. Thousands died with little food, and almost no sanitation. In some prison camps, prisoners were even required to make their own shelter.

As Bob Howland woke that first horrible morning on Johnson's Island, the awareness of a terrible stench, the cold hard bench he lay on, and loud banging noises shocked his senses. His aching bones seemed a minor pain compared to the pain of his ankle where a chain connecting him to other prisoners had pulled and rubbed for over a week. Through his ragged uniform, he could feel the rough wood beneath his hips, back, and shoulders. Opening his eyes, he saw that the only light in this prison was coming through a grilled window.

They had arrived in Kentucky a day or two before. A bit of bread and rations had been thrown at him for a meal. Somewhere along the way, he learned that the Yankees had won in Atlanta. Not good news. But now, he only wanted to satisfy the ravenous hunger in his belly.

It did not take long to learn the routine of this cold, cold site. Once a day, at noon, a small loaf of bread was handed out. That one loaf was to be shared by four men. A bit of pork and beans was sometimes added to these rations, but very little. That was it—just that one small meal at noon, then, nothing for twenty-four hours. The men were starving. How were they to survive? They had learned. Rats. Rats were the answer.

The prison was full of these rats; large wharf rats, and the prisoners were not shy about killing, and eating them.[166] "It's better than starving," someone may have remarked to the new prisoners.

The men made a business of catching these rats, which were "gentle and easily killed."[167] Joe Riley, a fellow Tennessean, was the prison's champion rat catcher. Joe caught rats more easily than many, and made a meal for the inmates. Half a dozen would be "dressed for the pot." Then, in the evening, the men feasted on them. "Rats are good eatin'," they said.

At the back of the barracks were "sinks or latrines" with "excavations eighteen feet long, and five feet wide."[168] Sheds had been built over these for privacy. The ground was mainly clay, and only 8 feet below the surface was bedrock. Thus, drainage was poor. The sinks could not drain, and within a few weeks were full. Then, it would be necessary to dig new sinks. Eventually, the drainage area formed one long sink. Sometimes, the excrement overflowed the seats, covering the floors. The prison had an almost unbearable odor.[169]

The rats fed off these sinks. As terrible as it was, the men had no choice—eat the rats or starve to death. In fact, the inmates of Johnson's island were so ravenous, one POW would later compare the men to "...a parcel of famished wolves..."[170]

Johnson's Island, at its fullest, had 3,000 men. Although Robert Howland may not have realized it, he had come to a much better place than he might have. The men were all officers, and civil to one another. They were a community. Life centered on finding enough to eat, and prayer. Even with the rats, the men were so ravenous; it was difficult for them to think of anything, but getting food.

Johnson's Island was well organized by the prisoners. It was like one great camp, and after a while, Robert got used to it. There was a debating society, a thespian band, and a Young Men's Christian Association, which looked after the sick, and needy prisoners, as well as those who were ailing mentally.[171] The men kept busy by whittling chains with the names of their troops on them. These trinkets and others were sold for money.

The summer passed, and in September the weather changed from balmy to cool, and then back again. During this time, a huge storm descended upon Lake Erie with pouring rain, lightening, and thunder. Then, without warning, the gale force winds turned into a tornado that ripped through the stockade fence. Some of the guards were carried away, and one wing of the hospital was also taken out.

When December arrived, Bob was aware that he had now spent half a year in this prison. With winter upon them, the air turned sharply cold. The freezing waters and winds on Lake Erie—only a few yards from the prison walls—caused the men to freeze. There were only two small stoves for each large room. The officers huddled together, trying to keep alive by sharing body warmth.

By early 1865, with the war nearing its end, the superiors of the prison began to release the men. The system they used for release was alphabetical order. Bob Howland was lucky he did not have to wait long.

Chapter 27

1865—Home Again

B EN BAUGH HAD BEEN SICK IN THE HOSPITAL FOR THE FIRST TWO MONTHS of 1864, but he returned after that, and was paid in March, and April for his service in the war. On January 25, 1865, Captain Rhea wrote under remarks: "Deserted." There were many other deserters now. Once they would have been shot, but it was becoming more and more apparent the war was lost. Tennessee had been completely taken over by the Feds. It was only a matter of time before the Confederacy as a whole fell.

The Confederate soldiers were tired, hungry, and freezing—without proper clothing or even proper arms to defend themselves. Some pushed on, but many just made the decision—it was time, they were going home.

Benjamin had wandered. Where he wandered, and for how long, even he may not have known. The roaring of the cannon in his head; the pounding of the shot; the faces and mangled bodies torn in agony flashed before his eyes. He was lost, dirty, and starving. He must have tried to find shelter where he could remain hidden and safe from both armies.

One day, he heard the news. The war was over! General Lee had surrendered to General Grant. This was on April 9th. Now, he wandered on until he found himself in a large city that somehow looked familiar. He was back where he had started four years earlier—Nashville! Home was not far away.

The Federal soldiers asked for his pass, and having none, he was taken before 1st Lt. William H. Bracken, the Assistant Provost Marshall of the Cumberland Army. He agreed to sign the Oath of Allegiance. The Oath he signed was dated April 25, 1865. He had been traveling for three months. Now he could go home.

All over the South, women were looking out their front doors, and across farmlands to see strange men walking toward them. They were men of skeletal figures; men so bedraggled in stinking, ragged clothing, they looked like paupers.

Mary Ann became one of those women that late April of 1865. A man appearing bent and old—with a face that was sunken in at the cheeks, and eyes that stared; eyes that had seen death—came walking down the road toward the house. Who was this strange man coming to the door? And then she knew. It was her son, Benjamin.

Tears, unlike any she had known must have come to her eyes as she held him. John was coming to the door now, embracing their son. The children, Clemmie and Rollie stood by, afraid, and in awe of the dirty man who was supposed to be Brother Ben. Aunt Ran, too, came crying, "Oh Lor', Massa Ben. Praise de Lor', you'se home!"

He sank into a chair, starved, gobbling down the food Ran placed before him; cherishing the bath of hot water and soap, which made him human again.

A hundred questions must have come Ben's way, but then he was too tired to speak. As with most men who have been to war, there would be no escaping the war's affects. The thing about this Civil War that would forever haunt men was the fact that this enemy was not a stranger, but rather brothers, and cousins; fellow Americans killing one another.

Benjamin had been wounded. Although we do not know where this wound was or how severe, it was likely around the head. His brother, Joseph Baugh, in an 1897 letter mentioned this wound.

One might imagine the candlelight nights in the old farm home as the family gathered together, and gave thanks to God that so many of them had survived. Of the six or more members who joined the Confederate Army, not one had perished. For the Baugh family, the women and children at home were the ones who paid with their lives.

In the time Benjamin had been gone, brother Charlie had grown from ten to fifteen, nearly the age Ben had been when he left. Sister Clemmie was now nine. Nephew Rollie, who had since become a member of the household, was five. The young people would have watched and listened with awe to the soldier's tales. Unlike her brothers and sisters, war and hardship were nearly all Clemmie had ever known.

～

When the news of Robert E. Lee's surrender to General Grant reached Murfreesboro (likely via telegraph), the Union soldiers were ecstatic, and began to celebrate. Guns were fired, and church bells rang for an entire day. That night, there were fireworks, and a torch procession.[172] Perhaps those in Old Jefferson and Old Millersburg could hear some of the noise. Likely, they had mixed emotions. The war was over, and their men would be coming home, but the cost had been tremendous, and the outcome was nothing they could have dreamed.

Only one week after the surrender, came the news that President Lincoln had been assassinated. The news was shocking, but not surprising to many who could not forgive him for his actions in the war.

～

By May 20th of 1865, Corporal Daniel Miller was preparing to leave Christiana and the South. The war was over, and the railroad had been turned back to the state of Tennessee. In one last letter to his parents, he wrote,

"Nothing much new except that we see a lot of Rebels on their way home. You should see them; they are as filthy as pigs and full of lice."[173]

In July of 1865, the Union soldiers gathered at the train station in Murfreesboro. They were going north by the hundreds, taking with them dogs, raccoons, and cedar walking sticks; and perhaps, belongings of the local residents—all souvenirs of their time in the South.

By mid-June and July, the balance of the Confederates—those who had fought to the end of the war—were returning home. Jack and Joseph Baugh were among those men. Both were Prisoners of War when their Captain, John L. Carney, surrendered at Citronelle, Alabama on May 4th, 1865. Many of the men would have liked to continue fighting for the "Cause," but now there was no choice in the matter.

From Citronelle, the 10th and 11th Tennessee Cavalry Regiments—which had consolidated in February of that year—traveled to Gainesville.

Here, on May 9th, General Nathan Bedford Forest addressed the troops who had gallantly served under him for the last three years. In his speech, he informed the men,

> "The armies of Generals Lee and Johnston have surrendered; you are the last of all the troops in the Confederate States Army east of the Mississippi River to lay down your arms. The cause for which you have so long and manfully struggled, and for which you have braved dangers, endured privations and sufferings, and made so many sacrifices, is today hopeless."[174]

Forest then asked his officers and soldiers to lay down their arms, put aside "bitterness" and "cheerfully obey orders" by the Union. He attempted to lift the spirits of his troops by stating,

"You have been good soldiers: you can be good citizens."

The next day, Joe and Jack Baugh were paroled.* Jack Baugh was still listed as a Private; Joseph as a Sergeant. From here, the men were taken to Nashville, arriving there on June 7th.

Joseph Baugh's military papers contain a record of his Oath of Allegiance before Provost Marshall, W.H. Bracken, Dept. of Cumberland at Nashville. John M. Baugh's military papers do not contain a record of the Oath, but it is possible the paperwork was lost. The delay in time between the parole, and the "Oath," suggests that the men were held as prisoners before being transported to Nashville. Some time may be accounted for as the time it took the men to travel. From Nashville, the defeated troops had to find their own means of getting home; even if it meant going by foot.

For the Confederate soldier, going home meant returning to the land where the war had been fought, and nothing was the same as when they left. The men returning to Rutherford County found the landscape had been greatly altered. A news reporter visiting Murfreesboro for a Boston paper described what he saw in this way:

> "Let this point (Murfreesboro) be the center and then make a circumference of 30 miles, and with me, we will stay a week in the womb of destruction. Whether you go on to the Salem, the Shelbyville, the Manchester,

---

* A pledge of honor by a prisoner that he will not seek to escape or will not serve against his captors. *Funk & Wagnalls Dictionary*, 1928

or any other pike ... what do we behold? One wide, wild and dreary waste
... The fences are all burned down; the apple, the pear, and the plum trees
burned in ashes long ago; The torch applied to thousands of splendid mansions the walls of which alone remain."[175]

Many men came back to find their homes gone. Some homes were
occupied by former slaves; the windows stuffed with old uniforms.[176] The
Southerner's sense of demoralization was intense, and the hatred rising
up in many hearts was fierce. Loss of their homes, only served to increase
the returning soldier's anger and resentment. The way of life, which had
brought prosperity, peace, and lawfulness, had been destroyed.

Hundreds of former slaves—black men, women, and children had
been set free. Many of them roamed the countryside, starving, with no
work, no homes, and nothing to do. Some built small huts to live in,
while others let loose their years of frustration, causing both fear, and
anger among the whites. Quite a few of the former slaves begged to stay
with their former masters, and work for pay—at least for a few years.

Millersburg was a tight area, where inter-related families took care of
their own, but in other areas, former servants were going door to door, asking for a pittance if they could farm the land, and live on it. In these uncertain times, however, most former slave holders were unable to pay anyone.
Some were happy to let their land to someone for a share of the profits.

Hundreds of men who had fought the fight they believed in came
home, worn, sick, and weary of heart. Many felt the war had been a
wasted cause, but a good portion of the South felt their cause had been
right, and honorable.

With the war officially over, Jefferson Davis was captured and condemned to prison as a traitor to the United States. Robert E. Lee, having
surrendered at the Appomattox Courthouse in Virginia, went back to his
hilltop home across the Potomac from Washington D.C., a broken man.
For those in the South, the end of war did not mean a return to life as
they had known it, nor did it mean peace.

Chapter 28

Reconstruction

THE WAR WAS OVER, AND THE MEN WERE COMING HOME. SOME CAME IN groups by train, and some any way they could. With both former masters gone, Willis Baugh was left to find his way home from Georgia. Many years later, when interviewed for "The Tennessee Civil War Veterans Questionnaire," he said about his trip home, "I walked home; took a long land and a hard road." Like the white man, but in a different way, on arriving home, Willis found that nothing was the same.

Once families had been reunited, they began to contact distant relatives to find out what had happened to them during the war. Down in Alabama, John Aldridge Baugh's brother, Richard, had owned a cotton mill on Shoal Creek. He bought the mill in 1860 with three other men. Water-powered by a dam, the mill produced osnaburg cloth and yarn. One hundred men and fifty women worked there. They lived in a village that was completely supplied by Richard Baugh, and the co-owners. There were forty cottages, a church, a school, and a company store.

In 1863, the mill was destroyed by Yankee Colonel Florence M. Cornyn, under Brigadier General Granville Dodge, who ordered the burning of all industry from Corinth to Florence. Interestingly, Dodge sent Lt. Risden Deford, the son of the area's previous Methodist pastor, to do the mission. Deford made sure all the workers were safe before he ordered the burning. Also, he did not do a thorough job. The mill was still able to produce some cloth until 1864, when General Hood came to Shoal Creek.[177] Meanwhile, the Baugh family in Alabama was safe.

Joseph Baugh's father-in-law, Ashton Butterworth had lost his Town Creek mills at Owls Hollow in a similar way. This was the third time the mills had burned, and Mr. Butterworth, now severely hurting for cash, decided to return to England in order to raise some capital. The South was bankrupt, and Southerners were considered traitors and disenfranchised.

Considering the economy, and loss of rights, Joseph Lawrence Baugh decided to take his family, including his wife, mother-in-law, and two sons to live in Delaware. Joseph would not see his parents or siblings for several years.

Most people in Rutherford County were lucky if they had food and clothing, let alone money for taxes, and other needs. The Baughs, on the other hand, seemed to be doing fairly well. In fact, many relatives came to John Baugh for a loan.

Along with John Baugh's careful planning, one reason the family was doing so well may have been due to the fact that Mary Ann Baugh's father had given her his money to take care of, and the money was probably in gold. At the beginning of the war, many had traded their U.S. currency for Confederate dollars, which were now worthless.

On February 27, 1865—just before the war ended—Bettie Baugh's father-in-law, Burrell Gannaway White, signed a Deed of Trust to John A. Baugh. The details in this note show the desperation of those in the South who had once been wealthy landowners.

At the time the men signed up to go to war in April of 1861, Mr. Baugh had lent Mr. White $147.72. Then, in August of 1862, he had lent him another $350.00. As security for these notes—yet unpaid—and for the sum of $5.00, Burrell G. White was selling John Baugh what appears to have been a portion of his household furnishings:

> Three featherbeds and furniture, three bed stands, one lounge and mat-tress, two divans, one center table, one large looking glass, small looking glass, twelve chairs, two old side boards, three wash stands, five small tables, one tin safe, two half-room home-made carpets, two half-room woolen carpets and one Bay mare.[178]

The Deed of Trust continues as follows:

Figure 22. Joseph L. Baugh with his wife, Anna, mother-in-law, Eliza Butterworth and sons, Ashton and Henry. This photo was taken shortly after the war, while the family was living in Delaware.
(Courtesy of Lawrence Hannah)

"The condition of the above obligations are such whereas I am justly indebted to the said J. A. Baugh in the sum of five hundred twenty-three dollars and sixty seven cents due by two notes."[179]

Mr. White states that if he does not pay the debt by the 15th of February 1866, Mr. Baugh may sell his goods. If he does pay the debt, then the obligation is "null and void." It seems likely that his goods remained with him, but this transaction leads to the question—what were the people in Christiana, and elsewhere left with after the war?

~

Not long after Robert Howland arrived back in Old Millersburg*—thin and worn from prison life—he asked John and Mary Ann Baugh's daughter, Mary—sister of his first wife, Mattie—if she would be his wife. She said "yes," and on June 20, 1865, twenty-nine year-old Robert and eighteen year-old Mary were married. However simple the wedding may have been, that day was the first joyous event for the Baugh family in over five years. Despite all the pain, loss, and hardship, it would be difficult to describe the joy had by family members the first time they joined together again.

It was decided that little five year-old Rollie Howland would stay with John and Mary Ann. They were the only parents he had known, and were quite attached to him. Besides, poor Bob Howland had a lot of recovering to do. He was little more than a skeleton, and it would take all of Mollie's (as Bob called her) time, just to nurse him back to health.

In August, Robert's father, John F. Howland sold 350 acres to John Baugh in order to pay the fines on three court cases he had lost. The amount owed by him was $5,736.†

The property John Baugh acquired bordered land he already owned, as well as land owned by B.F. Hoover, P.R. Runnells, Lewis Garner, James Lyones, R.P. Lowe, G.G. White, John Pruitt, and Stokely White.[180] This deed was signed on August 26, 1865.

Jack and Maria Baugh settled down to farm land on the Baugh property—a property which Jack would later purchase. Although he had

---

* Robert L. Howland was released with his Oath of Amnesty on May 13, 1865
† Approximately $70,946.22 in 2005.

grown up on a farm, Jack had never worked the land himself. Now, with only the use of one arm, it could not have been easy. Although the details are unknown, Jack Baugh must have found help, either from former slaves, or poor whites. Even so, John and Maria loved one another, and were very happy to live in peace at last. Their son, Thomas, was almost four years old when Jack Baugh returned from the war. In late 1865, Maria let Jack know it would not be long before another child arrived.

That September, John and Mary Ann Baugh were called to court for the purpose of settling Benjamin Marable's estate. It appears Mr. Marable had not made a will, or at least it had not been found. (If the house had been burnt, or taken apart by the Yankees, obviously, the will would have been lost.)

By 1865, Mary Ann was the only living child of Benjamin Marable, however, the children of her sister, Elizabeth Hicks, were living on the Marable land, and had claimed at least a portion of it as theirs. Possibly, they may have also suspected that Mary Ann had money from the estate.

The case came to the Rutherford County Courthouse as John A. Baugh, and wife, Mary A. vs. all of Elizabeth Hicks' descendants. The list, including Elizabeth's children, their spouses, and one grandchild was as follows: Henry H. Hicks, James H. Hicks, James Morton & wife Ann Eliza, Henry T. Prater & wife, Mary E., Sarah A. Hicks (widow of Isaac), Walter Sutton & wife, Elizabeth Henry Hicks, a minor, and James Hicks, a minor, and Louisa Elizabeth Hicks, (granddaughter), a minor, and Eveline Ward, (living separate and apart from her husband B. F. Ward.) The court appointed John A. Baugh and Henry T. Prater (husband of Mary Hicks) as Administrators of the will.

The court case stated that Benjamin Marable had left a tract of land containing four hundred acres in District 7. The land was surrounded on the north by Isaac Burlson, on the east by Levi Wade, on the south by George W. House, and on the west by Jackson Smith. There was also a tract containing thirty-one acres of cedar land. The court stated that Benjamin Marable had received this tract in two deeds, one from Luke M. Holmes, and one from James Bass.

In the end, the Rutherford County Court decreed that Mary Ann Baugh, as the daughter of Benjamin Marable, was indeed entitled to one-half of the land, and appointed Robert Cook, George W. House, and George W. Smith to partition the land.

John and Mary Ann Baugh may have considered living on their share of the Marable estate, but at this point in their lives they no longer wanted to farm. John was nearly sixty years old, and without the help of the slaves, he certainly could not farm the land.

As a result, the Baughs decided to move into the town of Murfrees-boro. In fact, an excellent property was up for sale on East Main Street, only three blocks from the town square and the Rutherford County Courthouse.

On June 3rd, 1867, John Baugh went to the Courthouse with Harvey Osborn, and made a down payment of $4,045.00 cash for the house. In addition, he signed a note to pay $2,000 more on March 1st, 1868 and $1,500 the following March 1869 for a total of $7,545.[181]

The lot he bought ran along East Main Street, south 320 feet to Maney Avenue, which led out to the Maney estate at Oaklands. The lot was 111 feet deep and backed up against land belonging to Mr. Clark. The only things on Mr. Clark's land were several former slave cabins—very small one to two-room wooden houses. The deed was witnessed by Robert Donald Reed, Mr. Osborn's brother-in-law, and Joseph B. Palmer, an attorney who had been a highly respected General in the Confederate Army. Mr. Palmer was in the process of building a home on East Main, in the middle of the next block down from the new Baugh residence, so they would be neighbors.

The house on the land purchased by the Baughs had been built around 1835 by Matthias Murfree, the son of Colonel Hardee Murfree—for whom Murfreesboro was named. Mathias Murfree had built the house in the Federal style; similar to the first addition Matthias' sister, Sallie Murfree Maney, had built at Oaklands.[182]

The two-story home was made of unadorned brick with walls a full twelve inches thick. The "off-center" entrance hall led to a nice-sized parlor on the right, and a door at the back of the hall led to the kitchen. The parlor opened into a large room, which could be used as a dining room, or sitting room. The stairs in the front entrance hall led to the upstairs where there were three rooms for sleeping, and above that, an attic. The house was quite elegant with high ceilings and beautiful mantles over the fireplaces in each room. This home would be a big change from the country living to which the Baughs were accustomed.

The seller, Harvey Osborne, was the owner of the carriage works. He had bought the house from Matthias Murfree in 1846, and moved into it with his young bride, Ann Read. By 1860, the Osborns had several small sons, and were living happily in the home.

Toward the end of 1860, the young Osborn sons had been in the country, and returned to town in an old wagon. Unbeknownst to them, the wagon had been used to transport the bodies of small pox victims. Shortly after that, the Osborn children broke out with small pox. As soon as this was discovered, the family was quarantined. To save their two year-old son, who was not yet sick, they lowered him from an upstairs window into a vat of whiskey, to sterilize him.[183]

Mrs. Osborn nursed her sons day and night. They survived, but she caught the small pox, and died. She was buried at Evergreen Cemetery, which had recently opened a little way out of the town proper. (Eventually, Evergreen would be used to bury many of the Confederate dead.) By 1867, Mr. Osborn's sons were grown, and he was ready to move to a new residence on Liberty Pike.

The Murfrees had asked that if the home was ever sold again, it be returned to them. However, after the Civil War, the Murfrees, like many others, were busy trying to recover from their devastating physical and financial losses. Even the Maneys at Oaklands were hurting terribly. Unable to pay their taxes, they would soon find it necessary to sell their beloved home, and move to a much smaller property on Maney Avenue.

The house on East Main was quite lovely, but apparently John Baugh did not consider it large enough. Whether this was due to the size of the family, because they hoped to bring in boarders, or because they needed living space on the first floor, due to Clemmie's disability, is unknown. What is known, is that John Baugh decided to double the size of the home by building another wing to the left of the hall.

The addition to the home contained two more rooms downstairs, and another three rooms upstairs. The downstairs rooms would be used by the family. The upstairs rooms could be rented. To finish the new addition, a balcony was added across the back of the house, with an outside staircase, so that boarders and servants might enter and exit without going through the main part of the home.[184]

The Baugh home was now the perfect combination of country and city. Although there were a few homes further down East Main Street, including General Palmer's, the land behind them consisted of country lanes and slave cabins. There was still farmland further out along East Main, surrounding the Baptist College. Going out Maney Avenue there were also corn and cotton fields until you reached the long and stately drive leading up to the Oaklands mansion.

Meanwhile, in the midst of adding on to their new home in Murfreesboro and getting ready to move, more of the Baugh children were getting married. In fact, the year 1867 was full of marriages. The widow, Angeline Childress had lived down the road from the Baughs for many years. Benjamin Baugh asked her daughter, the lovely Leticia Childress to be his wife, and the couple was married on January 8th. Ben was twenty-four, and Lettie, just twenty-one.

Six months after Ben's marriage, Fredonia, now twenty-one, married Dallas Polk Jacobs, a local merchant. The Jacobs family was from Beech Grove, where there was a large Jacobs's community. During the war, Mr. Jacobs had been a member of McLemore's Cavalry, Co E., which he joined in 1861 at the age of 18. In 1863, he was captured, and sent to prison in Baltimore, Maryland. Dallas Jacobs had quite a bit of money, and Fredonia was extremely happy. The couple moved only a few miles away, midway between Old Millersburg and Beech Grove.

Then, in September, John Pruitt, whose family lived a bit further down the road, not far from the Whites, asked for Eliza's hand in marriage.* Eliza was only eighteen, but had always been one to make her feelings known. Her father acquiesced, and on September 17th, Eliza became Mrs. John Pruitt.

It was a time of rejoicing, and sorrow for Mary Ann, as it is for every mother when her brood goes its own way. Even though they were, as Mr. Baugh said, "only down the road, a buggy ride away," the house must

---

* John Pruitt was the son of Henry Pruitt and Sallie Fox—the same family mentioned in the Civil War story.

have seemed empty. All the same, it had to be a huge weight off the mind of both parents. Their children were married happily, and all would be well provided for.

With all the marriages of white folks going on, the black folks were getting married, too. For the first time, they could marry legally, and be married by a minister, as well. In Christiana, the minister for the black folks must have come only periodically because the record shows that a large group of marriages took place at one time.

Among the names listed over the next several years, we find many of the former Baugh slaves:

1865: John Baugh to Celia Wright; Amanda Baugh to Harrison Frazier;

1866: Panny Baugh to Hiram Johnson; William Brown to Sylvia Baugh;

1867: Julius Greenlief to Elender Baugh;

1869: January 17th, Mirandy Baugh to Matt Miller, Fannie Baugh to James Washington;

1871: William James to Frances Baugh; Jane Baugh (Mirandy's daughter) to Van Hoover.[185]

In Tennessee, and the South in general, much had changed. Right or wrong, their way of life had been torn asunder. Those who had kept faith with their states found themselves disenfranchised by their country. Citizens of Tennessee, and most of the South, lost their rights, including the right to vote. Still, the government taxed them, and property taxes were too high for many who had lost their livelihood after the war. Without money or ability to farm the land, many people lost their property—sometimes these were farms that had been in the family for generations.

Now, Northerners—aware that there was money to be made in the South—came down in droves to prospect. Because of the cheap bags they carried, these men were often referred to as "Carpetbaggers." The Carpetbaggers bought family farms by paying past due taxes, and with bribes and graft bought their way into the government. At voting time, they scattered across the countryside, trying to influence the black vote. In this way, they gained wealth and power in the corrupt Reconstruction government. The Carpetbaggers' practices added greatly to the suffering of white Southerners, who were already hurting. Local citizens deeply resented the fact that these white Northerners were deciding their fate.

According to John Spence in his *Annals of Rutherford County*, the Carpetbaggers attempted to turn the black folks "against the white people of the county," and at the same time, were as apt to swindle them as anyone else.[186] Meanwhile, the black Southerner now had more power than their former owners. They even held positions in the government! It was difficult for the white citizen to see persons in charge who had once been their slaves, and whom they had seen as inferior.

There were also many former slaves who did not know how to live on their own. They were used to being given all their necessities, and being told what to do day-in and day-out. Now, they were free, but without money or structure to their lives. As a result, some resorted to crime and mischief.

One night in Pulaski, Tennessee, three young men fooling around, decided to don sheets and masks, and scare some of the black folks. The men knew that black people were very superstitious about spirits, and thought they would give them a good scare. It would be fun. From this idea, the Klu Klux Klan was born. Men—hiding their identities under the guise of sheets and tall pointed masks—would ride into a town, or into the countryside, leaving behind burning crosses and frightening messages.

What began as a lark soon became a means of taking back power. Along with trying to keep the black people in line, one of the Klan's purposes was to threaten and scare off corrupt Northerners. It seemed to work. Shortly after a visit from the Klan, many Northerners picked up and moved.

The old South had had many rules and codes of ethics. The Klansmen were seen as the moral providers in a South where there was no law or order. In Rutherford County, there was a man who had reportedly beaten his wife. The Klan paid him a visit with the admonition that he was not to beat her again.

Soon, in many communities, it was considered a matter of honor to join the Klan. Most persons in Rutherford County considered the Klan necessary to prevent crime and keep order. It is thought that some members of the Baugh and Gum family were also members of the Klan. If you were a gentleman, some said, that is what you did, you joined.

From 1867 to 1869, Nathan Bedford Forest was the Grand Wizard; a position to which he was elected. He was the only Grand Wizard in Klan history. Some said his leadership in the Klan was his vengeance for not winning the war. During this time and later, the Klu Klux Klan became the terror of the countryside, whipping, lynching, and committing other unspeakable acts toward blacks and others. In 1869, after a meeting with President Grant, Forest called for the disbandment of the Klu Klux Klan.

~

After 1867, the Baugh home was relatively quiet. Out of eleven children, only 17 year-old Charlie, 10 year-old Clemmie and 7 year-old Rollie remained.

Clemmie must have been a pretty little girl. Despite the fact that she was lame, she was a lively child, who charmed, and at times, demanded her way. She was her father's pet. Cousin Rollie was always a little gentleman with Clemmie, but the two did clash from time to time.

The grandchildren were always welcome in the Baugh home. Mary Ann took a lively interest in them, and their welfare, and she soon had many to be interested in.

By the end of the 1860s, Jack and Maria had Thomas Saunders, Mary Louise, John Aldridge, and little Lucy—though sadly Lucy died only four days after her birth.

After baby William died, Bettie and Robert White had another little boy, John. Benjamin and Leticia had a daughter named Mattie; Mollie and Robert Howland had two sons, Robert and Benjamin. Eliza and John Pruitt had a little girl they named Mary. From Delaware, Joseph wrote his parents that Anna had delivered a healthy, little girl whom they named Ida in 1866, and another little girl they called Mary Emma in 1869. By 1870, Mr. and Mrs. John Aldridge Baugh had thirteen living grandchildren (of the seventeen that had been born).

In November of 1869, two years after purchasing the property and home on East Main Street, John A. and Mary Ann Baugh purchased the land directly behind them from S.B. Clark for the sum of $1,000. The land in District 15 ran from the right side of the house lot, back to Vine Street and over to Maney Avenue. This purchase added another three-quarters of an acre to their property, giving them nearly the entire block from East Main to Vine, and from Maney three-quarters of the way to Spring Street.

One official difference for property buyers after the Civil War was that married women were given the rights to property along with their husbands, and began to be included on deeds. The purchase of land from Mr. Clark was signed the 9th of November 1869, and delivered to John A. Baugh on the 20th.

During this time—possibly to help pay for the cost of the new land and building, or because he did not want to be bothered with it—John Baugh sold two properties. The first property was three-quarters of an acre in the town of Christiana. The lot lay between the railroad, the road, and land that Mr. Baugh had previously sold to J. M. Miller. For this, J.A. Baugh received $264.50 from M.L. Fletcher.[187] On the 20th of November 1869, John Baugh appeared before the court clerk to finalize the deed.

Then, on December 17th, "John A. Baugh and wife Mary A. Baugh" sold 104 acres of Benjamin Marable's land to Pleasant T. Henderson and Delany H. Talley. The property was just north of the house Mary Ann intended to keep for herself, and bordered on the land of Burlason, H.H. Hicks, and Levi Wade. The Baughs received a down payment of $1,000.00, with additional payments expected each January from 1871 to 1873 in the amount of $1,355. A final payment of $1,476.95 was due in 1874.[188]

As previously mentioned, women were now being treated differently, with attention to their feelings and will. As a result, additional language appeared in the deed selling property that Mary Ann had inherited from her father. It read as follows:

> ... Mary A. Baugh ... having so appeared before me privately and apart from her husband the said John A. Baugh acknowledged the execution of said deed to have been done by her freely, voluntarily and understandingly, without compulsion or constraint from her said husband and for the purposes therein explained ...[189]

By 1870, Charlie was nineteen, Clemmie, now a young lady, was thirteen, and Rollie was ten. There had been no school for them to attend during the war years. They had only learned what the Baugh girls, and Mary Ann could teach. Since Rollie was a bright boy, he must have read whatever books he could lay his hands on, and learned much on his own. Now that the children lived in Murfreesboro, Rollie, Clemmie, and Charlie, all attended school. There was likely a school within walking distance, or a short buggy ride—for Clemmie.

Living in Murfreesboro after the war was truly a different way of the life. It must been a very, happy time for them to be free from the shadow of war. The children could walk down the street without the fear of soldiers, gunshots or having their home invaded. Perhaps by moving, the Baughs had wanted to get away from the unhappy war memories in Old Millersburg.

On March 12, 1870, John Baugh celebrated his sixty-fourth birthday. Likely the family gathered together during this time. Everyone was hopeful about good days ahead.

Four days later, John Baugh was stricken. Dr. J.B. Murfree was called, and a short time later the thirty-year-old county court clerk, who happened to be W. D. Robison—the same man John had gone to war with nine years earlier, and for whom the 2nd Tennessee was named—arrived to take down his will.

Coming into the house and going to his room, the men would have found John Baugh, a man who had always been hale and hearty, lying in bed pale and breathless. Dr. Murfree examined him, and listened to his heart. Then, as was his custom, Dr. Murfree knelt by the bed and prayed with John for his strength, and for God's blessing upon him and his family.

The children, who could get there in time, did. Eliza Pruitt, for one, was there. W.D. Robison took down John Aldridge Baugh's last wishes. He must not have had the strength to say much as the will was very short. It read as follows:

"I, John A. Baugh of the County of Rutherford and state of Tennessee do make and declare this to be my last will and testament and do hereby revoke all former wills by me at any time heretofore made. Having full confidence in the good sense and property management of my wife, Mary A Baugh, I do hereby give to her absolutely all my estate of every description with all the power to sell & convey any such property as she may deem advisable & to pay all my just debts out of the proceed of sales or from collections. And I further appoint her sole executrix to this my last will and testament and exempt her from giving any security as this 16, March 1870."

Figure 23. W.D. Robinson (Robison)

Then, Dr. Murfree and W.D. Robison, along with H.H. Clayton, witnessed what John Baugh had dictated. Privately, he requested of Mary Ann, as she hovered over his bed, that all of the children be given $1,000, and that she make sure Clemmie was taken care of for life. At 6 PM that night, John Aldridge Baugh left this world.

Chapter 29

The Greatest Loss

I
N THE NEXT HOURS, WORD SPREAD THAT THE "MAJOR," AS HE WAS affectionately called, was gone. His body was washed by the women of the house, dressed and laid out—in wait of the coffin.

Someone rode by horse to tell family members in Salem, Millersburg, and Beech Grove that Father Baugh had died. A telegram was sent to Joseph, who, by now, was back in Winchester, Tennessee. In addition, a notice was placed in the newspaper, and funeral notices were printed for hand-delivery.[190]

There would be much work to do the following day, but tonight, Mary Ann sat quietly with John's body. The lit candles flickered now and then in the dark room, softening the pale white stillness of his features. The house was strangely still without the ticking of the clocks, which as custom dictated, were stopped in the hour of John's death, and would stay so until after burial.

Quietly in the night, Mary Ann contemplated the forty some years she and John had been married, the eleven children that had come from their union, the five homes they had lived in, and their travels together. They had survived a war, and now had hoped for years of peace and happiness together. But nothing in this world was guaranteed.

What Mary Ann Baugh would remember most of all, perhaps, were the kind moments between them; his voice, eyes, and strong hands. Strange how, when at last they were about to share a peaceful life, God had taken him. Death was a common specter to most families, and Mary Ann knew that she had been comparatively fortunate and blessed in this regard. It was the Lord's will that he be taken now, and she must bow her head to that will.

The next day there was a bustle of activity as family members began to arrive. For each, there would be that heart-stopping moment when they saw the man who had represented strength and stability to them, now lying so pale and still; a body with the soul gone.

He was laid out in the parlor, with a small vase of flowers on a table nearby. Soon the coffin makers arrived with the box, narrow at the foot, then wider and curved at the top.

For Clemmie, aged thirteen, the loss of her father must have been the most heartbreaking of all. She knew that her father loved her, and had always looked out for her, treating her with special care.

The undertaker from Woodfin and Moore—who had his office on Lytle Street behind the square—came to the house to embalm the body. As he walked along East Main Street, he observed that the blinds were drawn, shutters closed, and a long strip of heavy, crinkled, black crepe was tied to the front door. Everyone who passed would know there had been a death in this home.

Eliza, Bettie, Fredonia, and maybe even Clemmie, had helped Mammy Ran, and the other servants decorate the doorways, mantles, and picture frames with black crepe. Mirrors in the home were either covered or turned to the wall. There was an old superstition that if you looked in a mirror during mourning, you would be the next to die.[191]

All this time, someone sat with John Baugh's body. Some said this was to ensure that rats did not get to it. But also,—as custom dictated—they wanted to make sure that the person was really dead. Meanwhile, food and drink were served.[192]

The sorrow and emptiness Mary Ann felt were difficult to describe. There stood Joseph, Jack, Benjamin, and Charles; all her sons. Two daughters were gone, but Bettie, Fredonia, Mollie, Eliza, and Clemmie remained. Each child held some part of John Baugh. Poor Clemmie was weeping! She was so young to see her father die.

Mary Ann's friend and neighbor, Mrs. A.R. Richardson came to pay her condolences. Mrs. Richardson had recently moved to town with her son, James Richardson, an attorney. They lived toward the square, on the same block as the Baughs.

A dress-maker had come, and now Mary Ann was wearing her widow's weeds. No one kept mourning clothing on hand; that was considered bad luck, and women did not leave the home after a death. They either had ready-made clothing brought in, or called for a dressmaker. Dresses often were made of bombazine; a combination of silk and wool. Most important though, was the black, crepe fabric—a gauzy silk, "heavily crimped."[193] The crepe easily became limp, and stained with a drop of water, making it look old. That was why woman's mourning dress was often referred to as "widow's weeds."[194]

On the day of the funeral, after the family visitation with the body, other visitors arrived for the funeral prayer services downstairs. If the Baugh family followed with custom, they waited upstairs in private, while others said goodbye to John Baugh.[195]

The long, black hearse with glass windows arrived in front of the house, and the men—perhaps those who were fellow Masons—with hats removed, bore the closed casket outside.

Figure 24. John A. Baugh monument.

Immediately after John Baugh's passing, Mrs. M.A. Baugh had purchased a family plot at Evergreen Cemetery, containing room for sixteen graves.[196] Evergreen was where all of the finest families in town were being buried now; rather than the family farms, as they used to do. Poor Mattie and Mary Ann's parents were all buried in unmarked graves.

If Mrs. Baugh attended the burial, she left the house with her widow's veil drawn over her face, and rode to Evergreen Cemetery in a closed carriage. The funeral procession traveled down Main to High Street, and then through the fields of newly planted cotton towards Oaklands. On the right was the entrance. The Baugh plot was not far.

Their Methodist minister, Rev. McFerrin, prayed over the grave. Mason rites were performed as well. Later, a tall Mason obelisk would be placed on the site. John Baugh was a well-respected man, who had taken on duty, when duty called.

When the burial was over, all returned to the home on East Main. That night—as was also the custom—there was music in the parlor, and possibly even quartettes singing. The most popular songs were "Rock of Ages," "Asleep in Jesus," and "Lead Kindly Light."[197]

Following this day, Mary Ann Baugh did not leave her home for a month—except to attend church. This, too, was part of the custom. She would wear black for the next year, and possibly—if it was her choice— she would wear it for the rest of her life. Her crepe bonnet had a long, crepe veil, which nearly reached her feet. Indoors, she wore a white cap, with only the white ruffle showing when she went outside. The only jewelry she wore was of dull or dark jet. After nine months, it would be proper for her to wear mauve, purple, lavender, or white. White bonnets and shawls were accepted, and were often part of women's mourning dress. It would be two years before she would return to regular society.[198]

In the days following the funeral, Dr. J.B. Murfree and W.D. Robison went before the court to swear that the signature on the will was indeed John A. Baugh's and that the will was according to his wishes.

When John Baugh's books came to light, it was found that a number of persons—including his children and some of Mary Ann's relatives— owed him money. Listed were:

- J.L. Baugh (son Joseph) due Dec 1858 $562.25
- J.M. Baugh (son Jack) due Jan 1866 $250
- H.I. & H.M. Prater* due Nov 1867 ... $375 & $375.00
- R.M. White, (son-in-law) .... $4,390 for land
- John Pruitt, (Eliza's husband) ... $1,550
- J.M. (son Jack) Baugh for land .... $1,100.00.[199]

* Relatives by marriage of Mary Ann's sister, Elizabeth

It seems possible that after John Baugh's death, Mary Ann left the debts of her sons and sons-in-law unpaid as part of the $1,000 that John wished to give them. Perhaps she was softer, and not quite as good with money as her husband had thought.

Meanwhile, Mary Ann Baugh completed the sale on some land in Christiana.[200] She was now a landowner and a businesswoman. Having survived most of the Civil War on her own, the role was not entirely foreign to her.

The 1870 census shows the occupants of the home on East Main several months after John Baugh's passing. Listed were Mary Ann, 58, Charles Baugh, 19, Clemmie Baugh 13, and Rollie, 10, who was also listed as a Baugh. All three young people were shown to be "at school."

Also living in the home were two domestic servants: Eliza Clay, age 40, and Walter Carter, age 20. Both were black. These persons were likely not their former Baugh slaves, but the former slaves of others, who were glad to work in a home in town for whatever wage. Possibly, they lived in the small cabins at the back of the property on Vine Street, or in the attic.

In January of 1871, Mrs. Baugh sold her son-in-law, John M. Pruitt, some land bordering on that of her son, Benjamin, and the Childress family. The following month, she sold a second lot, and then in August, a third. Mrs. Baugh must have had a need for additional funds, and did not want to bother with developing the land.

Once again in November, she sold another large plot of land to her son, Jack Baugh. The property was near that of Mathias Fox. An additional lot was sold to Nelson Wagoner.

It is difficult to know exactly how Mary Ann Baugh was faring at this time. The grief of having just lost her husband, and the unresolved trauma of the war years were still with her. She had given over most of the Baugh land in the Millersburg area to her children, and was well situated in Murfreesboro on East Main Street.

Now, with all her children married or out of the house—except for sixteen-year old Clemmie and thirteen-year old Rollie—Mary Ann decided to spend some time on the old Marable land. It was a decision that would change the future of the family, and bring a new dynasty into being.

To be continued . . .

Judy Garland's Gumm Family Line

Norton Gum—Sally Clampet
|
William Norton Gum—Malinda Nugent
|
John Alexander Gum—Martha Wade
|
William Tecumseh Gum—Clemmie Baugh
|
Frank Gumm—Ethel Milne
|
Frances Ethel Gumm

Endnotes
Book 3—Civil War

Note: RCHS = Rutherford County Historical Society

1. Baugh Family Bible
2. *The Millersburg 110*, by John Lee Fults, 2009, p. 7
3. Comment based on Robert White's short testimony in 1893 court case.
4. Interestingly, Maria's maternal uncle married Nancy Harwell, the daughter of Thomas, one of the relatives John A. Baugh may have come to see in 1828.
5. See Chancery Court case, *J.L. & J.M. Baugh vs. R. M. Howland & others*.
6. Quote taken from the Baugh Family Bible.
7. *Annals of Rutherford County*, Vol. 2, John C. Spence, RCHS, 1991, p. 129
8. U.S. Federal Census of 1860, Rutherford County, TN
9. *Annals of Rutherford County*, Vol. 2, John C. Spence, RCHS, 1991, p. 146
10. Ibid, Vol. 2, p. 146
11. Ibid, Vol. 2, p. 146
12. Ibid, Vol. 2, p. 143
13. Source Lost. See Bibliography—possibly *Call Forth the Mighty Men*
14. *Annals of Rutherford County*, Vol. 2, John C. Spence, RCHS, p. 144–145
15. This was a general comment going around; seen in many sources.
16. Letter from Joseph L. Baugh to his cousin, January 12, 1897, TN State Archives, Nashville, 1865–70. The Baughs had cash when most were poor.
17. *The Annals of Rutherford County*, by John Spence, p. 148
18. *The Life of Johnny Reb*, Bell I. Wiley, The Bobbs-Merrill Co., 1943, p. 15
19. *Call Forth the Mighty Men*, Bob Womack, Colonial Press, 1987, p. 12

20. Jimmy Fox letters, January 6, 2006

21. *The Millersburg's 110*, John Lee Fults, 2009, p. 2–3

22. Ibid, p. 3

23. Citation misplaced—likely, *Call Forth the Might Men*—see Bibliography

24. *A Diary of the Civil War*, John C. Spence, RCHS, 1993, p. 6

25. *The Millersburg's 110*, John L. Fults, p. 9

26. Ibid, p. 33–34

27. Ibid, p. 34

28. *Millersburg's 110*, John Lee Fults, 2009, p. 34–35, Also *Call Forth the Mighty Men*, see Bibliography

29. *The Tennessee Civil War Veterans Questionaires*, Vol. 1, The Rev. Salas Emmett Lucas, Jr., p. 294–295. Accounting for those who accompanied masters to war is described on p.78–79

30. This is speculation on the part of the writer.

31. Robert L. Howland mentioned (1893 Chancery Court) Mattie was given a slave at the time of their marriage, but not official ownership.

32. *The Life of Johnny Reb*, Bell Irvin Wiley, p. 21, New Orleans Daily Crescent, April 29, 1861. All references in the depot from this source.

33. While based on facts of the day, these personal moments are speculation.

34. http://en.wikipedia.org/wiki/Nashville_in_the_Civil_War

35. *The Millersburg 110*, John Lee Fults, 2009, p. 36

36. *Mothers of Invention*, Drew Gilpin Faust, University of North Carolina Press, 1996, p. 81

37. *Annals of Rutherford County*, Vol. 2, John C. Spence, RCHS, p. 149

38. *The Keebles: A Half Century of Southern Family Life*, Thesis, by William Foster Fleming, B.A., August 1951, The University of Texas

39. *The Millersburg 110*, John Lee Fults, 2009, p. 39

40. *Annals of Rutherford County*, John C. Spence, RCHS, p. 151

41. *The Millersburg 110*, John Lee Fults, 2009, p. 39

42. Joseph L. Baugh Letter, January 12, 1897, TN State Archives, Nashville

43. *The Mistress of Stoney Lonesome*, Mary Ann Burkholder, Oct. 1987, p. 6 Tennessee State Archives, Keeble file.

44. Notes on the Wade Family—Lucy May Lenoir

45. *The Mistress of Stoney Lonesome*, Mary Ann Burkholder, Oct. 1987, p. 9 Tennessee State Archives, Keeble file.

46. *FROW Chips*—RU CTY Historical Society, Vol. 34, No. 6, p. 9

47. *Cemeteries and Graveyards of Rutherford County, Tennessee*, compiled by Susan G. Daniels, Pub RCHS, 2005, p. 164

48. *A Diary of the Civil War*, John C. Spence, RCHS, 1990, p.13

49. *A Diary of the Civil War*, John C. Spence, RCHS, 1990, p.16–17

50. Ibid, p. 18

51. Ibid, p. 18

52. *A Diary of the Civil War*, John C Spence, RCHS, 1993, p. 18

53. *The Millersburg 110*, John Lee Fults, 2009, p. 41

54. *Annals of Rutherford County*, Vol. 2, John C. Spence, RCHS, p. 158–159

55. *A Diary of the Civil War*, John Spence, RCHS, p. 19

56. *The Life of Johnny Reb*, Bell I. Wiley, The Bobbs-Merrill Co, 1943, p?

57. *A Diary of the Civil War*, John C. Spence, RCHS, p. 20

58. Jim Lewis, Park Ranger, Civil War Symposium in Murfreesboro, 2005

59. Told to the writer by a descendent of families in the Old Millersburg area.

60. *The Annals of Rutherford County*, Vol 2, John Spence, RCHS, pgs. 163–165

61. RCHS, Pub. 25, Summer 1985, p. 81–83

62. *The Annals of Rutherford County*, Vol. 2, John Spence, RCHS, p. 164

63. Ibid, p. 160

64. *With Blood and Fire*, Michael R. Bradley, Burd Street Press, Shippensburg, PA, 2003, general comment

65. *Annals of Rutherford County*, John C. Spence, p. 162

66. *A Diary of the Civil War*, John C. Spence, RCHS, p. 40

67. RCHS, Pub. 26, Winter 1986, p. 37, other sources not mentioned

68. *A Diary of the Civil War*, John C. Spence, RCHS, p. 22

69. *The Millersburg 110*, John Lee Fults, 2009, p. 41–42

70. Ralph Pucket notes; Gum Family Archive

71. *A History of Murfreesboro*, C.C. Henderson, The News Banner Publishing Company, 1929, p. 7

72. In *Call Forth the Mighty Men*, Bob Womack writes that for a while some wives followed the troops, but it caused a split focus in the men. Soon, it was forbidden and the women sent home.

73. Original letter from Gum Family Archives of Ralph Puckett

74. http://www.geocities.com/Heartland/Acres/1257/shiloh.html?200531

75. Citation misplaced (p. 81)?

76. Information taken from many sources. Please see the Bibliography.

77. *The Millersburg 110*, John Lee Fults, 2009, p. 47–48

78. Ibid, p. 55'

79. *Call Forth the Mighty Men*, by Bob Womak, Colonial Press, 1987, p. 150

80. Ibid, p. 153

81. *Annals of Rutherford County*, Vol. 2, John C. Spence, RCHS, 1991, p. 170

82. Notes from a special tour of the Rutherford County Courthouse, 2006. On restoration of the Courthouse, a bullet had been found embedded in the wall.

83. It is assumed that Maria and baby Thomas stayed with her mother, Louisa Jarrett, in Salem. Mary Ann Baugh had more than enough mouths to feed.

84. Obit of Joseph Baugh, June 22, 1902, as found in *Glimpses into the Lives and Times of the Confederate Soldiers Known to Be Buried in City Cemetery, Winchester, Tennessee*, researched and compiled by Joy Quandt Gallagher, Peter Turney Chapter #1927, United Daughters of the Confederacy, 1998

85. Note from the Winchester Library historical card file. The cotton mill is mentioned in *Goodspeeds Tennessee*, Franklin County, p. 788

86. The Army of Tennessee, p. 78 p. 40–41?

87. Co. D, 11th (Holman's) Tennessee Cavalry. (Confederate) War records for J.L. Baugh and J.M. Baugh

88. Joseph L. Baugh's letter of Jan 12, 1897 states he was with Forest throughout the war. Tennessee State Archives, Marable file.

89. Anderson L. Crosthwait, Pension Application, Sept 28, 1917—His pension application is the one existing record of his war service.

90. Anderson L. Crosthwait, Obit, May 28, 1923, The Nashville Banner, TN, p. 13 states "Mr. Crosthwait's service in the Confederate Army was among his most cherished memories and his affection for his commanding general and his comrades …"

91. *Army of Tennessee*, Stanley Fitzgerald Horn, Univ. of Oklahoma Press, 1953 p. 78

92. Martha Fox Todd's application for The Daughters of the Confederacy

93. RCHS, Pub. No. 28, Winter 1987, p. 12

94. Spies of the Confederacy, John Bakeless, Dover Pub., Inc. 1970, p. 209

95. Ibid, p. 211

96. http://www.samdavishome.org/history.html

97. Ibid

98. http://www.tennessee-scv.org/Camp1293/samdavis.htm

99. RCHS Pub. No. 25, Summer 1985, p. 41-48

100. Ibid, p. 41–8 for entire paragraph.

101. Baugh Family Bible

102. No known photograph of Clemmie Baugh exists. We can only guess of her appearance from the features of her siblings.

103. J.L. & J.M. Baugh v. R.M. Howland & others Rutherford County Chancery Court, 1893, Testimony of Mrs. A. R. Richardson

104. Millerburg's 100, by John Lee Fults, 2009, p. 66

105. *Rutherford County*, Mabel Pittard, Memphis State University Press, 1984, p. 73

106. A.L. Crosthwait, as a scout for Wheeler, was a likely reporter.

107. *From Shiloh to San Juan; The Life of "Fightin' Joe" Wheeler*, John P. Dyer, Louisiana State University Press, Baton Rouge, 1941 & 1961, p. 66

108. Ibid, p. 68–69

109. *The Millersburg 110*, John Lee Fults, 2009, p. 71

110. Ibid, p. 74

111. Eyewitnesses at the Battle of Stones River, Compiled and edited by David R. Logsdon, 2002, p. 4

112. Billy Brown's story, http://home.flash.net/~coley/WCBrown.html

113. *Call Forth the Mighty Men*, by Bob Womack, Colonial Press, 1987, p. 202

114. Ibid, p. 204

115. Ibid, p. 211

116. Ibid, p. 76

117. Charles Batey, a descendent of the Batey and Bass families in Blackman.

118. From Park Service Rangers & local residents' passed down family history.

119. See Oaklands Mansion & others. Bloodstains removed from Manson home.

120. *Eyewitnesses at the Battle of Stones River*, David R. Logsdon, 2003, p. 84

121. Ibid, p. 71 & 84. It should be noted that Lt. Crosthwait, a descendant of Col. Hardee Murfree for whome Murfreesboro was named, had died trying to defend her. Cause of death was a severed artery which he attempted to stop.

122. Ibid, p. 84

123. *Call Forth the Mighty Men*, p. 216; W.W. Frazier, 5th Confederate Regiment, in Lindsley's Military Annals, p. 148

124. *Millersburg's 110*, John Lee Fults, p. 78

125. The exact location of Benjamin Marable's home has yet to be discovered.

126. *Hearthstones: The Story of Historic Rutherford County Homes*, Mary B. Hughes, Mid-South Publishing, 1942, p. 26; The Hiram Jenkins home was needlessly destroyed in June of 2006.

127. Letter of Joseph L. Baugh, letter to Cousin Marable, January 12, 1897, Tennessee State Archives, Nashville, TN

128. The Ridleys of Rydel, p. 521

129. Ibid, p. 521

130. Ibid, p. 521

131. Ibid, p.

132. Ibid, p. Entire diary was printed in the Tennessee Historical Quarterly of 1953?, but copy is presently misplaced.

133. Ibid, p. 522

134. *The Ancient Rydells*, from an article by Bettie Ridley, *Murfreesborough Monitor*, 1867, p. 519–522 (Also see *TN Historical Quarterly*)

135. *Liberty Gap*, John Lee Fults, Fults Publishing Co., 1996, p. 44–46

136. Ibid, pgs. 48–49

137. Ibid, p. 49–50

138. Ibid, p. 49–50

139. Ibid, p. 51

140. Ibid, p. 54

141. *Millersburg 110*, by John Lee Fults, p.78–79

142. Ibid, p. 82

143. Ibid, p. 83

144. Ibid, p. 85

145. http://americancivilwar.com/statepic/ga/ga005.html

146. *The Tennessee Civil War Veterans Questionaires*, Vol. 1, The Rev. Salas Emmett Lucas, Jr., p. 295, q. 17

147. *Mothers of Invention*, Drew Gilpin Faust, University of NC Press, p. 238

148. The Army of Tennessee, p. 78, p. 40–41?

149. http://www.rootsweb.com/~tngiles/cv1war/11cav.htm

150. *From Shiloh to San Juan; The life of "Fightin' Joe" Wheeler*, John P. Dyer, Louisiana State University Press, Baton Rouge, 1941 & 1961 p. 99

151. Ibid, p. 123

152. Ibid, p. 124

153. Ibid, p. 128

154. We know the results of his wound, and where it took place, but not the exact circumstances. These are only guessed at by the author.

155. *Great Battles of the Civil War*, John MacDonald, Macmillan, 1988, p. 156

156. *The Siege of Atlanta, 1864*, Samuel Carter, III, St. Martin's Press, NY 1973, p. 146–147

157. Ibid, p. 182

158. Ibid, p. 183

159. Ibid, p. 161

160. Ibid, p. 190

161. *Great Battles of the Civil War*, p. 161

162. Taken from the Confederate Army records, TN State Archives, Nashville, TN. Robert White appeared on a list of killed, wounded or missing in Cleburne's Division, December 31, 1863.

163. *Rutherford County*, Mabel Pittard, Memphis State University Press, p. 79

164. RCHS Pub. 26, Winter 1886, p. 18–19

165. Ibid, p. 37

166. *Portals to Hell*, Lorrie R. Spear, Stackpole Books, p. 184

167. Ibid, p. 184; Horace Carpenter, "Plain Living at Johnson's Island," *Century Magazine* (March 1891)

168. Ibid, p. 184

169. Ibid, p. 185

170. *Portals to Hell*, Lorrie R. Spear, Stackpole books, p. 184, quote from POW R.F. Webb.

171. Ibid, p.186

172. *A Diary of the Civil War*, John C. Spence, RCHS, 1993, p. 158–159

173. Rutherford County Historical Society, Pub. 26, p. 43

174. http://community-2.webtv.net/raycousins/NBFFarewell/

175. *A History of RU County*, C. C. Sims, Ed., 1947, p. 44 Prof. Hammer 1864

176. Ibid, p. 160

177. *Civil War Tales of the Tennessee Valley*, Wm Lindsey McDonald, p.70–71

178. Deed of Trust, February 27, 1865, Rutherford County, TN

179. Deed of Trust, February 27, 1865, RU Country Records, Murfreesboro, TN

180. RU County Record Book 3, p. 635–636, Minute Bk DD, p. 756–757

181. Rutherford County Record Book 15, p. 29

182. *Curry Wolfe Research*

183. Story told to the author by Mrs. Sarah King. Dates verified by *Cemeteries & Graveyards of Rutherford County, TN*, compiled by S. G. Daniel, p. 465

184. Per Mrs. Patterson. The back stairs were removed in the 1970s.

185. *History of RC African American Community*, Rev. Melvin E. Hughes Sr.

186. *The Annals of Rutherford County*, Vol 2, John C. Spence, p. 260

187. Rutherford County Court Record Book Record No. 688, Nov. 20, 1869

188. RC Property Records Book, No. 743

189. RC Property Records Book, No. 743, December 21, 1869

190. *Widows, Weepers & Wakes; Morning in Middle Tennessee*, by Janet S. Hasson, Belle Meade Plantation, Nashville, TN 2001, p. 5

191. Ibid, p. 7

192. Ibid, p. 9

193. Ibid, p. 18

194. Ibid, p. 18

195. Ibid, p. 11

196. This is according to Evergreen Cemetery records, however the original records were burned and they did the best they could to rewrite them.

197. Ibid, p. 13

198. Ibid, p. 22

199. Estate Inventory, 20 April 1870, Rutherford County, TN

200. May 20, 1870

Bibliography

Bergeron, Paul H., Ash, Stephen V., Keith, Jeanette, *Tennesseans and Their History*, The University of Tennessee Press, Knoxville, TN 1999.

Bradley, Michael R., *With Blood & Fire; Life behind Union Lines in Middle Tennessee, 1863–65*, Burd Street Press, Shippensburg, PA, 2003.

Brands, H.W., *Andrew Jackson, His Life and Times*, Anchor Books, 2005.

Carter III, Samuel, *The Siege of Atlanta, 1864*, St. Martin's Press, New York 1973.

Cozzens, Peter, *The Battle of Stones River*, National Parks Civil War Series, Text By, Pub. Eastern National 1995.

Daniel, Susan G., compiler, *Cemeteries and Graveyards of Rutherford County, Tennessee*, RCHS, 2005.

Daniel, Susan G., compiler, *Rutherford County Tennessee Pioneers Born Before 1810*, RCHS, 2003.

Denney, Robert E., *Civil War Prisons & Escapes; A Day-by Day Chronicle*, Sterling Publishing Company, NY 1993.

Fults, John Lee, *Hoover's Gap*, Fults Publishing Company, 2002.

Fults, John Lee, *Liberty Gap*, Fults Publishing Company, 1996.

Fults, John Lee, *Millersburg's 110*, 2009.

Gallagher, Gary W., Editor, *Fighting for the Confederacy; The Personal Recollections of General Edward Porter*, The University of North Carolina Press, Chapel Hill, 1989.

Jacobs, Harriet, *Incidents of a Slave Girl*, Dover Publications, 2001.

MacDonald, John, *Great Battles of the Civil War*, Macmillan Press, 1992.

Logsdon, David R., *Eyewitnesses at the Battle of Stones River*, 2002.

McDonald, Cornelia Peake, *A Woman's Civil War; A Diary with Reminiscences of the War from March 1862*, Gramercy Books, NY 1992.

Miller, Francis Trevelyan, *Armies and the Leaders, The Photographic History of The Civil War*, Castle Books, 1957.

Norton, Herman, A., *Religion in Tennessee 1777–1945*, The University of Tennessee Press, 1981.

Ridley, Elisabeth O. Howse, *Falling Leaves*, 1970.

Seigenthaler, John, *James K. Polk*, Times Books, Henry Holt & Co, 2003.

Sims, Carlton C., *A History of Rutherford County*, Rutherford County Historical Society, 1947.

Speer, Lonnie R., *Portals to Hell; Military Prisons of the Civil War*, Stackpole Books, Mechanicsburg, PA 1997.

Toney, Marcus B., *The Privations of a Private*, The University of A Press, 2005.

Wells, Carol, *Pioneers of Rutherford County, Tennessee, Abstract of County Court Minutes 1804—1811*, Ericson Books, Texas.

Wiley, Bell Irvin & Milhollen, Hirst D., *They Who Fought Here*, The Macmillan Company, NY, 1959.

Wolfe, Charles, K., *Tennessee Strings*, The University of Tennessee Press, Knoxville, 1977.

Index

As the owner of this book, you are entitled to purchase *From Tennessee to Oz, **PART 2*** which will cover Judy Garland's family history from 1870 to the mid-1940s and contain many family photos, previously unpublished.

Part Two begins with the meeting of Judy Garland's grandparents, Will Gum and Clemmie Baugh. It is a romance that soon becomes a dark and suspenseful mystery. The latter part of this book is a family story, with many happy and humorous anecdotes never before told to the general public. It is a never-to-be forgotten story.

Slated release time: June 2010.

You will be contacted, or you may contact us at **catsong2@netzero.net** or check our websites: **www.fromtennesseetooz.com** or **www.catsong publishing.com.**

Thank you!

Catsong Publishing

_____ From Tennessee to Oz, Part 1 . . . . $19.95

_____ From Tennessee to Oz, Part 2 (June 2010) . . . . TBA

_____ Made In America—Vaudeville Songs CD $10.95
(21 songs sung by the Gumm Family in vaudeville)

_____ Sabrina—The Autobiography of a Cat $11.99

_____ Lily: Through the Eyes of a Child (2/2010) . . . . TBA

The Gumm Family Songbook—purchase through the
Judy Garland Museum. _All profits go for benefit of the Museum._

_____ _Please add_ $3.50 _postage for any two items._

_____ Total

Visit our website for more information
http://www.catsongpublishing.com
HC1 Box 23Z-31, White Haven, PA 18661

CPSIA information can be obtained
at www.ICGtesting.com
Printed in the USA
FSHW012008041219
64777FS